SCOTT MESCUDI

CUDI

The Memoir

■■■

SIMON & SCHUSTER

New York   Amsterdam/Antwerp   London
Toronto   Sydney/Melbourne   New Delhi

Simon & Schuster
1230 Avenue of the Americas
New York, NY 10020

First Simon & Schuster hardcover edition August 2025

Simon & Schuster strongly believes in freedom of expression and stands against censorship in all its forms. For more information, visit BooksBelong.com.

SIMON & SCHUSTER and colophon are registered trademarks of Simon & Schuster, LLC

For information about special discounts for bulk purchases, please contact Simon & Schuster Special Sales at 1-866-506-1949 or business@simonandschuster.com.

The Simon & Schuster Speakers Bureau can bring authors to your live event. For more information or to book an event, contact the Simon & Schuster Speakers Bureau at 1-866-248-3049 or visit our website at www.simonspeakers.com.

Interior design by Lewelin Polanco
Interior insert paintings by Scott Mescudi © 2025
Interior insert family photographs courtesy of Scott Mescudi
Interior insert red carpet photograph of Scott Mescudi and Lola Abecassis used with permission from Getty Images
Act I, II, III illustrations by Keaf Holliday © 2025

Manufactured in the United States of America

10 9 8 7 6 5 4 3 2 1

Library of Congress Cataloging-in-Publication Data is available.

ISBN 978-1-6682-0133-6
ISBN 978-1-6682-0135-0 (ebook)

Dedicated to my daughter, Vada; my nieces, Zuri, Miyahn, and Vishay; and my nephew, Jabari. You guys are the future. I hope my story helps you along your way so that you don't make the mistakes I made. Learn from my bullshit, chase your dreams, and be the best you can be. I love each of you endlessly. You're my babies.

An Introduction from My Mom, Elsie Mescudi

Congratulations on a very special book about a very special young man that will bring insight into his blessed ongoing life and journey. I have known him for forty-one years, nine months, and a few days, and I am always still amazed at all of his accomplishments and his successes, and yet still moving forward while giving and sharing all of him.

I am more than just proud, which is ongoing. I am also a fan, and I am always in awe of everything he continues to share with the world.

I have not read the book, on purpose. I'm going to be just as excited and surprised, and in awe as the rest of the family, friends, fans, and supporters who are going to read it along with me.

I can't wait. I'm excited and I am so, so proud that he has another chance to showcase Scott Ramon Seguro Mescudi, a.k.a. Kid Cudi, a.k.a. The Chosen One, and he is sharing it with everyone including me! So when the reviews come out, mine will be along with the rest of you.

I would like to thank every single one of you that have been on this journey with Scott.

To my baby boy, I'm so proud of you and congratulations again.

You are no longer on a pursuit of happiness. You are happy. May God continue to bless you.

All my love and respect.

Love,

Mommy

Contents

PROLOGUE

I was at peace with dying. After doing more coke than I ever had in my life I was losing all sense of what was real. I'd been alone in my New York apartment, crying for hours, listening to the Lykke Li song "Time Flies" on repeat. It was a love song, but the melodies and her voice filled me with despair.

I tried to get up off the bed, but my legs wouldn't work, so I collapsed to the floor and started to crawl. Eventually, I gave in and just laid on the ground. My heart was racing. It felt like it was going to burst any minute.

I was a role model, but I didn't feel like one. People called me their savior. But who was going to save me? I was a lighthouse for others, but I couldn't find my own way. It was peace I was after. Here, crippled on the floor, minutes from overdosing, was the closest I'd ever come to finding it.

You made great music that people loved, I thought, *but this is the end.*

My eyes closed and the feeling of a warm blanket descended on me.

I awoke bathed in light.

This must be heaven.

The sun was pouring in. Everything was quiet.

I lived by the West Side Highway in Tribeca. You always hear some sort of traffic out there. But I couldn't hear anything. I looked out my window and didn't see any cars. *That seems strange.* I wasn't aware of the time of day. It was like some weird version of the afterlife that mirrored real life, like that moment in the movie *Vanilla Sky* where Tom Cruise wakes up. I was disappointed when I realized I was back to the reality I knew. The one I was trying to escape. I hadn't fulfilled my death wish.

I couldn't make sense of what was plaguing me. It was all happening so fast. The first *Man on the Moon* had been out for about a year and I was on a rocket ship. Grappling with fame pushed me toward cocaine, which I only ever did alone. I was drawn to it in isolation, and my time by myself was increasing. I was feeling shut-in and I could barely even leave my house. The coke felt like a necessary countermeasure for my celebrity, but it was wreaking havoc on my life, creatively and personally. I had become super volatile emotionally. My relationships were in shambles, and I couldn't get songs out like I wanted. The anger was boiling in me. My rage came from my reality not aligning with my dream.

I thought that my life was going to be perfect and that everything was going to be fine. I thought being set financially was going to save me and make everything all right. I thought being Kid Cudi would transform my life in all the best ways. It didn't. It didn't give me the feelings I had on the come up. There were so many fake people around me, so much phony energy. I was pissed. *This was not like anything I had imagined.*

I started working on *Man on the Moon II* a few months before I almost overdosed. The drugs were heavily involved in its creation; they put me in a dark mindset. I felt like I had demons latched on to me. I needed to soundtrack the moodiness I was feeling.

At first, I was doing bumps, but I had quickly worked my way up to heavier and steadier quantities. I'd make lines that were as wide as my pinky and do them back-to-back throughout the day, every day. When I would get after it, I would really get after it. I was a maniac. That's why that second album was so drug riddled, because that's what got me through. I wouldn't have been able to do it if I didn't have something to push me.

The fame was getting intense. The attention was starting to get to me, and I didn't like people having eyes on me all the time. It wasn't the celebrity I wanted; it was the music career, the influence, the impact. But celebrity came with it. Money was a motivating factor, because I wanted to take care of my family, but I thought I'd have a bunch of cool, critically acclaimed albums and I would still be in the streets, and not have swarms of kids chasing me down the block.

It was hard to get a sense of what people wanted from me, or who they were seeing when they looked at me. I didn't know what the attention was for. I didn't know if it was because they genuinely liked me or for my affiliation with Kanye. I hated how people treated me. I hated how I spent years of my life being a regular dude, not being noticed by anyone, being invisible, and then suddenly I was being noticed by everyone. It was a mindfuck. Bitches in my ear and all on my shit. Most of the people in my face were enthusiastic, seeming to want to be around me, but a lot of people around me were there for the excitement, for the hype. Everyone was wearing a mask, and I could see it, but I also didn't want to be alone.

When will the fantasy end? When will the heaven begin? For years, I'd sought answers to those questions. The lines between the two always blurred. Kid Cudi was built on the back of my dreaming, on my desire to transcend. I was reaching for another world, for an escape.

When I wrote "Mr. Rager," I had already realized my dream. But the dream hadn't been all I'd hoped, and the song was about me overdosing as dread was closing in on me, the surreal experience next to that silent West Side Highway. Neither the drugs nor the fame could fix me, and "Mr. Rager" stands as the remnant of that chaotic time, one where all that I had achieved could only be matched by the intensity of my wrath. Eventually, it grew to be too much. Death seemed to be hanging over me. In the thick of it all, I couldn't tell if heaven or the fantasy was the better option.

By the time I was writing *Speedin' Bullet 2 Heaven* in 2015, I'd come back to that moment, but in a much more real way. We had rented a house in Big Sur to get the album done. After we'd finished a session, I'd be alone Googling exit bags. I was thinking about a way I could actually do it. I was plotting it. There's a song at the end of *Speedin' Bullet* where I say good-bye, and that was meant to be my final album. I was going to kill myself at the end of that album, or before it came out, or during that cycle. I was not planning to live that year. Not many people around me expected me to either.

When I was a kid, I'd sit in my room by myself, daydreaming, drawing, thinking about what my life would become. It had become something, but this ain't what I expected it to feel like. My room was where I was most comfortable. Just me and my imagination. I would picture myself drifting into space, exploring. I was always imagining other realms, but I never imagined that I would spend so much of my life seeking a grounding force here on earth.

Act I

CHAPTER 1

My first memory was of drama and dysfunction. I was three years old, sitting in the backseat of a silver two-door Chevy Chevette with my siblings. Looking out of the rear driver's side window, I caught a glimpse of my mom and dad arguing on the front lawn. My dad was steaming, his face flush with rage. My sister took my hand and told me to look away. I found out later from my mom that was the moment she told my dad she wanted a divorce.

My parents met when my dad crashed my mom's twenty-fourth birthday party. She put him out, but he was relentless. He had just gotten out of a relationship and tracked down someone they both knew at the party and asked her who my mom was and where he could find her. He was just as persistent courting her. My mom was initially put off by his tenacity, but she decided to go out with him on the recommendation of a mutual friend. He could intrigue her with a conversation.

They dated for two years, but she told him he needed to keep his own apartment because she wouldn't live with a man she wasn't married to. They had a baby girl in 1976, and he kept asking my mom to be his wife, but she still wasn't convinced. Two years after the birth of their first child, she decided it was the right thing to do; her daughter needed her father. My mom married him on her thirtieth birthday.

My father, Lindberg Skiles Mescudi, was twenty-one years older than my mom. He served in the Air Force in World War II. After he came home from the war, he became a substitute teacher and a house-painter. He could paint a whole house by himself. He took my older brother to paint with him once, but I was too young. I didn't get to have those connections. My dad was a hard man, cold and funny at times. I'm happy he didn't come home from the service more fucked up than he was. I'm sure he had more issues that we didn't know about. But despite his hang-ups, he was still present and hung out with us. He didn't have any crazy quirks, other than his temper.

My mom, born Elsie Harriet Banks, moved with an elegance I have not seen elsewhere in all my life. She was a five-eleven woman with beautiful chocolate skin and the face of an African queen. She was born in Tennessee. She was strong, intense with her parenting, but also soft and loving. None of her siblings ever called her Elsie. Everyone called her Billie, because her dad wanted a son. My mom dreamed of being a singer and pursuing a career in opera. After transitioning to being a music teacher, she taught for about thirty-seven years, and she became a guidance counselor for about ten years. A lot of what I learned about music comes from her.

My sister, Maisha, was my parents' firstborn. My oldest brother, Dean, was born on January 29, 1980, then another boy, Domingo, a year later on January 31, 1981. After Domingo, my mom got pregnant again. She gave him a name—Dominque—and she planned to have her tubes tied after birth. Sadly, she lost the baby. A few years later, she decided to try again and had me. I came into the world on January 30, 1984. My birthday fell right between my brothers'. My mom got her tubes tied after. It's wild to think about, but I almost wasn't even born.

My name came from my dad's nickname, Scotty, which came from Skiles. My dad had a solemnity to him. It was almost as if being goofy was forbidden around him. Once, when I was four or five, he took my siblings and me to get some ice cream in Shaker Square. When my dad was a kid, they used to call him Limburger Cheese. We sat there, licking our cones, and they dared me to call him that name. They set me up. When I did, his hand was swift. He popped the shit out of me in my mouth, and I started crying. He dried my eyes and told me that he loved me, but I was wounded. For him it was an occasion to teach me, in his own bruised way, about respect. I never joked with him after that.

My dad could be a more than adequate caretaker for us, but Elsie ran the show—getting us ready for school, dinner, homework—all-purpose mommy, a choir teacher in Cleveland Heights, hustling, running a household. I never heard her complain. Not once. My mom gave up her pursuit of opera when my sister was born. She wanted to be a parent. Some people resent their kids, like they prevented them from realizing their dreams. That was never Elsie. But she was still a diva in her own way. Sometimes she would wear African dashikis and look so regal for something as routine as a parent-teacher conference.

My mom only dated one man after she left my dad, when I was

around seven or eight, but he didn't want to deal with kids, so my mom told him to fuck off. She was loyal to us. She was proud to be a mom.

In the early eighties, a housepainter and a music teacher could raise a family of four in all-right conditions, and we had a solidly middle-class life. But that changed after the separation. We started living a humbler existence in Shaker Heights, a city twenty minutes from Cleveland, Ohio. Our house on Chelton Road wasn't much more than a roof over our heads. My mom and us kids were just trying to survive. We had centipedes and ants everywhere. I would be sitting on the floor watching TV and there would be a juicy black ant crawling on my leg. There would be ants in the drawer when you went to get a spoon for some cereal. Once when I opened a cupboard, there was a dead mouse on a sticky trap. The house was overrun. The basement was the most treacherous. It reminded me of *Home Alone*. All kinds of critters down there.

I got a certain toughness from my parents. A take-no-shit mentality: Stand up for what's right; don't be a pushover; defend yourself; protect people. My parents weren't big-time lawyers or surgeons—not to say they weren't ambitious, but I didn't have lofty aspirations as a model to look to. There was no dream-big outlook to spur my own dreams.

My mom made sure we experienced nice things every once in a while. And that was the coolest shit: that I knew my mom would hold me down within reason and do her best. Every Christmas, I knew I was going to be happy.

There were situations where we got kicked out of a house and we had to live in a hotel for a little bit. I don't think I even knew what was going on. I just thought we were taking a little vacation. It was a modest hotel, but it had a little indoor water park that I played in every day. But despite the bitter truth, my mom provided a level of comfort for us. I never felt that we weren't going to figure it out. She kept the hardships hidden. We just knew our reality, which was a two-bedroom house with five people. My sister had to have a room by herself, and then three boys in one. So it left no room for my mom. She slept on the couch until I was maybe fifteen, and then she finally got a bed, but she put it in the living room. Whenever you walked in the house and looked to the left you saw a bed. That's why my mom never let guests in the house. She would let me bring only my close friends, because we were all fucked up. None of us had suitable situations. There was a shame there.

There wasn't enough food for us, and some nights my mom was missing meals. It was hard for me to stomach, but honestly, if I were a parent in that situation, I would make that sacrifice too. I wouldn't think twice about it: *I can't eat tonight. There's only enough food for the kids. It is what it is.* My mom was such a soldier—my hero then and my hero now.

My mom made us go to church every Sunday. It was a nightmare. I hated going. I hope God has forgiven me for that. I was a child sitting still for a long period of time, listening to things I didn't know about. I didn't have the best Sunday clothes and the people in the churches I went to were super judgmental, always up in everybody's business, always gossiping. It was more of a negative place than a spiritual one. The orthodoxy of religions turned me off. My mom and I used to argue about why I couldn't wear jeans and had to dress up. After a while, my mom stopped asking me to go. But I still believed in Him.

Even though I despised church, I was in there paying attention. And by the time I stopped attending as a teenager, I was a God-fearing man. Our reverend at the time, Reverend Lassiter, used to say a lot of stuff that connected with me about life and struggle and overcoming fears and the devil. Looking back, I'm happy I grew up in the church, because God is always behind me. My faith kept me alive in my darkest hours.

As long as I had a personal relationship with God and I spoke with Him, I felt I didn't need organized religion. Often when I was struggling, I prayed. There were a lot of times I asked God to guide me.

Living in Shaker Heights was like living in any midwestern town. It has an anonymous feel. Only our city was more segregated than most: Shaker is known for being wealthy, yet the five blocks that I grew up on were Section 8 housing. There were only two white families. And that's just how it was on that side of the road. The borderline between Cleveland and Shaker was right there: East 154th and Menlo. It was Chelton, which was my street, Hildana, Ludgate, Pennington, and Menlo. A lot of my childhood was growing up on those five blocks, kickin' it with my friends, going to the playground, getting caught up in all sorts of shit, you know?

My neighborhood friends and I would scurry around the streets, holding the ultimate hide-and-seek tournaments. You hide anywhere within the five blocks and they have to find you. We'd play all day and night. If we weren't playing hide-and-seek, we were playing basketball in friends' backyards. Being a kid meant being adventurous and having that freedom. My mom let me actually experience being a kid. She let me go outside by myself and enjoy myself.

When I entered school, I was forced to come to terms with the ways I was different. In kindergarten, I had a lot of friends, but being around others could be alienating. That was the first time I was around white kids or white people. My friend Charles lived by the school, so we would walk to his house, which was super fly because it had stairs. That muthafucka had multiple floors in that bitch. I was blown away. I was thinking, *I guess white people got money and niggas don't.* I figured that's what it was. I didn't know any better. I felt unlucky, like I was living the most fucked-up way. A bad lot in life. It was at that age I realized I wanted to be successful. I didn't know what I wanted to do yet, but I knew I wanted to take care of my family. It's crazy to put that burden on yourself at five or six years old.

When I saw *Stand by Me* as a kid, I cried at the end. Performing looked like the ultimate job. *These kids get a chance to pretend on a grand scale, make people feel something, and get paid for it. That's a job I would love to have.* I thought entertaining others could be the answer to my problems. I had a feeling it was possible. I imagined it as a way to provide. But it seemed so unrealistic coming from Cleveland, Ohio.

I've had only two real obsessions in my life: music and illustration. I was thinking about becoming a cartoonist a lot when I was a kid. There wasn't anyone funnier than me in the crew, and I was also the most artistic. Nobody could fuck with me when it came to my art or the jokes. I was on fire.

It was at this point that I first began to recognize the potential in the creative process—what it was like to envision something and then manifest that vision. I could feel myself beginning to create realities for myself to inhabit that didn't yet exist, even in simple forms.

In kindergarten at Mercer Elementary, I started drawing, and I noticed that I was pretty good, so I leaned into it more and got better and better. My mom was letting me lead and find what I loved, and then kind of nurturing that. She eventually got me the drawing tools, the airbrush kit, the table easel to airbrush on. She put me in art classes. That's what made me lean into it, because I had a mom that was willing to help me with whatever I needed.

Back in the day, I would pause movies and draw from the frozen frame. Anybody who was born in the eighties, raised in the nineties, remembers that when you paused the movie it didn't keep it still. It kind of moved and flickered with a static outline.

That's how I would draw characters—from movies like *Space Jam*. I think they used my drawing of Daffy Duck for my middle school yearbook. I'd do Ninja Turtles and other TV cartoons. Eventually, I began to build my own comics and cartoons. One of my favorite things to do was create stories and my mom would help me put together books.

That was my outlet back in the day. I was chasing the perfect picture, finding comfort in the process. My teachers knew what I wanted to be. My mom knew what I wanted to be. In school, I'd be pretending to listen, while my head was down, drawing doodles in the margins of my textbooks, on my folders and notebooks, or on my desk. I'd mark things up with the super *S* at every opportunity.

I've always been a creator. I've always been innovative. I always wanted to make something. I always had a boundless imagination. All I ever wanted to do was just explore. They say space is the final frontier, and that imagery resonated with me early—the astronaut floating out in the sea of stars, seeking to plant his flag where no one else has ever been. My true identity lies in those visions of the great beyond: storyteller, traveler, world-builder, Moon Man.

CHAPTER 2

When my siblings and I were kids, we hung out with each other, navigating Chelton and the Shaker world beyond as a unit. That dynamic changed when their teenage years hit. Suddenly they were doing their own thing, so I started spending a lot of time alone, entertaining myself—but when we were younger, we were close. I discovered early on that my own little universe could be found in isolation. And if I wasn't drawing alone, I was soaking in everything the era had to offer me. Music and the fertile grounds of nineties pop culture were both the refuge and incubator through which I discovered the power of creativity.

Video games were one way we found camaraderie. One year, for our birthdays, my mom got us Nintendo. It was an expensive thing— around $150. And that's a lot of money for my mom to be spending on all that when she's got four kids and she's taking care of us on her own, pretty much. I don't know how she did it.

The Super Nintendo came out in 1991, right when I was turning seven. It was a golden age of gaming. I'd amuse myself watching Dean play *Super Mario World*. We'd sit around the TV and escape from our universe into a different one, bonding on each adventure. For a while we were on that, and then we got into Sonic. My cousin had a Sega, so every now and then we would go over there to play. I used to be obsessed. I was maybe eight and *Sonic 2* was the only game I wanted to play. I could only play it at my cousin's house, because my mom was not about to buy two systems.

The speed of the gameplay of *Sonic 2* was unlike anything that came before. You got an adrenaline rush, zooming through the board. Then they added Knuckles. I thought he must have been Sonic's Black friend with dreadlocks. He was badass. I was obsessed. They created an adapter to *Sonic 3* that allowed for a character change and I always played as him. New systems started coming out—PlayStation and Nintendo 64—and I was still playing *Sonic 3*. When the Game Gear was released, it was the only thing I wanted for Christmas. It was $150. "We'll see," my mom said. Every time she went to the store, I was scouting to see if any bags looked like they could have a Game Gear in them, but I never spotted one. I was bummed. When Christmas morning came, it was under the tree.

My brothers and I used to take action figures and G.I. Joes and make imaginary movies—do a whole action sequence in front of the fireplace; there's a big fight and somebody ends up thrown in the fire, and then we'd watch it burn. We were inspired by the movie *Cliffhanger* with Sylvester Stallone, and we'd have a G.I. Joe standing on the edge of the bunk bed and he'd jump off onto a plane. I'd use my eyes as a camera and zoom in. We'd do club scenes and Naughty by Nature would be playing on the speakers.

The mind is the most powerful tool, and when I was playing I was sharpening it. Without even knowing, I was nurturing those instincts, feeding that creative beast inside me. That's how I know it's always been my destiny to make movies, because I used to do that shit as a kid all the time—make an entire film out of things I could find in my room. I was world-building.

My brothers and I bonded as kids, but, as they got older, boys in their teens, they started having other things that they were interested in. Me and Domingo are three years apart. Me and Dean are four. All the imaginative play went away, and I had to cultivate that in myself, but I still had my friends in the street, who I adopted as a family over the years.

When I wasn't outside, I was mostly solitary. I spent a lot of time alone in my room. I would dance in the reflection of my door—I didn't have a mirror—and I would put on music, put on clothes I thought were cool, and pretend I was in my own music video. When I wasn't dancing, I was at my desk drawing. I found it therapeutic. Time would go by and boredom would leave me. I was soothed by the stroke of a pencil. I would sit in my bed and dream about my life, my future, falling in love with a popular girl at school, doing a musical number, dancing around the school with her. It's one of the reasons I still spend so much time by myself. I enjoy my quiet time because at any given moment I could come up with a million-dollar idea. That's exciting. It allows me to plan, and I love to plan.

With my brother Domingo around, quiet time could be difficult to find. He was a confusing nigga. He was the neighborhood bully, always beating somebody up, getting into fights. He was always picking on me at home. His nickname for me was literally Faggot. The verbal and emotional abuse was brutal and relentless. My mom explained to me that he thought he would be the baby of the family, so when I was born, he was not happy. I think he carried that resentment in him. It was as if he always had something against me.

If he wasn't talking shit about me, he was attacking me physically, literally trying to beat me up. But he could also be sweet. If he found out somebody was picking on me, he would rip them apart. He was a contradiction—he loved me and would stand up for me but was controlling. It was like so many abusive relationships. Cyclical, up and down.

Eventually, I discovered that he had been diagnosed as mentally ill and that he wasn't taking his medicine. It was almost like, *No, I'm the only one that can fuck with my brother. Nobody else can fuck with my brother.* It was weird. I didn't understand it. I would think to myself, *You do the same shit.* I lived with the neighborhood bully my whole childhood.

On the opposite end of the spectrum, my sister, Maisha, and I were tight from day one. She loved me because I was a baby. She used to make me push a baby carriage around with her dolls in it. She's always taken care of me. Always been there. Always been a friend to lend an ear. She's really my best friend for real. Of all my siblings, I'm the closest with her.

Of the rest of my family, I only vibed with one cousin on my mom's side, Keanga. She was around my sister's age. She was autistic and nonverbal. She was capable and athletic, learning to skate, among other things, but she always needed assistance. She mostly communicated with sounds, but I understood her. We had a connection. We used to sneak into the kitchen at night and steal carrots out of the fridge.

Carrots, I know, random. But I loved carrots and so did she. She was always playful, and I loved that about her. Her energy matched my own.

Music was a love language in my family, keeping us together and connected. I was being exposed to everything along the soul spectrum because I had older siblings, and my mom, the choir teacher, was putting me on to her shit too. I was getting a taste of all the classic shit: Luther Vandross, Whitney Houston, Tina Turner, the Jackson 5, the Beatles. I was going through my mom's records, and I saw *Abbey Road. Man, what the hell?* I thought. *My mom got this record with these white men on here?* I was confused as hell.

I asked her, "Ma, why you got this?"

"That's the Beatles; boy, you don't know nothing about that," she said.

In my head I was thinking, *I sure as hell don't.* But my mom was plugged in and knew all the good shit. She was like Sister Mary Clarence in *Sister Act.* When that came out, it was my mom's movie. She used to have her students sing the songs.

Sometimes she'd be singing gospel, going all buck wild, singing these crazy-ass notes, and we'd yell, "Ma!" and she would go, "Shut up, niggas; this my house!" That's why I always get excited that I have my own place and my mom's over and she's doing something that gets on my nerves I tell her, "You gotta come on, now. This *my* house."

Before I wanted to be an artist, or had really developed my own taste in music, I recognized Michael Jackson's immense imagination. I saw in him a child that never got to grow up. I felt for him: an extraordinary talent put in an extraordinary position, world-famous before he even had an opportunity to discover who he was, then suddenly he's all things to everyone. We listened to his music as a family. He dropped *Thriller* in '82. I was born in '84. But when a hit record is a hit record, especially back in the day, shit's popping for years. It's not like that anymore.

People forget. You see people talking about new albums after a month or two weeks, and then it goes away. But back in the day, big albums, successful albums, people kept playing them. I got hit with Michael Jackson years later, at four or five years old. It felt like he just came out because it was such a big deal. My mom got *Bad* on tape and it became the standard play when we got in the car. Seeing him doing these incredible feats—as a performer, singer, style icon—made me appreciate the awe-inspiring power of being an entertainer. I never looked at him for a model. He was so impressive he didn't make you think, *Oh, I can do that.* He was superhuman.

The first music I ever heard was the same music ringing out in most households at the time. MC Hammer was a big deal for us. He was a fucking megastar. I rapped his songs all the time at home. I knew one song he did called "It's All Good" word for word.

I was maybe four or five years old when I saw my first music video, watching MTV at home on our floor-model TV, lying on my stomach with my feet kicked up. It was Aerosmith and Run-DMC's "Walk This Way." It wasn't the video that blew my mind; it was hearing Steven Tyler scream and sing, and then Run rap, and then DMC rap. It was the fusion of styles. My brain melted, and it trained me to want to break down any borders that felt restrictive. I thought that was how you were supposed to do it: Be creative, blend genres, cross boundaries. Take shit where people aren't taking it. Music videos are becoming a lost art. My label is always telling me nobody watches them.

Every time I try to do a music video, they never want to. It's always a fight to get a budget. Michael Jackson used to drop videos in prime time after *The Simpsons*. Now no money comes back from a music video, so labels feel like they're burning cash. I'm grateful that I came up in an era that prioritized great visuals. From Missy Elliott to Jay-Z to Busta Rhymes, there was a sense that the videos you made were part of the story you were telling.

One of my favorite movies as a kid was Michael Jackson's *Moonwalker*. My mom had the VHS tape because she would play it at school for her students—she'd often take a movie in with a musical angle and then bring the tape home after. I would rewind his acrobatic moves over and over. He had such an incredible feel for composition and navigating space. The choreography was fucking out of this world. It felt like one of those things that you'd never see again. No other artist will ever do something quite as epic as *Moonwalker*.

He was the greatest in my eyes. A beam of light cutting through culture. He was bigger than life but also had a gentleness that made him seem like a real pure human. There was something sacred about how he spoke to us. When he did the song to the *Free Willy* soundtrack "Will You Be There," I listened to it nonstop. I was on the back porch during summer fucking jamming on the picnic table with my Walkman blasting that shit. (Walkmans were funny, because when the batteries were low they slowed the music down.) I was a student of Michael, and eventually, when I became an artist myself, I tried to emulate the ways he translated his humanity to his audience, the way he crafted himself as a superhero-like figure. He never did his fans bad and I always aspired to be that way. If I ever got some success, I wanted to be like Mike.

Everyone in my house had their own thing musically. Domingo listened to the hood shit like Brotha Lynch Hung, UGK, No Limit, Snoop

Dogg, and Jay-Z. Dean listened to backpack rap: A Tribe Called Quest, the Pharcyde, the Roots, Mos Def. Maisha listened to the R&B of the moment like SWV and Boyz II Men. She was like the fourth member of TLC. She wore guy clothes and Nautica button-downs and baggy jeans and high-top sneakers. She was super "cool nineties girl." She loved New Edition, Al B. Sure!, Tevin Campbell.

I was getting everything mainstream but country. Then Billy Ray Cyrus made his way into my life with "Achy Breaky Heart." That song was huge—a crossover pop hit that became the biggest country song in nearly a decade, going platinum and charting No. 5 on the Hot 100. Even when I was a kid, I thought, *If I had a song like that . . .*

I was mostly soaking in Top 40 radio, but eventually I got to buy my first CD, Crash Test Dummies' *God Shuffled His Feet*. This is 1994. I heard one of the singles in the *Dumb and Dumber* movie, then again on the radio, and I thought to myself, *I need this album.* So I had my mom take me to go get it from Sam Goody at the mall. I listened to it over and over on cassette. I had my Walkman and I also had a boombox. There's still two songs I listen to to this day: the album's title track and "Mmm Mmm Mmm Mmm." That band informed my songwriting, my storytelling: thinking about formatting, character building, and the ways an arc can unfold.

"Mmm Mmm Mmm Mmm" tells three different stories about these children. They go through these experiences, and it feels like somebody's telling you a fable but in melody. I tried to incorporate that structural concept in my first album.

I was as drawn to rock as I was to hip-hop, two sonic worlds that didn't seem as cut off from each other as everyone around me seemed to believe. Listening to both genres made me curious about the various shapes and colors artists can conjure. I would take cassette tapes and put tape over the holes at the bottom so I could record over them and make my own mixtapes. They collected all my favorite songs on the radio. Every time the Celine Dion song "My Heart Will Go On" from *Titanic* came on the radio, I would stop everything and turn it up and just be jamming: "Near, far, whereeeeever you are!" I was a young dude that was so wrapped up in the melody. It was the most beautiful song I'd ever heard. I would never tell my homies that I was bumping Celine Dion at the crib, but she made it to the mixtape.

There were two stations in Cleveland: 93.1 played hip-hop and R&B and 92.3 played Top 40. I was listening to the 92.3 station more because musically it had more to offer. I was obsessed with melody and emotionality, the way a tune could course through you and recalibrate your mood. Domingo would have called me a faggot if he heard me listening to Celine Dion. I was ashamed that I had these interests, so I would always keep this stuff to myself. The only people on the same shit I was on were my little crew.

CHAPTER 3

My childhood was spent trying to reconcile conflicting emotions: humor and sorrow, a yearning for direction and a distaste for authority, being outgoing yet feeling cut off. Enduring isolation made me long for companionship even more, and I was lucky enough to find that in a few close friends and in shared experience through laughter.

I met my best friend Dennis in third grade. Dennis was in the second. I had peanut butter and crackers, because I didn't want to eat the lunch I had. My juice box and my apple had smashed my peanut butter and jelly sandwich, and it was nasty, which is the worst thing. Dennis was at the table eating peanut butter and crackers too and we hit it off. We took the bus home together and discovered we lived on the same street. From that day on, we were hanging out all the time. That was my boy. He was a serious kid. A little fucker at times, but I loved him. He was just a real nigga in a pint-sized body. Around the sixth grade, though, he suddenly became the silliest muthafucka. It's one of those things: You meet somebody as a kid and they become your person. Dennis loved the music I loved and it bonded us. We were always on the same wavelength.

The summer of 1992 we would be outside all the time, day and night. Me, Dennis, DeAndre, Steve, all of us kind of just kickin' it. Steve was this kid that lived on the block with us. His dad didn't take no shit and was always outside looking for him. DeAndre was the athlete in the crew. He played basketball and football, and we would always hoop in his backyard, until his mom kicked me out because she said I was always cursing. We were thick as nails, man. A tight-knit crew. The outcasts of the neighborhood. We were nerds, roller-blading together through construction sites and attempting tricks off shit.

I always wanted to take care of people—take care of my friends and be the provider. I don't need much to make myself happy. I'm always shopping and buying some shoes and shit—but I don't need those things. As long as my family is cool, my loved ones are cool, my friends, I'm straight. That's all that matters. It's always been like that. When I get money, I spend so much on those around me because I can't be the only one experiencing this.

At school, I was pretty popular. I was a goofy kid. One thing I always did, something I do to this day, was quote lines from movies and TV shows. *Wayne's World* came out and I was obsessed. Amazing performances and characters. My teacher at the time, Mrs. Lanham, loved the Mescudis. She had two of my other siblings in class before me, but I was her favorite. I asked her, "Can me and Jeremy after class do a little skit that we have?"

"What is the skit?" she asked.

"It's *Wayne's World*."

"Sure!" she said.

So after recess she let us get in front of the class and do these skits where I'd be Wayne and Jeremy would be Garth. We'd be up there riffing in character. It was the first time a teacher supported my goofiness and the performer side of me. My classmates loved it and that was my debut as an entertainer, feeling what it was like to make people laugh. It was infectious. The class clown Scott was born.

I was always emulating something that I saw on *In Living Color*. Fire Marshall Bill was the shit. The character had *Ace Ventura* vibes. Seeing Jim Carrey and all them guys—Jamie Foxx and the Wayans siblings—I thought, *Man, these niggas is magical.* Those dudes are once-in-a-lifetime talents—that came at the same time! And I witnessed it. I was raised on it. We came together as a family to watch that show. That was the greatest comedy, and it was my education. My taste level was so out there because I was soaking up the work of the masters.

Out of all the great comedians of the nineties, Jim Carrey was my god. He could do no wrong in my eyes. When I saw *Ace Ventura* in 1994, I actually shed tears laughing my ass off. I feel lucky to have come up when I did, in the eighties and the nineties. It was a golden age of popular culture and art. The era made Scott *Scott*, and consequently made Kid Cudi *Kid Cudi*. The endless pool of inspiration I have in my mind ultimately comes from this era, all nineties influenced and grungy, that energy.

Nickelodeon, *Saturday Night Live*—those types of things fueled my desire to want to be an actor. I would see the neighborhoods on Nickelodeon shows and I would think, *Damn, I want to live in a neighborhood like that with a cul-de-sac. That'd be so fire.* With *Saturday Night Live*, I discovered Adam Sandler and Chris Farley and Phil Hartman and Tim Meadows and David Spade. These guys were my heroes. They were in their twenties. That era of comedy rocked my soul. When I was thirty-eight years old, I even got a Chris Farley tattoo.

It was goofy shit. Absurd. In your face. I loved how much it relied on hijinks and mischief, how little it took itself seriously. Especially Adam Sandler. That muthafucka was goofy as hell. And he's still goofy—that's what I love about him. He still does his brand of comedy and has his friends involved. He does his thing, gets his check, keeps his head down. It's a beautiful thing to get a chance to be silly and get paid for it.

When *Billy Madison* came out in '95, it immediately became my favorite movie ever. My friends and I would talk about it in the cafeteria, laughing our asses off, quoting it left and right. I knew Adam Sandler was going to be my favorite actor for the rest of my life. Straight up and down, this nigga is the coolest. He was already big bro from *Saturday Night Live*, so he became the ultimate big bro with this. The juvenile, stupid nature of *Billy Madison* was the best shit. It was the dumbest humor and I loved it. Something about it resonated with me.

That slapstick energy has always been a part of my life, and, as I was discovering comedy, life would sometimes imitate art. When I was about seven, I accidentally pissed in my mouth. Back when I was younger, I would always try to hold it. When you're a kid you're holding it and then suddenly it hits you: *Fuck, I gotta go now.* I pulled my pants down and my penis was sticking up and I pissed and it went straight up. It was a total disaster. I had to gargle with soapy water. My babysitter at the time had to call the poison agency. She was watching me and that was embarrassing. But I was only a kid, still trying to figure things out down there.

At eight years old I was already starting to think about my life as an adult and the career I wanted to have. I wanted to be a cartoonist. I used to draw pictures of Ninja Turtles and sell them to my classmates for fifty cents apiece, and it was one dollar for something front and back. I would come home with mad money after school and get me and my friends candy and shit. I was on my hustle, trying to get this money.

As I was learning the power of performance and illustration, it became clear pretty early that academics likely wouldn't be the path for me. Just as humor is often considered lowbrow and simple, my jokester nature left me unfairly mistaken for a half-wit. When I got to the second grade, I had a teacher named Ms. Smith, a Black lady with a little Jheri curl. I was having a hard time with the assignment one day—a pop quiz on multiplication—and I raised my hand for help. She was working through it with me and I was still having trouble. She asked me what the answer was, and I gave her the wrong one.

She said, "Are you stupid? You do this, this, and this and you get this answer." I felt so low. I came home and I told my mom. The next day, she dropped me off at school. Now, mind you, the elementary school was about thirty-five minutes away from where we lived. It was way, way the opposite direction of where my mom had to go to work. So she made herself late that day to take me to school. I was down the hallway and couldn't hear what was said, but I saw my mom going off on Ms. Smith. The teacher looked shook. My mom came up to me after that and said, "Have a good day, baby, I'll see you when I get home."

Ms. Smith didn't say shit. I felt like I had support after that, that somebody had my back: my mom. But the idea that I was stupid was planted in my mind and I carried that through the rest of my time in school: Second grade, all through high school, I thought I was an idiot because of Ms. Smith. I never applied myself in school, and that was a big reason why.

■ ■ ■

As one authority figure in my life had shaken my confidence, another seemed just out of reach to reassure me: my dad. I wanted more of a relationship with him than I had. He would watch us on weekends and come pick us up from school sometimes. When he wasn't with us, I don't know what he was up to. I didn't know much of his life, and that was always weighing on me. When I would leave my dad's house, I would look out the window as I drove away and see him standing there. He'd wave good-bye, then walk back into his apartment. I'd be like, *I wonder what my dad is going to do right now.* It was always a big mystery. When I would be out with him, there would always be some woman coming up to him like, "Hey, Scotty, how you doing? I don't see you out no more." They'd walk up to him in the street showing him love. He wasn't necessarily removed from us, but he never felt particularly close either.

Movies remained a lifeline. My dad would rent them and rip them to blank VHS tapes. It was one of my favorite things. He would always get the newest movies, and then when I would come over to his place he would have them on tape so I could take them home. My dad had all the cool little electronic hookups. He had a laser disc too, that was fucking gnarly. You had to flip that bitch over to get to the second half of the movie. When he gave me the *Teenage Mutant Ninja Turtles* movie, I must've watched it a million times. Those VHS tapes were one of the ways I stayed most connected to him.

The rest of us carried on as a unit with my dad floating off on the periphery. A few times, we took trips together as a family. I went to New York City when I was a kid still in the stroller, so I don't remember that; in '94, we drove to North Carolina for my uncle Bey's wedding; and then we went to Disneyland once when I was sixteen. We went to Disneyland because my mom's job was taking her there. She was doing some type of retreat with teachers. She brought me with her. It was the first time I flew on a plane. I was scared shitless.

Of those few trips beyond Cleveland's borders, South Carolina resonated most. It was extremely hot and country. But it was a lot of fun, seeing something other than Shaker Heights. We saw a lot of open road. I spent a lot of the time looking out at the mountains, daydreaming. There were no devices to play on, and you couldn't watch a movie. You pretty much sat in the car and chilled. I always loved road trips because of that. It was some of the best times. I played little games in the car with my brothers as the Boyz II Men album *II* played on repeat for most of the drive.

South Carolina felt a world away. In the hotel, I was eating with my siblings and this guy came up to my sister and asked, "Does your food taste like gun smoke?" in a thick southern accent. We were like, *What the fuck?* My sister didn't even know how to respond. How would we even know what gun smoke tastes like? That was the most country shit I'd ever heard in my life. I got a Davy Crockett hat as a memento from the souvenir shop as we were leaving. That was my prized possession for a while.

Back at home, things were more mundane, and run-ins with toxic disciplinarians continued to damage my view of authority figures. When I was ten years old, I was introduced to this bitch-ass nigga named Lieutenant Tompkins. He was a Black cop in the Shaker Heights police district, and he was the most fucked-up nigga you could think of.

One day in fifth grade, I was coming home from school on the bus. There was a rule to keep the aisle clear, but at that age kids rarely listen. I was leaning over the seat talking to my friends behind me when the bus pulled over to the side of the street for like ten minutes.

I went up to the front and I was like, "Hey, why'd we stop?"

The bus driver said, "'Cause I called the police. They're coming for you. Because you don't know how to follow instructions."

What the fuck? "What did I do wrong?"

"You were standing in your seat and I told you sit down."

The driver had told me to sit down, and she told another kid to sit down, but we're kids. It's not like you've gotta call the police on us. It was a Black lady too, which was disappointing. So I go to my seat and wait. I'm like, *What the fuck is going on? What is this?* Next thing I know, bitch-ass Lieutenant Tompkins walks on. The bus driver pointed to me: "There he is right there."

I stand up.

He said, "So you don't want to follow instructions, huh?"

He pushed me. I told him not to touch me.

"So you don't want to listen when people tell you what to do. You wanna stand up in your seat."

He kept pushing me. I tried to get up and he pushed me into the seat. Every time I kept trying to get up, he kept pushing me down and pushing me down and pushing me down to the seat. I was helpless. He was a grown-ass man and I was a kid. He towered over me.

Finally, he grabbed me up and got me off the bus.

My mom picked me up from the police precinct and she checked his ass. She always had my back. But I knew I was gonna see him again. I had to watch my back for that muthafucka. It was the first of many cases in which I was unfairly branded a troublemaker. I wasn't one; I was simply a carefree spirit looking to goof around, and I wasn't given the space to do so. Far too often it felt like adults weren't being patient with me, at a time when a young person needs guidance but also the freedom to learn and grow from their mistakes. I coveted the security of being watched over without reprimand, but instead my path would get much harder.

CHAPTER 4

End of '94, beginning of '95, it was all bad. My father was getting very sick with pancreatic cancer in August and my mom had to step up. She would go over to his place and check in on him, bring him food, clean him up. I often prayed to God that I would find one woman in my life that would take care of me on my deathbed, if, God forbid, I got sick or something like that happened to me. I prayed that He would bring me someone who could be that loyal like my mom was.

After the divorce, they spoke, but it's not like they were talking. It was uplifting to see her step up like that. *Damn, my mom is a ride-or-die.* Her efforts put things in perspective for me. *That's what I need when I grow up. Even if a woman becomes my ex-wife, she's still holding me down.* That's the real shit. It don't get realer than that, bro. My mom was our eternal anchor through the storm.

During my dad's cancer journey, I was having a real hard time in school. I'd be in class and just break down crying. Sometimes I'd come to school in tears. The day I found out my dad was sick, I was crying next to my locker. My teacher Ms. Johnson came up to see what was going on and I told her, "My dad is dying. He's probably not going to make it through summer." She comforted me. That was a rough year. The hardest part was knowing that I was eventually never going to see my father ever again, and having to face that reality as the months went on. I was worried that I would forget him, that I wouldn't remember his voice. If I heard it now, I'm not sure I'd know it. You're not supposed to have to face death that young, especially of a parent. I was living with this wound on my heart. Over the years, it gradually healed, but the scar remains.

I was looking for any refuge from the misery of home life. Ms. Johnson was my favorite teacher. I had a huge crush on her. She was twenty-five, Black, and fly. Fit. Kind of tall. She gave off supermodel vibes, and I thought that she was so ill. What was crazy was that she lived on the street behind me. Sometimes I would pretend I needed help with homework and I'd go to her house after school and wait for her to come home to work with me. Just so I could smell her perfume. Or hear her voice. I loved Ms. Johnson. She was everything.

One day she was giving me a ride home and the Raphael Saadiq song "Ask of You" played on the radio. She said, "Oh my god, Scott, this is my song," and she turned it up and started grooving to it. I'd never heard it before, but in that moment, it was me and Ms. Johnson's song: "Ask of You" by Raphael Saadiq. To this day I always remember that song as being our song.

I needed those distractions. As things were getting worse with my dad, I was trying to pretend like there wasn't anything wrong. I was confused. He was sick for about a year and a half. I didn't realize my dad was truly dying until he got into hospice. My mom explained to me what that was: a place people went in their final days. It leveled me. My dad was so sick that he couldn't even speak. I tried to act like it wasn't happening.

When we went to hospice to visit him, I would go into the TV room and watch Nickelodeon. We didn't have cable at home at the time, so I'd zone out in there. I didn't have anyone to talk to about what I was feeling. I was broken, as if half of me was dying alongside my dad. My mom was comforting, but I didn't know how to articulate the ways it was affecting me. I was in denial, and as his death approached I was at school having emotional fits. I couldn't contain the pain anymore.

After two weeks in hospice, my dad died. It was the summer of '95. My sister handled the funeral. She was eighteen. She took it especially hard because she had the best relationship with my dad. For weeks after he died she would break out into shakes for hours. She was trembling through the whole funeral. I was eleven. It felt like my grief existed in the shadow of hers. I couldn't mourn how I wanted to mourn. I wanted to think about him more. I wanted to dwell on what he meant to me, and my new reality without him. I didn't because life around me was going on. There wasn't enough time. *I gotta be strong and be a little soldier because other people are going through it.*

The funeral was in this church that I grew up in called United Church of Christ. Everything was white, including my dad's casket, which was closed. I sat there feeling hurt because I knew that I would never see the man in that casket again. The last image I had of him was this gnarly one of him at the fucking funeral home. It fucked me up. I just kept thinking, *Damn, my dad is dead. I'm only eleven years old.*

Not long after he died, I started having night terrors. They were unsettling dreams about my dad's corpse. When everybody was viewing the body at the funeral home, I said I didn't want to see, but I wandered by out of curiosity and peeked into the room when nobody was looking. I had spent so much time denying the inevitable. I needed to confront my new truth. We didn't have the money to get the best mortician, so it didn't look like him. The cancer took him. That image of his face traumatized me. It gave me intense nightmares. I started to also think about my mom dying, being worried about her, feeling like I would lose two parents.

In the fall of '95 I was transitioning into the sixth grade. I had this teacher, Mrs. Lane, this Black lady who was friends with my mom. She looked after me and treated me like I was the favorite. She made me feel special at a time when I needed someone to attend to me. If I was struggling in class, she was there to give me help. The summer before I started class with her, she was giving my mom extra math assignments that I could do to get ready for school. She's the auntie I never had as a teacher. I didn't fuck around in her class. I didn't give her a hard time. I didn't give Ms. Johnson a hard time either. Two Black ladies. I had a lot of Black teachers, actually. There was often this respect factor. They cared about me: *You Elsie's son. I'm going to look after you.*

The year kept dealing me blows. Long before my dad's death, my uncle Bey had gotten clean off crack. He got his life together, moved to South Carolina, married this woman, got her pregnant, and finally had his life in order. He became a reverend and everything. Then he got cancer. So fucked up. He would still be alive to this day. He was the baby of the family, and my mom was the oldest. So it's the same dynamic with me and my sister.

My mom wouldn't let us go to the funeral, because we would've had to fly. We couldn't afford to have all of us go down there and we couldn't drive like before. I only knew my uncle when I was a kid and then he moved away. I didn't see him at all after that, really. He was the coolest, most fun uncle ever. It's one of the reasons why I pride myself on being Uncle Scott. I wanted that title: the Coolest Uncle. I wanted all my nieces and nephews to know that I was the uncle of all uncles. He used to pick us up and be playing Bobby Brown, bumping it loud as fuck. He was the smoothest muthafucka. Super handsome. He was the best uncle in the universe. His death felt catastrophic. I wasn't even close to recovering from my dad's passing.

The year after that, my favorite cousin, Keanga, died during the school year. She was maybe twenty-one and out of nowhere had a brain hemorrhage. Just like that. Gone.

I was brokenhearted. We drove down to Mississippi for the funeral. The cloud that had been looming over my head was growing. I started crying in Dean's arms. "Why does this keep happening to us?" I repeated. Three years in a row. Three people gone. People I loved. People that meant the most to me in my family. It was dark. I was making sure I was spending time with my friends to cope with things and keep my mind off shit, but it was hard not to lash out and be an angry kid at school.

I was still just being a kid, kind of pretending my dad's death didn't happen, trying to enjoy my childhood, going about my life. I would go to sleepaway camps. My mom did a computer camp that I would go to. She was a computer teacher on the side at Roxboro Middle School for a couple years. So we would always have the newest computers. It was the illest shit about her job because she got the latest Apple products to stay up on tech so she could teach the kids. It was absurd: We were living in this fucked-up-ass house with this fancy-ass Macintosh. I used it mostly for games. I mean, this is the nineties. What else can you do? There's no internet.

Experiencing so much death as a kid darkened my soul. It felt like I was always thinking about death, about losing people, about my mom dying, about my own demise. I had a phobia of dying in a car accident. I thought that it was some kind of prophetic vision. I had no real reason to think that would happen, but death suddenly was everywhere, so I was faced with the prospect of my own mortality.

Around that time, I started to write my first poems—mostly about my father and being a fatherless child. I felt lost without his guidance. It was the perfect way for me to express what I was feeling at the time.

I went into overdrive. When I got dark, the comedy turned up. It kept me from completely falling. I started to become more of a disruption, not paying attention to my work and failing classes. Over the years, I just got worse. But comedy is what kept me from sinking into my darkness. I loved making people laugh and just having that escape. I returned to my refuge of movies. I'd escape into *Bill & Ted* or *Tommy Boy*.

A simple conversation with someone at home might have gone a long way at the time. But I think the trauma of those losses, the pain of it—there was nothing that could have really healed that wound. There was a gaping hole in my heart, and talking about what I was feeling would have reminded me of the pain. I needed real therapy. I needed somebody outside of the situation to sift through it. I didn't have an outlet to express myself, and have somebody ask the right questions, poke a little bit. My mom's not a therapist, so she's only gonna go so far. She said all the right things. She told me that everything was going to be OK, and that my dad was in a better place. But that shit didn't make me feel better.

Before the deaths, I sort of related to being alone in my imagination.

But after the deaths I started to fear it. After my father died, being alone became much more difficult for me. As much as I would try to sweep it under the rug, it would linger. The actual thought wouldn't be in my mind, but the mood was present: the sadness. It was like that for the first couple years and then it began to feel like a permanent fixture in my life: I mastered the art of bottling up those feelings and got back into being a kid. I'd known my dad as a serious disciplinarian. Suddenly he was gone. There wasn't anyone who could teach me how to be a man.

CHAPTER 5

Transitioning into middle school in the wake of so many deaths left me searching. For consolation. For company. For a sense of self.

A new setting meant new challenges but also a new opportunity to stand on a new stage. I entered this phase lost and isolated, but I started to find comfort in comedy and performance, in the craft of eliciting a reaction. Showmanship was my release.

When I went into the seventh grade at my mom's school, Roxboro Middle School, there were only two options: You were either in the choir or in band. And my mom was a choir teacher. I didn't want to be in her class, so I forced myself to learn an instrument. I picked up the trumpet because my older brother Dean played. Back in those days, I was still trying to be like him. I was still that younger brother that was thinking, *Oh, my older brother did this. I think that's cool.* I was having a hard time learning the sheet music, and so the teacher went and told my mom, "Hey, Scott is about to fail. It might be better if he's in your class," and they switched me.

I was so stressed out being in my mom's class. I sat in the back of the classroom and kept my head down, pretending that wasn't my mom up there. Sometimes my mom would proposition me: If I sang a solo in the school concert, she would buy me some Jordans. She was always trying to get me to sing a solo. One time, she had me come down in the middle of class and sing for everybody. I can't remember what song it was. But I couldn't perform in front of them, so I had to turn my back to everybody and sing. When I was done, everybody was clapping and cheering. But it was a wild experience. I wasn't nervous or anxious, because I felt confident with my solo and I felt confident that I was gonna get those shoes. I'd never had anyone praise me for something I did. *People think I'm good. Holy shit.*

One year, I performed "I Believe I Can Fly" at a school concert. I fucking sang my little soul out. I got a standing ovation. It was the first show I ever did, and the first time I saw a real audience cheer for me. Just imagine, ninety-pound Scott up there: "I think about it every night and day / Spread my wings and fly away. . . ."

As my mom was helping me embrace my inner entertainer, I was still looking for ways to define my masculinity. Despite being small for my age, I went out for the wrestling team. I was terrible, but I thought it would teach me some discipline. My art teacher, Mr. Holiday, was also the wrestling coach, and he was a mentor to me.

He told me, "Yeah, you should join to teach you some things."

I was thinking, *Well, Mr. Holiday is the man, the man of all men, so let me just follow his lead on this and maybe this can teach me how to be tough.* And it did. It toughened me up. But even more so, it made me realize that sports wasn't my calling.

I only won one match. We were at Wiley Middle School in Cleveland Heights. This kid was whupping my ass. He was throwing me around. You get points for escaping and shit, so I was getting points from breaking out, but he was taking it to me. All of a sudden they stopped the match. We were standing there, the ref holding both of our hands, and he lifted my arm up. I was looking confused: *What the fuck—this dude been handing it to me this whole fight; what the hell is going on? How did I win this?* We found out that the dude was not in my weight class. He was twenty pounds heavier than me. He lost because he cheated. That's how that kid was handling me. But that's the only match I won. It seemed clear that machismo was not my path.

My mom was the one who linked me up with Mr. Holiday for private art lessons. She knew I was drawing a lot and she knew that it would be a great thing for me to be connected with him. I would meet with him outside of class at the school and work on cartoons. Then when I went to Roxboro, I had him as a teacher, and it was the best experience ever. He was the coolest muthafucka, man. He had a young spirit. His swag was unbelievable. It was two teachers that I had in my life that had crazy swag. Later, there was Mr. Hutch. But with Mr. Holiday, it was the way he carried himself. He was more like an uncle giving you guidance than a teacher. The way he talked. His mannerisms. He was so laid-back. He was a fucking character.

I had begged my mom and sister to give me some dope-ass clothes. That was the first Christmas I wasn't asking for toys. I asked for Tommy Hilfiger and Nautica. I wanted these hiker Timbs and my sister got them for me. I was so geeked when I went back to school after Christmas break, because that's when niggas pull out all the new shit that they got during the holiday and stunt for two weeks after.

I was so excited to come back—to be stuntin' hard. Because I knew niggas ain't got the fucking hiker Timbs. Niggas ain't got the fucking corduroy khakis with the navy-blue Tommy Hilfiger fleece with the Tommy sign on the chest. It was a whole fit. I was super fucking swagged out with the Nautica polo plaid button-down with the fucking baggy jeans and some Jordans.

I used to watch Martin and Fresh Prince and the Wayans brothers, and I thought, *Yo, these muthafuckas is always fresh in the muthafuckin' house. These niggas is too fresh.* So I always told myself, *When I get money, I want to start my day being too fitted.* During the day, I ain't going nowhere and I'm dripping. If somebody saw me right now, they would go, "Oh, this nigga's fit is crazy." I got that from them. I want my life to feel like a sitcom—super fresh at all times in a ballin'-ass house like the Fresh Prince for real.

Years later, I got my first job at Wendy's because I wanted to buy fly-ass clothes. My mom was still trying to put me in Old Navy. I thought, *Something's gotta give. We gotta switch it up.* If Mom's buying the clothes, we stuck. So I got a job to be able to take care of myself. My first check, I bought this Sean John outfit (much more on him later)—this gray shirt with the rubber Sean John logo, and some dark baggy denim blue jeans. I loved wearing that shit in school. The pants were way too big for me. They had this gap in the front. But that was the style.

■ ■ ■

At Roxboro, there were a lot more Black students. It was much cooler. The students were just good kids. I made a lot of friends that year. It's a shame I lost touch with everybody I went to school with there. I had some good buddies.

One time, in my mom's class, this kid was talking shit to her. I had to stand up and go, "Yo, what the fuck? Who the fuck are you talking to?"

My mom went, "Nope, nope, nope, Scott."

I was like, "Nah, fuck that. Who are you talking to, nigga? You know that's my mom." He ain't say shit at all.

My mom told him to leave the room and he did. She was stressed out that I said something, but I said, "No, fuck that; you're not gonna tell me to shut up when this nigga is acting like this. He knows you're my mother and he's my age. I will whoop his ass right here."

He was in the same row as me and all I had to do was walk down and that was the next step if he said anything. That nigga wasn't trying to hear it. As soon as I said something, he ain't say shit at all. That whole class was silent. Like, *Oh shit, Scott got the juice in front of his mom.* I was cursing and everything, like so what? I don't give a fuck if my mom there, nigga. What's she going to do, put me on punishment? I'm in seventh grade. She can't give me no whooping no more. My mom used to give me jailhouse beatings—not so often, but often enough that it kept me straight. Just knowing that if you did something bad there would be a repercussion was a scary thought. But that shit came to an end one day when I grabbed the belt, took that bitch out of her hand, threw it across the room, and said, "Stop." She said, "I'm tired of this shit. I ain't about to have a heart attack beating these kids. These kids too grown."

And grown was how I was feeling. Maturing meant becoming more independent, which came with self-confidence, personality, style, and the pursuit of manhood and romance. That was when I started to like girls. This one girl used to come to school wearing these sundresses. She looked so pretty to me. I would sit in class and stare at her legs. It's that age where you are experiencing your body and feeling things: *Oh, I get an erection if I just think about this girl's leg.* I was thinking sexual thoughts. Things got real, and the fantasies got a little bit more extreme.

In an effort to attract the finer sex, I harnessed performance skills I'd sharpened in school to entertain the girls I was into—singing Ginuwine's "So Anxious," or some 112 song, or some other R&B song. Sing it to them, put on the show, and then just laugh. Any time I got a girl, I got her because she fell in love with my goofball side. The icing on top was that I happened to be cool and, to them, good-looking—thank God. I was a hopeless romantic. To me, performing a song was a way to profess my love.

My first real girlfriend was in eighth grade: It was this girl named Ashley. In seventh grade, it was all innocent. It was simply that you liked a girl. I wasn't having sex. It was more adolescent: I got a boner, but not, *Oh, I'm gonna stick it in her vagina.* I knew I was horny and was thinking, *I want to make out with her, maybe.* That was the exciting thing for me with girls. I would sigh and go, "I haven't French-kissed a girl in like months. I can't wait to French-kiss a girl again." It was all about French-kissing a girl, the excitement behind it.

When I dated Ashley, she was a new girl in school. She was accepting of all my quirkiness. We dated for a little bit, but I broke up with her because I heard that she was gonna break up with me for this other dude. I thought, *Fuck that. You not about to hit me with the whoopty whoop. Let me get out of this before she comes to me with the bullshit.*

I broke up with her and then she asked me why and eventually I told her. She said it wasn't true, but she eventually started dating the dude I thought that she was gonna break up with me for. It was cool, though. I ain't have no beef with Ashley. We became close friends, actually. She was my first real homegirl. Part of maturing and becoming a man is learning that your first love isn't necessarily the one.

When it came to masculinity, I had a clear model: my Advanced English teacher, Mr. Hutch, who was the swaggiest muthafucka. He was a young Black man teaching in a white school district coming to school wearing white-and-blue Jordan 13s. I'd never met a teacher like him. Even his teaching approach: His demeanor was very real nigga. He was the type to put a big F at the top of your paper, and then write a paragraph about how he was disappointed in you in a red Sharpie. He believed in us as students and wanted us to be the top versions of ourselves. His motto was "Be the best." That simple idea wedged its way somewhere deep inside me, and it's part of why I still always push myself with my work, or anything I'm doing. In some way I owe my illness and my confidence to Mr. Hutch.

Mr. Hutch's motto stuck with me, but his words were constantly competing with those ingrained in me years earlier by Ms. Smith in second grade: that I was stupid. I wanted to be a better student. I wish I didn't think I was so dense. I didn't want to apply myself, because I didn't think I was good enough. Ms. Smith's bitch ass had poisoned any hopes of me becoming more of a scholar. My report card told the story: failing, failing, failing.

I just chose my moments to pay attention. I wanted to graduate and get by. I never wanted to flunk out. I didn't study as hard as I could have. I was getting into trouble and going to detention, having to be there all day. Eighth grade was whatever. I was ready to go to high school. But even if middle school hadn't been all I'd hoped for, amidst the hardships I'd begun to find my place. My confidence was growing, my style was budding, and my creative instincts were sharpening. A duality of spirit was coming into focus: outwardly easygoing but inwardly haunted.

CHAPTER 6

Two Scotts were emerging. I appeared fun loving, happy, and sociable, but at my core, I was deeply depressed. When I was in school, I loved being around my friends. I loved making people laugh. I was just on. Being in crowds, dealing with people face-to-face, that was when I felt somewhat normal. But when I would be alone in my room at night, the sadness would surface and overtake me. I thought something was wrong with me, but I was suppressing it. I got good at wearing a mask. And in the Black community, then and now, there is a stigma around mental health. There was no getting a therapist. They'd simply put you on Ritalin or some other medication. I didn't want to be a burden to my family, because they already had it hard enough, so I was minimizing my pain: *My shit is not that deep. I'll deal with it. I'll be OK.*

All in all I was a good kid. I was cool with everybody—the jocks, the skater kids, the nerds, the theater kids, the goth kids, Black, white, Asian, all sorts of backgrounds. I didn't really belong to any one group. I was an outsider, which made me adaptable. A lone ranger, rolling to the beat of my own drum.

I wanted to find my tribe, and high school seemed like the perfect place. I was excited to start ninth grade at Shaker Heights High School. It was a whole world of new opportunities.

On the first day, I was walking in the hallway when I saw somebody—a familiar fucking face. He turned around and said, "Mr. Mescudi, we ain't gon' have no trouble this year, are we?"

It was Tompkins.

"Nah," and I walked right past that nigga. I couldn't stand it. *This muthafucka*, I thought. *I got to deal with this muthafucka. He's security at my school now? This nigga is the worst.* I was always ducking Tompkins, who was always around, lurking.

Not even Tompkins could keep the pleasures of adolescence at bay. In the summer of ninth grade, going into tenth grade, I lost my virginity. Summer of love, baby. It was a nice warm, sunny summer day. It was around 7:00 p.m. I met up with Vanessa. Her dad's not home. It's the perfect time. She lived ten minutes down the street, walking. She's playing Drag-On's "Down Bottom" on repeat in the next room, and that was the song that set the scene. I went straight to it. She took off her pants. We kissed. She took off her panties. She didn't give me head or anything, and I didn't go down on her. We weren't doing that yet. That was a scary-ass notion. Niggas used to say "you pussy-eating-ass nigga" and you'd be wanting to fight. I put on a condom not knowing how to put on a condom—putting it on regular without pinching the top. She bent over and I started having sex with her and after, I'd say, four strokes the condom broke. I went, "Oh!!" and I pulled out.

I told her, "I'm done," out of fear that I got her pregnant. I was so scared. I asked her, "Can you walk me home?"

As she was walking me home, I was thinking, *Oh my god, I got her pregnant. I got her pregnant. Oh my god. I know there's such a thing as pre-cum, and I know that I've got pre-cum inside her. I'm fucked.*

I was talking to her, and I said, "You know, there's places you can go to anonymously to talk about abortion."

I was super scared that at fifteen years old I'd got some girl pregnant. She said, "Yeah, I heard stuff like that."

That was an awkward walk home, because I kept thinking about her getting pregnant and then it was a wrap for my life. She eventually got pregnant a couple of years later, but it wasn't by me.

The second time I had sex was with this girl named Aaliyah. We went into the bathroom inside the small auditorium at school, and I sat on the toilet and she sat on top of me. It was one of those times when I figured it was a good thing I kept a condom in my pocket. The sex was way better than the first time. That was the first time I actually nutted. And I put the condom on right this time. It was exciting because we were in the middle of the school doing something we shouldn't have been doing. My shirt got wet in the toilet. I don't even think Aaliyah knows that she was only the second girl I had sex with, but I thought she was so beautiful. It wasn't just her looks that made her beautiful. She had a spirit about her. I was in love with her, but I don't know if I could have dated her. She liked the jocks. She was one of those hot girls that hung with the popular kids in school. I don't think I was Dating Material. I was kind of a cool nerd, but I was no athlete, and that's who got the chicks in school.

There was this other Black girl named Cheney who I also obsessed over. Super sexy, oh my god. She was stunning. To be in high school and to look this good—it didn't make sense. She looked like a fly-ass, grown-ass woman in her twenties. She was only sixteen or seventeen. She was a grade older than me. Every dude in school—every jock, all the little fly popular dudes—they were all hollering at Cheney. I knew I didn't stand a chance. But in study hall, I wrote her letters and shit. We'd talk there and write back and forth.

In Ohio, we have our own special day called Sweetest Day, the third Saturday in October. It's like another form of Valentine's Day, and in our school you could get carnations for somebody. You could send the flowers anonymously or you could let them know who you are. I sent her a bunch of carnations. She was so happy and wrote me a little letter thanking me. I thought to myself, *Oh my god. Cheney wrote me a letter. She liked the carnations. Oh my god.* I was crushing on her mad hard, but she was way out of my league. There was no way in hell this beautiful older girl was fucking with a freshman boy. All them senior niggas were on her. Dudes with cars. It was not happening.

I reconnected with a girl named Penny Chang in high school. We'd met at elementary school when we were younger, and at Shaker I would see her in the library. She would always try to hook me up with her homegirl. I was never interested, but Penny and I had a great relationship. She had a calm, even energy. She was obsessed with the Spice Girls and I thought that was ridiculous. I mean, they were hot, but c'mon. I thought that was the cool thing about her, though: She didn't give a fuck what anybody thought about that, or anything else. She was just herself.

One day, I was walking to school with my buddies Damon and Charlie. We were walking past the library, cutting through, walking past the side lawn, about to cross the tracks, and then we saw something that looked like a body face down on the ground.

We were about to walk close up on it, and the police came out of nowhere. "Step back! Step back!" We were like, *Yo, what the fuck is going on?*

Somebody had been killed. I thought, *Holy shit.* They let us go around, but they had caught whoever it was that did it. They had tackled that muthafucka. It's crazy, because the police station was literally one hundred yards away. It was right there.

Later that day, they announced over the PA that somebody had been shot. It was Penny Chang. The whole school was rocked. The school district reached out to other school districts to have teachers come and console students, and my mom was one of the teachers from Cleveland Heights that came and talked to some of the students. I don't think I ever coped with that. At that point, my relationship with death had morphed into a sort of "it happens" type shit. But I was still heartbroken by the news. I protected myself from death by figuring, *Well, they're in a better place. Heaven is a much better spot than this shithole.* That was my mindset.

It came out that Penny was killed by the dude that was stalking her. Super deranged. I hope that muthafucka never gets out of jail. If I have another daughter, I want to name her Penny.

Her death haunted the school. I had to walk past the scene of the murder every day. Even to this day when I'm in Cleveland I drive past that train station and think about Penny. It's a stained image that can't be blotted out.

Another person in my life gone. It only fed the aches inside me. Retreating further into the darkness forced me to turn to my usual coping mechanism. At home, in school, trying to lighten the mood was my natural reaction to negative things. That's why I became such a goofy dude. But high school was when I became the goofiest. Sixteen years old, Black, no father figure—it's rough. Outside of a few teachers, no positive male influence, really. No respect for authority, especially with the police, with whom I'd already had a few run-ins, all of which were unpleasant. But I made sure to stay around friends.

Loss makes you want to find people to latch on to. I would adopt outside people to take the place of an auntie or uncle or cousin or a brother or sister because I didn't have that many strong relationships with my outside family like that. I always wanted an aunt that I was cool with or that was there for me in ways that every kid wants. A grandmother that was cooking Sunday dinners and all that.

This young woman, Vita, who lived across the street became my aunt, and her daughter Arielle, who was, maybe, twelve, became my little sister. They lived with Vita's mom, Nan, who was the sweetest old lady. Always in there watching the news. She never had a problem giving up the TV so we could watch pay-per-view wrestling. Back then we were into The Rock, so we'd be watching him all the time on Sunday nights.

I could always count on Vita. There would be days where I would go over there and hang out with her on the porch. She always had her cigarettes and her Heineken in hand. A total badass. She worked in construction and would be the only woman in the crew. Just rolling with the dudes doing manly-ass work like a G. I looked up to her, man.

When I think of strength, I think of a woman. I've seen more women be strong and tough in my life than men. The thing about Vita was she had dealt with some things in the streets. She was rehabilitated and came out of that, and she was making an honest living. Taking care of her daughter—Arielle got everything she wanted. Vita held it down, and she was there for me.

I needed the support because my home life was chaotic. My mom kicked Domingo out of the house when he was eighteen. She just couldn't take it anymore. He was being disrespectful, calling her out of her name, putting holes in the wall. My mom would get the wall fixed and he would punch another hole in it. He was uncontrollable and inconsolable. I was so young that I felt like I couldn't intervene. If Dean was around, he'd intervene, but when it was just me, I felt hopeless. My brother was a big dude, and I found his size intimidating. He made everybody in that house's life a living hell.

My room was in the back of the house, and when you looked out, you saw the porch. One intense snowy day, I saw Domingo out there sleeping. It was sad seeing my brother like that. I went out and brought him some food and stayed there with him for a little bit.

We found out later that he was a paranoid schizophrenic and he was dealing with all these mental health issues. We kind of already knew he was. He was supposed to take medicine when he was younger, but he never did. Learning that diagnosis made things make sense for me, though. It gave me some peace. To understand what he was dealing with specifically gave me closure. It helped me to not be so mad at him. He couldn't control it. He had a sickness. I was able to find a little more compassion for him in my heart.

CHAPTER 7

n '96, my mom took me to see my first concert. The Fugees were headlining on the Smokin' Grooves tour at Blossom Music Center in Cuyahoga Falls. It was so funny because I guess she thought she was gonna hear Lauryn Hill singing "Killing Me Softly" all night. She didn't know what she was getting her ass into. The bill was Busta Rhymes, Cypress Hill, A Tribe Called Quest—it was packed. That was the first time I smelled weed in the air, but not even knowing it was weed. The whole fucking space smelled like the shit. My mom was struggling. She was standing there with these earplugs in, stressed out. I felt so bad for her.

But the show blew my mind. Watching Busta Rhymes do "Woo-Hah!!" He had on this blue fit like he wore in the video. Nas doing "If I Ruled the World" with Lauryn Hill. Crazy shit, bro. In that moment, something happened to me just looking over the stage. Being that close to those superstars, going from seeing them in music videos to seeing them onstage, breathing the same air—it wasn't lost on me what I was witnessing, what I was getting to be a part of. Thanks, Mom. She didn't let me go to concerts, but I pleaded for her to take me. That was the first and last concert she took me to. It was so rowdy in that bitch.

There's a freedom of expression in hip-hop, and I was seeing myself in the other Black brothers doing it. I saw it as the perfect outlet to amplify my voice. My earliest rhymes were like poems, and then they became raps. I figured I can tell my story in a way I can't in any other genre. I gravitated toward the coolness, the I-don't-give-a-fuckness, the swagger. When I was young, niggas was rapping about whatever. That's what drove me into wanting to have a career of my own—watching the Hot Boy$ in 1999 and finding out that Lil Wayne was seventeen. I was fifteen, thinking, *Man, this lil nigga is like me.* It motivated me.

I was recording demos with my friends. In high school, I had buddies who had equipment and I was recording at their houses. These two kids from Philly moved to Shaker. Ernie and Vernon. They were mad cool. We hit it off and started rapping together. I would go over there and record demos and make beats myself and do a bunch of shit.

I also recorded some shit with one of my older brother's good friends named Fred, who lived a couple houses down. Fred was an East Coast hip-hop head. Obsessed with Wu-Tang.

The first beat I ever recorded on was Wu-Tang Clan's "Itz Yours" at Fred's house. The rap was simple. I can't remember the verse, but the hook was:

It's the Jr. Don Dada
It's the Jr. Don Dada, that's me, that's me
It's the Jr. Don Dada. It's the Jr. Don Dada, that's me

Most hip-hop was street shit at the time. There was some conscious rap out there, but I was gravitating toward the street shit. Rough and rugged. But honestly, I grew out of that style. When I started recording, I began to listen back to my voice. I could feel myself slowly becoming a fully realized artist. We were recording our songs on a karaoke machine. Same thing with Ernie and Vernon's setup. That was some of the first times I heard my voice outside my own head. I didn't think that it would be such a shocking thing: *Shit, that's what I sound like.* I felt like I could hear a transmission from another world.

Once I was out on the porch writing raps and Domingo came out. I told him, "Hey, man, I'm having trouble writing my rap. I don't know what to write about."

I was maybe twelve or thirteen.

My brother was like, "Man, write about what you know. You go to school, don't you?"

I was like, "Yeah."

"Write about that."

I started writing about walking to school with my Eastsport back-pack and missing homework, liking girls in school, and shit like that. From there, a rapper was born. I talked about my day-to-day life as a kid. In the short term, my raps were imitations, but Domingo's words informed the artist I would become: Writing about my life. Telling my story. Being honest.

Hip-hop was taking over the culture at this point. 2Pac and Biggie were megastars on opposite sides of a widely publicized bicoastal feud. A Tribe Called Quest and the Native Tongues were making jazz and Afrocentricity cool again. Wu-Tang Clan sampled martial arts cinema into a cross-borough-defining street rap. And Nas had made the rap album a statement piece. My ninth-grade math teacher, Mr. Slauson, went by Slau Dog with the students. He used to make rap part of his curriculum. He had a rap that he did to "Gangsta's Paradise," but it was all about math. He was tapped in and relatable. He made it fun. I feel bad because I never applied myself in that class either. Part of me felt like I let Mr. Slauson down as a student, because I knew he liked me. By that time, I was excited to be in high school, but the older I got, the more schoolwork became less and less important. Ms. Smith, man. Fucking Ms. Smith sent a ripple effect through my life for the rest of my academic career.

By tenth grade, I was committed to being an artist. I wanted to have a rap career. I had a natural ability with freestyling and writing rhymes, and I felt confident that I had a shot. If I just got with the right producers and worked with the right people, I'd be straight. In your mid-teens, you start to think about your future. I was imagining where I wanted to be in ten years. The answer was touring the world.

One day, I was sitting in algebra and all the kids were taking a test. I didn't study for it. I looked around the room, and I saw everybody working hard and stressing out over this fucking thing. In my mind, I was thinking, *I'm gonna be a rapper one day; I'm going to be fucking famous. I don't need fucking algebra. What the fuck am I doing? I don't need to be here.* I filled in random answers on the Scantron and turned the test in. It was almost as if I was so sure of what my fate was going to be.

Even telling that story, I feel like such an idiot. That's my biggest regret in life: I did not show up in school. That's why whenever I hear about anybody graduating from high school or college, I have so much respect for them. Especially college. It's like, *Yo, you fucking graduated from college? Sweet Jesus!* That's so impressive to me. People probably look at me and go, "Oh my god, you performed for sixty thousand people and do this for ninety minutes and you have them all enjoying themselves," and blah blah blah. "That's so impressive." But I'm going, "Yeah, but graduating from a four-year college seems a little bit more impressive, if you ask me." That's something I'll never be able to experience. I guess I could go back to school. I've thought about that a bunch of times. Take some online classes or something. We'll see.

At the time, though, rap was the only thing on my mind, and I'd take any opportunity to hone my skills. We had freestyle battles at lunch, somebody making the beat with a pen on a table and shit, tapping. That's when I homed in on my freestyle game. Around that time, fourteen, fifteen, sixteen, Dennis, Steve, DeAndre, and I spent a lot of time out on the porches of our friends' houses trying to come up with the illest shit without fumbling. We'd be out there for hours, trying to be witty and sharp. I got nice with that shit. That's why, when it came time and I was doing open mic battles, I was good, because I had years of practice in school. Developing that muscle memory helped me grow into the song maker and artist I wanted to be, laying the groundwork. It's like basketball: You have to know the fundamentals before you can play the game.

I was starting to have this wacky idea to become a rapper, in part because there were a couple albums that fucked me up that year. *The Slim Shady LP* came out and I was obsessed, and then *The Chronic 2001* came out and blew my mind. I listened to Eminem on my CD player on repeat. He was the most remarkable MC I'd heard in my life. I would study these guys like, *Damn, I want to do this. I want to be an artist. I want to make rap songs. Hard-ass rap songs.* Those turn-of-the-millennium albums established rap as both a big commercial product and an avenue toward the breakthrough of new sounds and perspectives, weirder samples and big personalities.

With an introduction to *The Chronic* came an introduction to the drug that inspired the album. The first time I smoked weed, I was sixteen. My homeboy Damon lived across the street and we smoked in his garage. We didn't know what we were doing, so we smoked weed out of a Black & Mild. I was a little high, not high enough to ensure I'd start smoking permanently. It was shitty weed; I couldn't be high in front of my mom anyway, so I just packed up and headed home hoping the faint aroma wasn't clinging to me.

Beyond Em and Dre, I would listen to Hov and zone out. When "Hard Knock Life" came out, my brother Domingo would sit on the front porch blasting it. *Yo, this is the most amazing-sounding shit I've ever heard.* There was something about that bass line; it felt good and Jay skated on that bitch. He tap-danced all over that muthafucka, man. I played that song over and over and over and over and over again. '96, '97, '98, '99. Those are great years for music. At night, I was consuming all that shit. By the time I became interested in making my own jams, I had already soaked up so much iconic rap. Snoop and Dre. It was the street life shit. My earlier raps were riddled with shit that I knew nothing about. I was just trying to emulate what I was listening to.

But soon I was taking my own approach, one with a more East Coast tone and leaning. Finding your voice as a kid from Cleveland was tricky, especially when the primary influences were the dominant national sound. But in a way, that would prove freeing. Having no true pattern to follow forced me to embrace my individuality.

CHAPTER 8

Just as things were starting to make sense, boom: My mom moved me from Shaker Heights to Solon, an uppity white suburb of Cleveland. I was sixteen and she wanted me to stay out of trouble. For her it was a welcome change, but for me not so much.

I think this period of adolescence is super hard for most people, and it certainly was for me. It was a time when I was at my most angry and confused, but I was also feeling excited and optimistic about my growing sense of self and independence. I was experiencing the entire roller coaster—the emotional turbulence of growing up, falling in love, being heartbroken, lashing out, finding my voice. I was pushing through it all in a messy attempt to become someone I knew deep down I could become, someone great and someone I was proud to be.

Being at that age without a father figure is what fucked me up.

Fifteen, sixteen is the time when you're changing. You're in the middle of high school and you're gonna graduate soon. You're suddenly forced to confront your future. Do you go to college or not? I didn't know what I wanted to do. I knew I liked music, and that I wanted to pursue making it because I was passionate about it. But I was fifty-fifty with that. Part of me wanted it, and knew I could do it, but the other half was thinking, *But you're from Cleveland, bro. You're just Scott Mescudi. You're not meant to be a big artist. You're just Scott. Be OK with that.* In hindsight, my name itself is marquee ready: unique, singular, anything but ordinary.

When my mom told us we were moving, I was pissed. It meant moving away from all my friends. I had been in Shaker my whole school life. All my friends grew up with me, and to just move me at the last minute—I was upset. She was trying to make a better life for us. The house we were living in was not a good place. We needed more space. My mom needed a bedroom. I understood. I got it. But I wasn't happy about it.

The new crib was much better, much roomier, with two floors. Or one floor and a half second floor. I was excited to be living in a better space, but I was not excited about the new school, which was way whiter than the district I was coming from. I imagined it was going to be like something out of *Clueless*. The schools I had attended were always majority white, but this was extreme. There were almost no Black students at my school in Solon. I was worried it was gonna be the worst situation. But when I got there to the spot where everybody would hang out when school started, I saw this crew of Black kids all migrated to one section and I started making friends. They all kind of stayed together, and I became cool with them. They adopted me into their inner circle. I was coming from Shaker and Shaker was a cool school district. It was a cool flex.

■ ■ ■

Being sixteen comes with a swirl of emotions—the fear and joy of finding out about yourself, a process that can only happen alongside others. It is in those moments that you discover autonomy and shared interests, and the future seems bright and full of unknowable possibilities. Finding your tribe kick-starts every journey of self-realization, and I met some great kids. There was this one dude named Darryl Adams, who lived in the cul-de-sac opposite my house. He was this muscular, beast wrestler, but he was funny too. We had a lot of good times together just hanging out at his house downloading music. My homegirl Tiffany Glass lived down the street from me in Solon. She was a chic Black chick. Mad swag. A real bad bitch. She was about her business and she stood on business. She was the first homegirl that I had since Ashley, and gave straight sister vibes. She'd drive me to school some days, and pick me up playing OutKast. We'd jam to school every morning, blasting that shit loud as fuck. Her mom was cool. Her whole family was cool. Her, Darryl, Darryl's sister Brenda, and I all stuck together. We were some of the few Black kids in that school.

There were also these two brothers, Demetrius and Denny. They were both pretty boys—two metrosexual brothers. They were the prettiest niggas I ever knew. They inspired me. They used to get all the girls, straight up. They were the smoothest niggas. I don't understand how these niggas were so smooth.

This one boy Deontay, he used to wrestle too—and that muthafucka was cold in wrestling. Him and this other dude, Vinnie di Giovanni, them niggas was baaad, man, they were the illest wrestlers, amazing athletes but also amazing dudes. Dominic Rizzo was this Italian kid that was a super tough guy. Always had his fucking shirt off. He was macho, but he always showed love. We all bonded early on. This other kid Joe Minardi had an interesting voice that was colored by a country twang. He drove an Infiniti that he kept super clean, and he used to listen to Arabic chants in his car for fun. I loved Joe. Him and my other dudes Mel Whiskey, a.k.a. Romel, and this kid D, who had the nicest car out of anybody in the crew. We were all homies. I had so many friends in Solon. Sitting here name-dropping them all, I wonder how everybody's doing, man. It was a family of us. Some of us got into trouble, but for the most part we were all good kids that were just trying to pass the time. And we were always looking to party.

I was in eleventh grade when I first started drinking. I was a social drinker, only getting drunk at parties. I never went out of my way to get it. I wasn't smoking that much either. I didn't buy weed, and I wasn't sneaking around and bringing it home. Friends would have it, and I would partake. I wasn't using substances to cope; it was just a way to be around people. Obviously, this part of town had more money, and a lot of spoiled kids. Niggas had Benzes. They were pulling up to the schoolhouse in luxury cars. Some balling-ass shit. I used to ride my bike around town and I'd see kids drive past me and they'd beep their horn. I would go, *Fuck.* I mean, I had a nice bike and all, but still; I felt like a fucking idiot. I was the only one that didn't have a car. People were having to come pick me up all the time. It was the worst.

But it would also be kind of exhilarating: Homies come get you; you come outside; the car is bumping music; you get in; they got weed for you, smoking. We're all in the whip; we're 'bout to go to the club. We're drinking forties on the highway, throwing the bottles out the window. Bumping Three 6 Mafia, getting fucked up, starting fights in parties. It was crazy. It was reckless. It was fun. Solon was rowdy. That place got turnt up. You would think that in this white suburb it would be more tame, but it was wild. We used to get into shit all the time. At house parties getting fucked up. Just straight madness. The Rager was born in Solon.

We used to drive out to this club for teenagers called the Boot Scootin' Saloon, and you would pretty much go there just to fight. Not even to pick up girls. Everybody that was in my crew played sports or did something aggressive. The testosterone was through the roof. These dudes were like, "Let's fight somebody!" every weekend. Nobody was focused on getting chicks—I mean, I was, but I was always having to get into some shit: "Hold on. Excuse me, babe. I gotta go handle this shit. I gotta go be with my boys." Even in the moment, you knew you would probably get into a fight. Probably going to jail. Getting jumped. Some wild shit. There was the feeling that you could be getting into it at any given point going out with these dudes in high school.

My focus on getting chicks eventually led me to a girl that I'll call Monica. We hit it off immediately. It was instantaneous. We met at school the first day and hung out later at the football game. After that, we were inseparable, hanging out all the time.

The first time I ever ate pussy was with Monica. I was terrible at it. Once, we were having sex in the car, I was going down on her, and she made me stop immediately.

"It's OK," she said.

"What?" I replied.

She said again, "It's OK, it's OK."

I realized she just didn't like when I ate her out. I felt inadequate, like I couldn't give her what she needed. I was like, *From this point on no girl is going to be unpleased with my eating-out game ever again. I'm going to make sure that I'm the best at it.* So girls later on in my life can thank Monica for being so ruthless because it lit a fire under my ass.

I was in love with this girl. And she had the fattest ass. Oh my god. It made no sense how fat her booty was. I was a lucky young man. We were together my whole junior year.

My best friend was Kenny. He got me a job at Papa John's once— that was my favorite pizza—and we went everywhere together. He would pick me up from school and we'd smoke mad weed and listen to Three 6 Mafia. That was my guy. Working there was like a teenage dream come true—learning how to make my favorite pie, making my own cheese sticks with extra cheese and pepperoni and all sorts of shit on them, making my own little special pizzas.

One day, it was just me and my manager, handling the store on a busy Friday night. The phones were going off the hook, back-to-back, ringing like crazy. We were answering them, I was responsible for making the pizzas, and there were thirty orders backed up on the screen. So I stopped answering so that I could make a dent in the mounting pizza orders. Otherwise people wouldn't get their pizzas for three hours. I thought, *Let me knock out some of these and put them in the thing so they can be fresh and we can send them out.*

My manager told me, "I need you to answer the phone."

I replied, "Well, we can't be answering the phone. We're backed up in orders and we need to make some of these pizzas. We got all these orders coming in."

"Answer the goddamn phone!!" he screamed at me, loud as fuck.

I ain't never had no white man talk to me like this ever. My Blackness could not believe this white man would talk to me like this. I thought, *This nigga's crazy.* So I took off my apron and walked out.

"Just so you know, you don't have a job anymore," he said.

I looked at him sideways and said, "I quit, fool," and then left.

I never looked back. Papa John's was one of my favorite jobs, but when I quit Kenny got me another job working with him at this fine-dining restaurant, a bar and grill in this hotel. Then I eventually got a job at the movie theater, which allowed me to dive headfirst into film. I had many jobs over the years, but I would never stray too far from the cinema.

If friends are one avenue to greater self-discovery, there is perhaps no greater developmental milestone than young love. It can be a powerful force for good, but also a destructive one. I was a sucker for Monica. One day, she called me and said she'd just got in, and then suddenly, Kenny was at my doorstep. Now, Monica lived five minutes away a few streets over.

I told her over the phone, "Kenny is at my door."

"Oh, he just gave me a ride home," she said.

"Oh, you were with Kenny. OK, cool."

I didn't think anything of it.

A few weeks later, she told me that she cheated on me with Kenny that day and that she let him eat her out. In exchange, she let him fuck her. I was crushed. Learning my girl cheated with my best friend broke me.

Despite the fact that she had cheated on me, she was able to make me feel like we shouldn't break up. We stayed together after that, maybe because I felt like I couldn't be by myself. We got along so well, better than I had with any other girl. She was my first older girl; we had chemistry and drama, and it was my first passionate, powerful love. I thought it would never end. But it clearly wasn't right.

About a year later, as she was going off to college, we broke up. I was losing her. I was clearly not OK, and I could not reconcile the fact that she was so OK with our relationship ending, knowing how much that would hurt me. As I walked to my ex's house to give her back a locket she gave me, I took about twelve Tylenols, intending to kill myself. I called my friends Darryl and Brenda and told them to come pick me up. They saw I was fucked up and we stayed on this corner of the street until the police came.

The paramedics took me to the hospital and my mom arrived shortly thereafter. Within thirty minutes of taking the pills, I was on a gurney. The doctors were using this black tar to pump my stomach. I bit down on a white plastic clamp they put in my mouth. A water hose–sized tube was then pushed through a hole in the mouth guard and slowly inserted down my throat. They warned me I would gag but told me to relax my throat and let the tube run. The tube was inserted deeper and deeper, past my gag reflex, and it felt like I was gonna throw up. You see black shit coming in your body and you're going, *What the fuck?* Then they pump your stomach so you actually see the fluids coming out of the tube, little pieces of pills swirling around in the bag. My mom was standing there, watching, on the verge of tears. As it was happening, I was thinking, *Scott, what did you do? This was stupid. Over a girl? C'mon, man.* A realization started kicking in almost immediately: What I had done was not worth it.

I woke up the next morning in the hospital with an IV in my arm, thinking, *OK, I'm ready to go home now.* I went out and talked to the lady at the front desk: "Hey, when is my mom coming to pick me up?"

"Aw, I'm sorry, honey; your mom's not coming back to pick you up for a while. You're gonna be with us for a little bit," she said.

"What?" I asked.

That shit rocked my world. I was stuck in the psychiatric wing of the hospital because they felt I was potentially at risk of trying to kill myself or hurt myself again. They wanted to make sure I was good before they let me go back into the world.

I had to go through this rehabilitation program before I could get discharged. There were other kids there dealing with different things like eating disorders. How you did in the sessions dictated how long you stayed in the facility. There were kids who had been in there for a minute. I was not trying to be one of those kids, so, as most kids in that situation would, I told the staff what they wanted to hear: that I was not a threat to harm myself anymore. They were having us listen to Nelly Furtado—"I'm Like a Bird" and stuff. Using her lyrics in therapy was kind of dope. I wanted people to do that with my music. I wasn't taking in what they were telling me, because I was so young, but I didn't want to hurt myself either. As the days went by, I was in a better place psychologically. I was confused and regretful, but I was feeling hopeful. I was no longer an urgent risk. I was scared straight. I almost left my mom and siblings; that was a big mistake.

I snuck and used the phone to call Monica on Friday night. She answered.

"Hey, it's Scott."

"What's up?"

"I'm in the hospital. I gotta be here for a little while longer."

All she could muster: "Oh."

Cold.

"What are you doing?" I asked.

"I'm about to go out."

"Oh, OK."

"I'll talk to you later."

"OK."

She said bye and just hung up. I thought, *Fuck, this girl doesn't give a fuck about me.* That freaked me out, the idea that someone could be so cavalier in the face of such despair.

When I was leaving the facility, they made me promise that I'd never try to take my life ever again. They heard what they needed to hear, but I didn't actually mean it. Keeping that promise would prove difficult, but the silver lining is that nothing happened to me. When the urge came to me later on in life, I went and sought help. I want to be here, truthfully. I'm so glad I decided to stay.

After I went to the emergency room my mom was watching me much closer, but I told her it wouldn't happen again. She understood, and soon I was back in the swing of school. Things went back into order pretty quickly. There wasn't time to dwell on the fact that I tried to commit suicide.

Coming out of that—coming home, getting back into my life, getting back to my happiness, getting back to Scott—was what made me realize that Monica wasn't worth all the energy I was putting into her. She wasn't the right one for me. From there it was easy to move on. Rebounding meant chasing my ambitions. Music was starting to become more of a reality for me, and there were more and more signs of what was to come.

As a bit of a contingency plan, I had decided on applying to the University of Toledo at the top of senior year. If I was to go to college, I didn't want to go too far from home. Toledo was like two hours from Cleveland, so I thought that would be best. And they had a film program. I wanted to be a film major, so I decided I would go there. I filled out the application, and they accepted me not long after my birthday. But that seemed like a backup for if show business didn't come calling.

When I was seventeen, my mom entered me into a local talent contest. At first, I was a little upset, because I was thinking, *What the fuck kind of shit is this? Why would you do this?* But she knew I was passionate about my music, and she thought the exposure would be good for me. I decided to ride with it and see what would happen. Worst-case scenario was that they didn't pick me, so no big deal.

I was in the fifteen-to-eighteen age group. There were two auditions. You had to perform your own original song. I had taken the beat to Ja Rule's "Holla Holla" and made my own track. I put that on my demo with a couple other ones and I submitted it. They picked me to audition again at the Rock & Roll Hall of Fame. I did it and passed that round. I didn't know if I was doing a good job, but I kept getting called back, and soon found out that I won in my age group. It was some small amount of vindication for the path I was beginning to commit to.

The prize was to perform at the Cleveland Browns stadium in this little banquet area. I made sure my fit was on fucking point: I bought this Rocawear denim set with navy-blue accents—the jacket and the jeans to match, which I paired with a Cleveland shirt. I had this Carolina-blue headband to go with the fit. I was up in that bitch dripping, you know what I'm saying? For that time, that fit was too cold. I was up in there and I had them old folks dancing. I performed a medley of songs that I put together myself, me rapping on other people's beats. It was exciting to see people fucking with the music. Preparing me for that final performance, the people behind the contest got me a performance coach to work with me on stage presence.

I went to this lady's house in the inner city for a couple hours, and she gave me the tools for putting on a great show—working all angles of a stage, breath control, interaction with the audience, all things I still use and keep in mind. The seeds for the performer I would become were planted prepping for and participating in that contest. So all that stuff definitely paid off in the moment.

Around the same time my mom put me in Barbizon, a modeling talent agency that teaches runway and acting techniques like posture and improv. They taught you how to walk on the catwalk, pose in photo shoots, carry yourself on camera, all that shit. At first it seemed like a scam, but looking back, I learned a lot, particularly about the importance of being confident and relaxed in front of the camera.

I was balancing these newfound extracurricular activities with just being a teenager, which, for me, meant getting wasted. Once I went to one of the high school football games and I was drunk, because that was just what we did: got drunk and went to games, just kickin' it, hanging with our homies, trying to talk to girls. I was kind of running around, wild'n' out, hanging out with my friends, but you could tell I was on something. This cop saw me joking around and I was obviously drunk, so he told me to come over.

"You seem drunk," he said.

I said, "No, no, I haven't drank tonight."

He asked for my ID and I gave it to him. On it, I'd tried to alter the year on the card so that the 4 in '84 would read either '80 or '81, to make it look as if I were twenty-one.

"What is this?" he asked. "Looks like you tried to alter your ID."

I said, "Oh, nah, it just got scratched."

The cop smelled my breath and said, "We're taking you in."

I went, *Fuuuck.* They arrested me right there on the spot in front of all my friends. I was so wasted I couldn't even argue. I was just caught.

My mom picked me up from the police station. She didn't talk to me all night. When she was ashamed of me, she went quiet.

When you think about it, it's standard kid shit, man. If a kid doesn't do shit like this when they're growing up, that kid's gonna be an asshole.

He's not gonna know how to live. He's not gonna know right from wrong. He's not going to learn from those mistakes and get better.

Unfortunately for me, the powers that be in my adolescent life would come to see that kid shit as a sign of delinquency. They weren't giving me the benefit of the doubt. There was this program for minorities that I was a part of after school. We were doing stuff in the community, and there was this one trip that they had planned for us to go camping. There were some kids smoking cigarettes and weed on the trip. I started smoking cigarettes my junior year, not long after I got to Solon. By the first football game of the year, I was smoking Newports. I wasn't smoking a pack a day, but I was smoking enough that everybody in my school knew. Back at school that following week, the teacher that ran the program gathered us together. He'd received a bad report from the people that were on-site at the camp: Kids were smoking and it was bad representation for the school. I knew who they were talking about, and it wasn't me, but the teacher knew for a fact that out of all the students in the class, I smoked. So he was putting the blame on me, as if I were the one who needed to be held responsible. I wasn't smoking weed with anybody. I was smoking my cigarettes, but not even out like that. I was chillin', but I was getting blamed for something I didn't do.

I don't know why she came, but I guess she was coming anyway, because the principal showed up to the room, and the teacher went, "Oh, Ms. Short, so happy you're here."

Ms. Short was explaining that there were some kids behaving inappropriately on the campgrounds. The teacher said, "I'm having a conversation with Scott and he's getting a little upset."

I said, "Yeah, because you're blaming me for everything. You don't even know it's me and you just know I smoke, so you're saying it's me."

Ms. Short said, "Come with me."

"Nah, I got my ride here. I'm good," I replied.

She said, "I'll take you home."

"Can I smoke in your car?"

"No."

"I'm good then. I got a ride."

"Come with me now or I'm gonna call the police," she told me.

So I said, "Call them and I'm stealin' on the first one that walks through that door and if you come in behind them I might just steal on you too."

"All right, I'm calling the police."

I left before they could get me. When I went to school the next day, I was pretending as if everything was fine, but they called me down to the office over the PA and I could sense it. I got suspended in that meeting that morning, which wasn't news, but then a bigger bombshell dropped: I was being recommended for expulsion.

I had been suspended twice before, so I guess they were treating this as my third strike. I had been kicked out of Solon once and put in the alternative school, but I convinced them to let me come back because I was doing so well. They let me come half day first for a while, then full day; then this happens. I walked out of the meeting when they said that they were going to expel me. My mom and my sister were there and my sister just said, "Let him go, let him go." I left and I started crying. I started crying because my life was over. I didn't want to ever flunk a grade, and now they wanted to kick me out of school. I was disappointed in myself.

My counselor came in—because she was supposed to be in the

meeting, but she arrived a little late—and she asked me what was wrong.

I told her, "They just said I was expelled. I don't know what I'ma do now."

She said, "Scott, you already got accepted to college. All you gotta do is get your GED and you'll be fine. You can still go."

"Really?" I said.

"Yeah, pass the pretest and they'll pay for your real test. Take the test for free."

In Ohio, every student has to pass a ninth-grade proficiency test in order to graduate. It was a pretty routine standardized test that measured a baseline understanding of the major subjects: math, science, English, history. The GED was a similar test, only passing the GED meant that even if you were missing courses from the ninth-grade proficiency test, you could still go to college.

That following week, I put myself in class for a GED pretest—you study all week and then you take the test. I passed that. Then I took the real test the following week. Passed that. Got my GED, and ended up getting my diploma a couple months before school was over. So I was chillin'. All my classmates were still in school struggling, studying for finals, stressing out. And I was done. It was perfect. I'd taken the roundabout way to end up in the same place: waiting for college. In my spare time, I just wrote raps. My desire to be the kind of student that could make my mom proud was conflicting with my need to become the most next-level rapper that I could be.

CHAPTER 9

Curiosity and obligation were the only things drawing me to college. At the very least I could make my mom happy. I knew she wanted her youngest to go the distance and try and put himself out there. Plus, it was an opportunity to be on my own. I got a shitty apartment off campus because we registered too late for the dorms. Music was top of mind, but I still had to figure myself out as an artist.

My freshman year at the University of Toledo was one nonstop party. I had a ball at dorm functions, smoking a ton of weed. I got a chance to experience freedom for the first time—staying out late, coming and going when I wanted, eating whatever I wanted, having sloppy-ass fast food all day. The George Foreman grill was my best friend. I was using that muthafucka left and right. I'd have my homies come over and we'd have Burger Night. I was holding it the fuck down. There was no Postmates or any of that shit. Maybe you order a pizza or Chinese food, but I ain't have money like that, so I had to play it smart. I'd spend my days sitting in my living room playing *Vice City* on a little TV for hours, listening to Scarface's *The Fix*, zoning out, cleaning my house, smoking mad weed.

I was staying in this little development called Kenwood Gardens. We used to chill in our complex, shoot dice, get high, and listen to 50 Cent's mixtapes with DJ Whoo Kid and his album *Get Rich or Die Tryin'*. All I did was sell weed, smoke weed, and hang out in my apartment complex. I was mostly meeting up with cats or doing drop-offs at people's houses. I was selling nicks and dimes. I wanted word to get around that Scott hooked up the sacks when you bought from him. I thought if I got the clientele then eventually I could go back to being exact. That wasn't a great plan, because I was ruining my money. I was smoking most of my supply and giving it to my friends, and then I ended up having to pay back for the shit I smoked. It wasn't good. I had become too much of a stoner.

I loved the feeling that weed gave me, the peace. It brought me a serenity that nothing else could. As an artist, I found that smoking allowed me to tap into new flavors. Pretty quickly it became part of my creative process. The clarity it offered me let me work at a much higher level and unlock my true self.

My friend Sheffield was out in Toledo with me, and Jeff, one of my homeboys from Solon, came with us too. Jeff would pick me up at Kenwood Gardens and just drive on the lawn. I would look outside and his car would be right on the path by the door. Though it may have felt like we were wandering around aimlessly, being at school did have a purpose: doing film. The ambition was to make movies, tapping into the essence of all the comedies I'd admired growing up, but also to make me a full-fledged actor.

Other patterns from my youth continued too: Just as I'd spent a lot of time alone as a kid, I was often solo in college. But, like before, I stayed social. I went out a lot, but I was by myself more, in my thoughts, thinking about my future. I was having fun my freshman year, but the reality that I was not going to do four years of this was already starting to sink in. By the same token, I didn't know if this music shit was going to be anything, if I was going to make it. If I didn't do school, I didn't know what I was going to do outside of that. I enjoyed my English classes. Writing essays got me a B+. But as the school year went on, my other grades were coming in and they were bad. Thankfully, I was feeling good about the music I was making. I was writing raps in my house by myself, getting inspired, listening to the Clipse.

College was where I found myself as an artist. I went by Kid Mesc, and started discovering who I was creatively and realizing the type of songs I would make. When I did my first records as a freshman, I would start them going, "Kid, Kid Mes, Kid Mes-*cudi*!" One day, it went from "Kid Mes-*cudi*" to just "Kid Cudi," and the name stuck. Even though the flows were very East Coast, the Cudi sensibilities were there: the raw singing and the melodies.

I recorded my first demo at the University of Toledo working with this dude named Chris. He had a whole setup in his bedroom to record in the closet. The beats he made were sample heavy and knocking, super East Coast vibes. At the time, I was listening to a lot of Bone Thugs-n-Harmony. Their melodies and realness were key to the development of the Kid Cudi sound, and they were the rare hometown rap act that had broken nationally, showing that it was possible.

Chris and I crafted the first bits of the demo. It took a little under a year to finish. It was ten songs total. Some of the songs I did in Cleveland in a proper studio later, and put them together with the rest of the songs I did in college. I was really confident in it because it felt like such an effective representation of who I was. The motivation was to simply have people recognize my talent. The bars and hooks were both strong. I started singing my hooks because I didn't have a singer to sing them. Initially, I thought I was recording reference vocals that someone else would rerecord later. But then I was like, *Fuck that. I'll sing it myself.*

I passed the college cut around to anyone who would take one. The resulting buzz made me a little popular on campus. People would be coming up to me singing my songs and shit. It was a good feeling. But by Christmas break that's when I knew: I thought, *Man, this ain't for me. I can't be in school.* Having heard a full piece of work from myself, I realized I had a knack for it. I knew I could create an album. I had a voice. That's why I felt I had to leave college, because I saw I had something. I thought, *I need to go ahead and do this for real.* I felt like my story was unique to me and only me. If you can bring something new to the table that hasn't been heard before, and nobody can do what you do, you'll have a presence. And if you work at your craft and make sure it's right and perfect it, just being yourself is enough.

At the end of the first semester, I came home. I had time at home to reflect on the half a year that had passed, and I knew I wasn't eager to go back. *Fuck this. I'm not coming back to college, so I need to figure out the next step.* I gave it an honest shot. I just couldn't do it. It wasn't for me. But I didn't want to waste my mom's money. So I finished up the year. Ultimately, I didn't feel bad about my decision to leave. My mom was understanding too. I spent the rest of my time at the University of Toledo polishing my music. I was still going to classes, but I was going through the motions. When I left that summer, I was gone for good.

CHAPTER 10

Going back home to Solon felt a little like being back at square one. College wasn't for me, but at least there I was on a track. Now I had to figure out what my whole future looked like.

Dean was a cook at Applebee's in Solon and I started working there too. This was the second time he and I worked together—we worked at Arby's when I was in high school. We were never very close. We worked at the stores together and just never talked to or interacted with each other, not at work or at home. We kept to ourselves. As much as I wanted a relationship with my brother, it didn't seem like he wanted one with me. I was around. I'd be in the house chillin'. He never wanted to do anything with me. It was kind of weird. But oh well. I was figuring, *It just is what it is.* I love him, I care about him, but we didn't kick it.

At Applebee's, the bartender was this beautiful, light-skinned chick named Jackie. She was my brother's age and also grew up in Shaker. My mom knew her mom, and my siblings knew her siblings. We started to hang out all the time after work, smoking cigarettes as we counted our tips. She was twenty-three at the time, and I was nineteen, so sometimes she would take me to bars and get me in. I would order a drink as if I were of age and they never guessed it because Jackie looked older, so it was always in the clear. Eventually, we started dating. Dean couldn't believe it. I knew it was the ultimate flex. I bagged the girl from his grade. What an accomplishment.

My boy Sheffield started working at Applebee's too. He didn't go back to school either. He was a tall, slim, dark-skinned dude. We were both on this "get this fucking money" type shit. Sheffield was slick talking and silly. He came up with his nickname that he called himself: Mr. Bubble. He'd always say, "I'm fucking bubblin', man. I'm fucking bubblin'." He was a character, probably one of the coolest niggas out in Solon. I want to smoke an L with Sheffield right now. Just thinking about all my old homies makes me miss them. Life is crazy. Everybody goes their own way, follows their own path. Some people you connect with again; some you never see again. Thinking about Sheffield, I miss that dude. I miss everyone I kicked it with in Solon.

I was working at Applebee's four to five days a week, and I eventually also started working at this restaurant in this hotel, a bar and grill called the Bertram. Jackie and I dated for about eight months, and then she broke it off. She gave me the excuse that her life was crazy and she needed to figure things out. She told me she wasn't in a place to date anyone. I was heartbroken. I couldn't understand it. As she was this mature Aquarius woman, I thought she could show me the ropes. She was being the OG in the situation and being like "Scotty Don't"—from

Austin Powers; you know, that was our joke: "C'mon, this is OK. We're meant to move on and do other things. We'll always be in touch. We'll always be friends." Blah blah blah. I didn't want to hear it, but I eventually accepted it. From that point on, it was fuel to my fire. I was gonna show Jackie what she could've had. I was gonna be successful, and she was gonna see that she made a mistake and realize that I was the one.

Success was going to require a plan. I was working overtime at my job to get money for studio time to try to complete a demo. Completing one would allow me to shop my music with labels in New York. As I started thinking more seriously about moving to a big city, I knew I wanted to show up with something that I could give people should I stumble into somebody. I wanted to record it in a real studio, not in somebody's fucking basement or closet. So I got enough money together and started recording songs. I got beats from these local producers that were doing shit in the game already named Alex and Matt, who went by the name The Kickdrums. They sold me a couple incredible beats for two hundred bucks apiece. The best production I'd ever rapped on at that time—some crispy, fully mixed, properly produced shit, not no shit that was made in nobody's parents' house. It was legit. And I knew if I put the right shit on it I was gonna sound official.

So I locked in and for a couple weeks I banged out a few demos. I ended up having maybe ten joints. I used some joints from college mixed in with some new joints. That became my first mixtape, *Rap Hard*. I had a whole theme: I was gonna do *Rap Hard* and then the sequel would be *Rap Harder* and the sequel after that was gonna be *Rap Hard with a Vengeance*. It's kind of a dope idea. I might still want to do it.

I was definitely still in the novice stage of my game. The raps were competent, but the beats that I made myself were super amateurish. It was very sample driven. With song names like "Pimpin'" or "I'm Not the Average," my lyrics ranged from braggadocious bars to me speaking my destiny out into the world. I think of "I'm Not the Average" as the first *Man on the Moon* song, letting people know what I'm about: that I'm different and I'm gonna fuck the game up. Inspiration was key to process, but I refused to be a copycat. I always took my many inspirations and mixed them up in the pot. That was the only way to create something new. I never wanted to sound like another muthafucka doing what I do. Even in those early songs, my distinct voice was emerging. It had a rasp that exuded both exertion and perseverance. Sitting and writing those songs was invigorating. Even though I wasn't signed, I thought, *Man, I'm making an album.* Hearing a body of work that I put together myself, watching it reach completion, was extremely gratifying.

I was busting my ass going back and forth between the Bertram and Applebee's every week. Getting it on. My sister lent me one of her old cars, a blue 1984 Honda Accord stick shift, to get around. I learned to drive stick in that, and that was my whip. It was fucking old, but that muthafucka got me from point A to point B. The Accord allowed me to see my friends and got me over to the theater when I wanted to go see a movie by myself—I did that a lot of times, especially as soon as I got that car. It was my main thing to do when I wasn't making music: see a movie on a Tuesday night.

I spent a lot of time with my sister at her condo in the summer of 2003. I loved how she handled her business. She was super smart and driven, and it seemed like she had things all figured out early on: graduated from college, went and got a job as a mechanical engineer, bought her own condo, had her own fly-ass Mitsubishi Spyder back when that was popping. She had a dog named Butch Romeo, a pit bull that looked like Petey from *The Little Rascals*. I used to go over there, smoke weed, and watch MTV all day, staring at music videos. When *Speakerboxxx/The Love Below* came out, we were bumping that shit all the time. That was our shit, and we bonded over music. When I was younger, she put me on to all the essential New York hip-hop, like Big Pun and Biggie. She taught me all the dope shit.

I was putting the knowledge to good use. When I was nineteen, we went downtown to a freestyle battle. I was just going to spectate, but as we were watching the battle, my boy Hubert told me, "Yo, bro, you should be up there."

I was like, "Naaah."

He said, "You'd body these niggas."

"Man, I don't know . . ."

"What the fuck. You would totally win this shit."

So I'm standing there and I'm watching a couple more people lose and I'm listening to these bars that people had and they were weak. I thought, *You know what? Fuck it. I'm gonna enter this and if I lose this, cool, but let me give it a shot.* So I entered the battle and round after round I'm winning—making it to the next round, winning, winning, destroying niggas left and right. Finally, I got up to this one dude who was the reigning champion for eight weeks straight. Nobody could beat this muthafucka. We did three rounds.

First round: body him.

Second round: body him.

Third round: body him.

It was a unanimous decision that I had won. I couldn't believe it. I wasn't a freestyle master. I would only freestyle with my friends. It wasn't like I was in other competitions. But there I was: the new champion.

I was wearing a sky-blue or turquoise oversized Lacoste polo with khaki shorts and black Chucks. When we were walking out, he saw us and said, "Man, I can't believe I lost to a nigga in an IZOD shirt." I didn't say anything, but I was laughing to myself: *Yes, you did, muthafucka.* My prize was an Ashanti calendar or some bullshit. I did all that rapping my ass off thinking I was going for like $20,000. I was sick. But I knew I was nice.

The prize proved that rap couldn't pay the bills (yet), so I was getting anxious. It wasn't just that I needed money; I needed purpose. Because even though I had music, I was still fundamentally adrift—a college dropout with a dead-end job and no secure housing. So in 2004, I attempted to join the Navy. I had this wacky idea after watching *Antwone Fisher* to just go. I must have watched it way too many times, because I was thinking, *This is my destiny.* And I thought they could teach me how to be a man. All these things that I did in my youth were because I didn't have a father figure. I was trying to fill that void.

This is a move for me. This could teach me some discipline. So I met a recruiter, this young Black dude, and we started to hit it off. He would come over and talk, and I enthusiastically told him I wanted to do it. So, I went through all the tests—the physical, the written test—and passed everything with flying colors. For the physical, they took me into a room, made me strip down to my underwear, then crouch down and squat. I was told to spread my butt cheeks and cough. They checked to make sure I didn't have flat feet. The written portion was like the GED. This was the second standardized test I had to take, and it's two years after high school, so I'm thinking, *Man, I haven't studied. I'm not sharp on any of this shit.* But I passed it. After all the years of feeling like a second-rate student, passing my second big test in a row was validation that I wasn't an idiot.

There was one final thing that I needed to do: I needed to talk to this lieutenant. They had questions about two assault charges from high school that were apparently on my police record. I had been watching a fight as a spectator and dudes in the fight getting beat up were dropping names after, and everybody knew me in the schoolhouse so they dropped mine: "Scott Mescudi was there!" I had to go to court for this and it was supposed to be expunged from my record because all I had to do was get good grades and stay out of trouble.

But it wasn't. So the lieutenant brought it up. He asked me what happened and I explained the situation. They reviewed it, but they denied me entry. They told me they didn't feel comfortable, and it seemed like they were hinting that they felt the incident was a sign of delinquent behavior. It broke my heart.

I found myself in a lost, hopeless place. I got home and I was feeling like a failure. I went through this whole process only to come up short at the very end. The days went by, and I was unsure of what to do. I thought, *What do I do now?* Then it hit me. The music. I have the music. I started to realize that I had to pursue it. I had nothing else to lose. School was out. The Navy was out. The path forward was there.

I knew I had to get out of Cleveland, for the sake of my music. I started to think about where I could go. There were two places: LA and New York. I thought New York would be best because I wouldn't need a car. I could get around on a train or bus. I just felt like that was where I needed to be. I had an uncle there, so at least one person would know me.

That summer, my friend Ashley's boyfriend, Ronnel, was planning to move out to the city, so it felt like an opportunity to do some scouting. He had a cousin, Jovan, that we linked up with out in the city to show us around. I fell in love with New York on that trip—walking around Times Square in the middle of the summer, hanging out in Union Square, going to the Virgin Megastore, Greenwich Village, Alphabet City, Fifth Avenue, the Lower East Side. Just exploring. Jovan went to school in Staten Island, so that was where we were staying. We'd leave his dorm and go into the city and I was like, *This is where I need to be, man. This is where I need to be.* It seemed like they were on different time in the city. Seeing the vibrancy, it was like a huge playground with infinite possibilities. As we stood outside the Virgin Megastore, the sun glancing off the buildings on a beautiful day, everyone walking past seemed to be thriving. Right then and there it struck me: *I want this to be my home.*

I came back to Solon after about a week and told my mom I wanted to move. I guess she thought it was a joke. She didn't laugh at me in that way, but she didn't know how serious I was—and also she was afraid for me to leave home. Any parent would be. I'm the baby. So I never gave my mom shit about her having reservations. But as soon as I got back, I started to put my plan in motion. Taking doubles left and right, working overtime. I worked at Applebee's serving tables. At the hotel, I was a busboy, a valet, a host. I was everything. Food expediter. You name it. I was on room service. I did everything in that bitch.

My daughter likes to make fun of me because she's like, "Dad, you worked everywhere. You worked so many damn jobs." We were hanging out one day and there were like three instances where I was like, "Oh yeah, I remember when I was working at Applebee's. I remember when I was working at Wendy's. Oh man, I remember when I was working at Arby's. I remember I was working in Papa John's." That was my life.

What I wanted now was to follow my dream. I got all my money together, around $500 or $600, and I reached out to my uncle Kalil Madi in New York. I met him when I was a kid, before I was old enough to remember, and I wanted to reconnect with him anyway. So when he told me that I could live with him in the Bronx, it was perfect.

I jumped at the opportunity and set my date and my flight. I didn't have money for a real ticket. One of my friends had a connect to the airport, so I got a buddy pass. I flew out of the Akron airport going to LaGuardia at 1:35 p.m. I packed some clothes, my rap books, my CD player, and some mix CDs with instrumentals on them. My mom dropped me off at the airport. As I got out of the car and grabbed my bags, she came up, and she gave me a big hug.

When she turned to me, she said, "You know, if you change your mind right now, we can just go right back home."

She pulled back and I said, "Mom, I have to do this."

She said, "I know."

She was crying, but I was on a muthafuckin' mission.

I walked in the airport, getting ready to go through security, and looked back, seeing her standing there, watching me go through to the gates. She waved. I waved back. I could feel the space between us, and it was only growing wider. She had been my lifeline for so long, but there were things that I couldn't learn about myself, or my music, in Cleveland. As we said our good-byes, I was dedicating myself fully to my rap vision for the first time, pursuing it without a tether. At that moment I became a man. I left the nest. I was on my own.

Act II

CHAPTER 11

was hit by the commotion of the Big Apple right off the plane. My uncle Kalil picked me up from the airport on October 7, 2004. I was meeting him for the first time that I could remember. Kalil was a famous jazz drummer back in the day. He worked with Billie Holiday, Eddie and Vickie Barnes, Sadik Hakim, Mongo Santamaría. A tiny old man traveling in this brown big-body Oldsmobile. I got in the car, put on my seat belt, and feared for my life the whole way home. *Yo . . . this nigga shouldn't be on the road!* I thought for sure it was an accident about to happen at any minute driving with this man. It was the scariest shit. But I had some good conversations with him. Talking to my uncle Kalil— those were some of the best times. We had a chance to bond on the way home. He gave me his bedroom and he slept in the living room on a La-Z-Boy chair. He lived in a small apartment in the Bronx. It wasn't the best living situation. My uncle had a lot of clutter. He was too old to keep up the place. But it was somewhere to sleep, a way I could get started in New York and try to get my footing.

My uncle's son, Ralph, who I'd never met, had a family in Brooklyn. I connected with them whenever I visited with my uncle on holidays, so they got to know me. My Puerto Rican family. I loved being around them so much because I was getting in touch with that side of myself for the first time. It was so much love. They were so happy to see somebody else from the family. Ralph's son Richie and I hit it off. We were around the same age, but Richie was mad hood. He was always in the streets fighting niggas. He was a fucking soldier, a big stocky nigga—him and Tito, my two cousins. Tito was bald and swole as fuck, looked like he'd break somebody's face off. These dudes were in the trenches. And this is my family. I was so proud to be like, *Yeah, these are my people right here. These are my fucking soldiers.*

Richie and I would hang out sometimes. He did construction and he would come pick me up in his work van. We were always vibing, always joking around. We'd ride around and go to his crib and hang out and shit. As we would cruise, I started coming up with this song, which Richie and I always used to sing together. We'd hum and beatbox it all the time. There was another song that we made up too, called "Sweet Tangerine," which was the most ridiculous shit ever. But this other song—we just kept coming back to it.

I went to Times Square on the first free day I had. Walking around, I was in awe of all the excitement, seeing kids my age kickin' it with their friends. I thought, *I can't wait until I have friends in the city that I can hang out with.* I went to the Lids there and got a Yankees fitted so I could blend in. I figured, *I'm in New York now, time to rep it.*

There were two theaters across from each other in Times Square at the time and I would go see a movie in one and then cross the street to see a movie in the other. I'd watch movies all day—everything from the Will Smith romantic comedy *Hitch* to Frank Miller's gritty comic adaptation *Sin City* to the horror franchise installment *Resident Evil*— dreaming of being an actor having my own movie playing one day.

People in the city could come across as detached, but there was a real sense of community too. I loved that everyone got to know me at the corner store, at the McDonald's, at the bodega, at the barbershop, all over. I had my guy at the barbershop who used to cut me all the time. It was all love, and that's what it is when people start to see you enough times. Because the streets are always watching and they see you going into a building enough times, you're obviously staying there. So, OK, you must have family here or whatever. I never got robbed or pressed in my New York days, and I was always out at the wee hours in the most fucked-up situations, drunk in the worst neighborhoods, and nobody ever fucked with me, because I kept to myself. Plus, I was living that famous Chris Tucker line from his first standup: "I was so broke if a nigga tried to rob me, he'd just be practicing." They would have been disappointed with that lick they tried to hit.

I didn't have money, but I had a lot going on, and on any given night, Jovan would have us on missions, man. He'd go, "Yo, I know about a party over here in the Lower East Side," and we'd go and we'd all be walking for blocks, walking around in circles, looking for this party.

Then all of a sudden he can't find the party. Anytime he came up with plans it was a gamble. But he always knew where the action was. He was in the streets, and since he went to school in the city he was connected with everybody; he knew about the proper shit happening in the scene with young, cool, artsy kids. I started wearing my belt buckle to the side because of him. I felt like I was camping in various scenes:

hipsters, skaters, clubgoers, rappers. I'd been an outsider for most of my life, but now I was a literal outsider in the city sampling its fringe cultures.

I picked up skateboarding and started riding around in Union Square. I had kids who were skating teach me tricks. It was fun for a while there, about a year and a half. But after falling and busting my ass a bunch of times, I started thinking about breaking a bone or something and my mom having to pay for the medical bills. I didn't want to put her through that—have her drive all the way from Cleveland to come to New York to take me and pay. So I gave it up.

Trying to find a job in New York in 2004 was a job in and of itself. I applied everywhere. Eventually, I found this boutique on Broadway in SoHo called the Bee's Knees that sold all the fly shit—a bunch of North Face jackets with Gore-Tex, Timbs, the Beef and Broccolis, everything. It was the one-stop shop that everybody went to. I interviewed at the store and ended up getting the job. Initially, I was working the floor, getting sizes for people. Then I started doing shoes in the stockroom— unloading them, scanning them into the system, getting them organized in the basement. I knew how to talk to people, and I was styling customers sometimes, which could be fun. I loved helping people get what they wanted, like a sneaker they'd been trying to get their hands on for a long time. It paid every week, but I was working a few days and it wasn't real hours. So the checks weren't that great. I was working for just over five dollars an hour, and making about fifty dollars a week. But it was one of those important things, man, because I started to learn the culture.

Being in Cleveland and then being thrown into New York is a

whole 'nother muthafuckin' ball game. Even with the culture shock, being where I'm from made me a well-rounded kid. So I'm the type of person who can be in any room and adapt, and that's what I did. Everybody would ask me questions about back home at work, and they knew I rapped. Some days, I would play my demos in the store. I was already more backpack than street, a downtown kid with hipster vibes.

There was a manager at the store named Faruk, this Indian dude. He was always on my back about getting to work on time, doing things properly, and talking on the floor. He took his job far too seriously. Sometimes he'd be cool, but most times he wasn't. Part of it seemed to come with the title: Managers were taskmasters by nature. I was at the mercy of Faruk. He was my boss. I had to do whatever he said. I knew one day I wouldn't have no boss, so I was dealing with the shit that I had to deal with. It was all a part of the plan.

When I first moved to New York, I used to go to these little storefronts and buy J Armz mixtapes with instrumentals from all the hottest rappers out: Nas, Cam'ron, Nelly, Mobb Deep. I would freestyle over 'em to make songs, approaching the beats like they were my own. That's pretty much how I learned how to make hit records. The tapes would always feature the most buzzed-about record on the radio and in the streets. These J Armz tapes were super poppin', and seemed to come out every week. I stayed copping that shit. I used to put my headphones on, be in the mirror dancing and performing and rapping, studying my moves, and trying to get my swag right, so that whenever I hit the stage, I knew what the fuck I was doing.

Before I got the job at Bee's Knees, I hung out with my uncle at a spot where he played jazz. It was awesome to see him do his thing. Hanging out with him down in Alphabet City, watching him playing with a bunch of other old-school dudes in a little jazz band, jamming out—it was cool as hell. I thought, *This is about to be me when I'm his age. Still doing music.* It put it in perspective for me too: that this is running in my family. This gift. I'm not the first Mescudi with this natural talent for music, and I'm not gonna be the last. That's for certain.

When I was leaving work, I'd always walk up to Union Square to catch the train. If I wasn't ready to go home, I would stop in the Virgin Megastore—one, because it was a cool-ass fucking store; two, so I could imagine my shit being in the store one day; and three, because I liked to listen to new music that they had on display. The store itself was ginormous. Two stories with an escalator. On the outside, next to a bright neon sign of the swooshing Virgin logo, they had album covers in the window that functioned like huge billboards.

They had those listening stations where you could go and put on headphones and play tracks. Once I was there, just like any other day, looking at CDs. I was in the alternative rock section, looking at a Coldplay CD, and then out of the right side of my eye, I noticed some type of glare. I saw this Jesus piece. I looked up, and it was Kanye West, who had recently transitioned from Roc-A-Fella beatmaker to trailblazing star. I snapped my head back to look away, and under my breath I said, "Oh shit." Before I could think of another word, I turned to him with my hand open for a handshake.

I said, "Hey, what's up, Kanye? My name is Scott. I'm a big fan."

He was on the phone. He had an earpiece in, and he went, "Hold on, one second."

He was looking at CDs at the same time, and he stopped doing both to talk to me. He asked, "What's your name?"

"Scott."

"What's up?"

I told him, "Nothing, man, you know, in New York trying to do my thing. I wanted to know if you are looking for artists?"

"Aw, man, I already got a lot of artists right now. Unless you on some Biggie or 2Pac shit," he said.

I laughed. "Nah, nah, but I have that potential for greatness."

"OK, OK," he said.

Security came up to him and whispered something in his ear. At that point, I was taken out of the fantasy and I was able to look around to see a crowd of people watching us talk.

When I turned back to him, he went, "Hey, man, my security says I gotta keep it moving, but what's the name again?"

I said, "Scott, but my rap name is Kid Cudi, and we definitely gonna work again one day."

He said, "All right, I believe it," and he walked away.

I called my friend: "Man, I just met Kanye West."

They couldn't believe it. "What happened? What you say?"

I told them what happened: "I asked him to sign me. He said he couldn't, but I told him he gon' see me one day, we gon' work."

My friend was all excited for me, but then I thought, *Man, it's going to take me forever to make it. Oh my god, I just moved here, man. How am I gonna get to that level?* My friend was giving me advice and telling me it was gonna work out, so I went home and I laid in the bed with the lights off that night and just dreamed—dreamed of my success. I saw myself being driven around by a car service, pulling up to an award show, living in a mansion in Hollywood. I could taste it; it was right there within my reach. I woke up the next day with a new hunger.

■ ■ ■

In December 2005, I went to Atlanta to spend Christmas with my sister because I wanted to see family. She told me beforehand that she wanted to connect me with André 3000. She had befriended his mom through church. Because Maisha was cool with the family, his mom invited us to go over to their house for the holiday. Walking in, you could see all of André's awards from OutKast. There are huge cases filled with MTV awards, American Music Awards, Billboard Awards, everything. My mom was looking at it, and I told her, "I'm gonna get this for you."

"I believe it," she said.

That's why I was so hell-bent on awards, because I went into André's mom's house and saw that. The ambition was embedded there.

I holed up in the back playing Xbox. I was dressed the part, donning this pink Abercrombie & Fitch sweater with a pink striped button-down shirt underneath and some jeans. André came in the room and just went, "Yo, what's up? What you playing?"

I was like, *Oh shit!* OutKast was among the most respected rap acts of all time, a futuristic funk duo whose most recent album, *Speakerboxxx/The Love Below*, the same album my sister and I used to bump in the car together, had just gone Diamond. Here, right in front of me, was the group's smooth, bohemian whiz. I showed him the game. We were just talking. I told him that I did music and he was showing love. I can't remember what he said, because I was so in awe of him. It was early on in my career and I had not met that many famous people. He was as I imagined and he was right there. Being in proximity with someone so beyond comprehension made me yearn for access to the plane he was on.

To do that, I needed a steadier check. Back in New York, I got wind that Abercrombie & Fitch did weekly open interviews for hires. It was nine dollars an hour, which was some real fucking money, and I knew that I would be able to change my situation if I had that job. So I went to the Seaport store for an open interview call. It's pretty much a group meeting with a bunch of other young people. You get to know everybody. It was chill. A couple days went by, and I didn't hear anything. The following week, I got off the train and saw I had a voicemail. It was one of the managers that was hiring people and she offered me the job. I'd got off the train at the 161st Street–Yankee Stadium station and I was ready to catch the bus back home to my uncle's crib. I was so thrilled that I screamed, "Yes! Yes!" in the streets. Everybody was looking at me like, *What the fuck?* but I thought, *Finally some real fucking money.*

I was also amped about potentially making friends. Abercrombie was great because it was filled with kids my age. Everybody there was pretty much in college or doing something. It was a lot of cats from the hood that worked in the stockroom or worked overnight. But I met one of the coolest muthafuckas I've ever met in my life there: this kid named Rillawan.

The Seaport store was popping. The inside was dim lit. Music would be blaring as if it were a nightclub. Rillawan and I always used to rap in the stockroom. That was our thing. One day, he said, "Aye, man, you should meet my dude Dot. He's a producer. He's really fucking dope."

I was like, "OK, hell yeah."

He set it up and Dot and I met at this dude Endo's house at 80 John Street, just upstairs from where the Roc Nation executive Kyambo Hip Hop Joshua lived. We came over; he played some beats. I didn't commit to any, but I heard skill in the production. Rillawan explained to me that Dot was a classically trained pianist, pretty much a child prodigy. His dad put him in lessons when he was a kid and he knew how to write sheet music by the time he was seven. Dot was in school still living with his parents in Brooklyn, in New Lots on Cleveland Street, but he was the real deal. I knew he would be capable of crafting something from the ground up if he worked with me. We got in the studio a couple days later. We made a song. Then another song after that. Kept working. Made more songs. Across the next three years Dot and I made hundreds of songs together. We were on fire. Our chemistry was instant and undeniable, the beginning of a lifelong partnership that would travel to the moon and back.

CHAPTER 12

My uncle Kalil eventually kicked me out. Sometimes he would tell me about his days coming up in New York's jazz scene, but for the most part I kept to myself. He was an old man, and when he was watching his TV shows, I would be writing my raps. We didn't get a chance to connect as much as I wanted to. I was so caught up in dealing with my own shit. Ultimately, I had overstayed my welcome. He'd done his service, and he wanted his bed back.

With no other options, I had to move in with Ronnel on Staten Island. Ronnel had dated my ex-girlfriend turned best homie Ashley in Cleveland and we scouted the city together before moving, but he wasn't really my boy. Still, I had exhausted all of my other options. He was someone I knew, he was in New York, and when I had my situation I asked if I could move in with him.

I was sleeping on this floor with a fucking blanket folded hot dog–style. The floor had carpet, but it was thin. Shit was not comfortable. I had back problems for a minute. It was all fucked up, but that was my situation. It was what I had to do. I was bitter with my uncle for sending me packing. I didn't have the money to move somewhere else. It was as if he was kicking me to the curb in a crazy-ass city despite being my only safety net. But a part of me understood it.

As I lived in Staten Island, I was splitting time between picking up shifts and trying to find industry connectors who could take me to the next level. Staten Island was crazy. It reminded me of Cleveland a little bit, mostly suburban, but the hood was right down the street from a regular residential block. Being there felt a little special because I stayed in Shaolin, word to Wu. I used to take the 40 bus all the way down to the ferryboat every day to go to work at Abercrombie. Three forms of transportation: bus, boat, and train. I had to leave more than an hour in advance to get there on time, and that was assuming the bus would arrive on schedule. It was intense, but I enjoyed seeing my friends, being young, chasing my dreams. Every day was a step closer.

At the time, when I was working with Dot, I met these producers Jerz and Clay at a talent search that took place in a little audition room in Manhattan in 2006. They had connections with Bad Boy and were close with this guy named Prez who ran stuff for Puff for a while. There were hundreds of people there. I walked in thinking, *What the fuck is this? This is crazy. I don't know why I'm here. This is some* Star Search *type shit. I don't know what the fuck this is, man.*

There were all sorts of people, all ages—adults, young kids. *There's no possible way anything's gonna come out of this, but I'm gonna do this because I just fucking feel like I should.* So I did the audition and I got a call a few days later. They said that Jerz and Clay wanted to work with me. My voice was the differentiator, how raw and hypnotic it was. Out of those couple hundred kids, I was the only one that they picked. I couldn't fucking believe it. Jerz and Clay were in the business, working with artists, who knew the ins and outs, and I thought I could learn from them. Partnering with some producers in the game was exactly what I needed.

I started working with Jerz, taking the bus to his crib out in Jersey. He instantly became big bro. He looked out for me. He made sure I ate every time I came over. I felt taken care of. We made some decent songs, but the stuff that I was making with Dot felt more like me. Jerz knew I had the ability; he knew I had the gift. But he was trying to force me to make records that I didn't want to make, or rap on beats that I didn't genuinely love. It wasn't that he was pushing me toward a sound that felt inauthentic; it just felt dated, and I was looking for something fresh. I was doing shit because I was like, *This is gonna get me to where I need to go and I think I need to do this because he's telling me I need to.* I was trying to get from one point to another. I wanted to grow. I thought, *This is just what I have to do then.*

But in the meantime, I'd be leaving Jerz's crib and going back and working with Dot and banging out shit. That was my life for months. I was never truly making the songs with Jerz that represented who I was. I mean, they did—they were, in some ways, still me. It wasn't like I was talking about shit that wasn't Scott. But I don't know, man. If you guys could hear those records you would be able to tell it is a drastic difference between that stuff and *my* stuff. I could feel the difference, but I also knew that Jerz was gonna get me into the label meetings.

■ ■ ■

In his capacity as my manager, Jerz had set up meetings for me with damn near every major label. And no one would sign me. Weeks went by and we got no calls. We weren't getting any feedback either. It was discouraging, but there was one meeting we took at Def Jam that I felt went well. It was with this guy named Patrick Reynolds, but the world knows him as Plain Pat. He was an A&R (artists and repertoire), a label position focused on developing artists, and he was working with Kanye. Pat seemed to be into the music, and it felt like he understood it. He was comfortable with me and he asked, "Yo, do you want to hear some new Ye instrumentals that I got?"

The answer was obvious: "Uh, yeah? Holy shit."

Ye was like a god to me, and the most forward-thinking rapper in music then.

I looked at Jerz like, *Oh my god, this is crazy! We 'bout to hear some unreleased Ye shit.*

He played me one of these joints—which, as it turned out, would end up being "The Glory" off *Graduation*, an LP released the following year. He played the beat, and the sample—this soul sample—and this bass line came in, and the drums came in, and it just felt so good. My life flashed before my eyes. I imagined I was on and I started rapping my ass off like I was trying to make the absolute most of my shot. *I'm at Def Jam, rapping over a Kanye beat. I got Plain Pat the god here. I'm about to fucking go off.* I rapped so long Plain Pat finally had to go, "All right, all right, all right, all right," and cut it off. I was in the zone. I told myself, *This is my opportunity. I'ma fucking go off.* I was good at that type of rapping off the dome. That was the one meeting I left feeling good about.

Months passed, I didn't hear anything from Jerz about any label meetings, but something told me to ask him about Plain Pat. I couldn't believe that Pat wouldn't reach back out.

"Yo, you heard from Pat?" I asked him.

He told me, "Nah, I ain't hear from Pat," blah blah blah.

Something about it didn't make sense to me. One day I was out in the city kickin' it, talking to my homegirl throwing this party. I was in the hallway coming into the spot on the Lower East Side, and I heard a familiar voice outside the front, beefing with the doorman. I went out there and it was Plain Pat.

"Yo! Plain Pat!" I called out.

"Yo! Cudi! Cudi! What's up?" he yelled back. "Man, I've been trying to get up with you."

"What?" I couldn't believe it.

He said, "Yeah, I've been hitting up Jerz. I've had your demo in my car. I listen to that shit all the time."

I don't even trip. "Yo, man, what's your number?"

I hit Jerz the next day: "Guess who I ran into?"

He said, "Who?"

"Plain Pat. He said he was reaching out for months."

"Oh word? What he say?"

"He said he's tryna work."

"Oh, OK," Jerz replied.

I could sense that Jerz was kind of standoffish about bringing in Plain Pat. I didn't know why at first; then I found out that Pat didn't work at Def Jam anymore. Jerz probably thought, *Man, he can't do nothing for us; he don't even work at that label anymore; he got fired.* Turns out Pat had been filling his time supporting the Kanye machine, producing and serving as his A&R, which was its own full-time job. But me—I knew if I was going to the Promised Land, I needed Plain Pat. He was the key to everything.

The spring of 2007, I found out that my uncle was sick. He'd been diagnosed with cancer and nobody knew how much longer he would last. It was painful. I was still so bitter that he had so casually forced me out onto the street. Before he got sick, he was leaving me voicemails asking me when I was gonna come pick up my stuff that I left over there. He said he had it in a box for me. I ignored the messages and never wanted to go get it and see him. I completely shut him out.

When he got sick, things happened so suddenly. The cancer sprung up quickly and took him in a flash. My uncle was Muslim, so he didn't want anything special at his funeral. All he asked for was a pine box. I went to the funeral and the cemetery, and I waited there while they buried that pine box and I just stood there thinking, *Something's gotta change. I gotta do this for my uncle, for all of the sacrifices he made for me here, for letting me stay with him, jump-starting this whole shit. I gotta get it on, for him. I gotta make him proud.*

CHAPTER 13

While living with Ronnel on Staten Island, I lost my job at Abercrombie, got a job at American Apparel, lost that job too, and then started working at Dean & DeLuca on the Upper East Side in the coffee, candy, and dried fruit section. My homegirl Ashley, who I had dated in eighth grade, was still Ronnel's girlfriend, and worked there too. It was the most boring job ever: You'd have to fill a bag with candy and weigh it. That's what I did: put shit into bags for people.

I was always on my lunch break smoking, people-watching, thinking about life and what the fuck I was doing. In those moments, I'd reflect on my journey, all my dreams; seeing all those rich people coming in there and buying shit, the more I saw, the more I'd dream, getting hungrier and hungrier. I knew that the life I was living wasn't gonna be for me forever. I knew I had to stick with it.

People-watching was one of my favorite things to do. There were days at work—whether it was Dean & DeLuca, or Abercrombie & Fitch, or American Apparel—on my smoke break, where I'd just sit out on Broadway or at the seaport, think about what everybody was doing and where they were headed and what their lives must be like. If they were married, divorced. If they had kids. I'd fantasize about being success-ful, having everything I wanted. The more I was progressing with my music and hearing the things I was making, the more sure of myself I was becoming. I was breaking molds—for sound and scene and image, standing at the center of a bunch of different cultures that had rarely interacted before. There was no precedent for what I was doing and that was exciting. It was as if I was making the future.

All of the pieces of the puzzle were starting to come together. I had my producer. I had a manager who saw my vision, who had demon-strated impeccable taste, and who had brought me one degree of sepa-ration away from Kanye. It wasn't a question of if I would make it at this point; it was only a matter of when.

One New Year's, I was getting ready to go out and my neighbor at the Staten Island crib came down. Joey was a white kid from the family that lived next door. They were the coolest white family ever. They al-ways looked out for me. Always. When I wanted some food, when I was hungry, I couldn't feed myself, they held me down. We were all in it to-gether. It was a unity-type thing. But looking out for me, as they always did, they got an eviction notice that had been left for me by the landlord and brought it to me, right before I was about to go out.

I thought to myself, *What the fuck?* I'd been paying rent, giving Ron-nel a couple hundred dollars every month. *Why are we getting evicted?*

What the fuck is going on? We're not loud in this bitch, and it's not like we blast music. We super chill. I was so stressed out. I had already been kicked out at my uncle's place and now I was being booted again, only this time it wasn't my fault. I was starting to settle in and the rug was being pulled out from under me once again.

To take my mind off potentially being homeless in the new year, I went out by myself to this party in the city to link up with some friends. We were all hanging out, and I met this white chick. Superbad. Thick, short hair, and we started chopping it up. Next thing I knew we had a few drinks and she wanted to come back to my place. Ronnel was not coming back for the night, so I had the crib all to myself. I brought her home, and we hooked up. It was one of the most magical experiences I've ever had on New Year's. I went out not expecting much, and it ended up being the time of my life: Being on the ferry coming back out to Staten Island, then getting on the bus, and her taking this whole trip with me back to the hood. Everything. It felt representative of the dramatic shifts in fortune possible in New York. I never saw that girl again. But it felt magical—two in-tune people meeting and connecting, for one night, at a time when one could truly use the companionship. She was a rapper too. I thought that was cute. Suddenly there's this shitty night that turned into something special. It took my mind off being evicted.

Before I got put out in Staten Island, I called my sister to ask her for some money, and she said she couldn't help me. She felt bad, but she just didn't have it. I told her I understood and it was OK. She asked if I was going to be OK and I told her I'd be all right and that I'd figure it out. Then I told her I loved her, got off the phone, and collapsed on the floor of the bathroom. I cried in a fetal position for hours, hungry, not knowing what I was gonna do.

Later, I came to find out that Ronnel had been taking the money from me and spending it instead of paying the rent. I was fucked up about that, and I was pissed at him. The eviction notice said that we had to get out by the thirty-first, which only gave me a few weeks to figure out what was next. I was at Dot's house one night recording, and I thought, *Man, what am I going to do?* I was telling him about my situation and what I was dealing with. I told him, "Hey, man, you know, if I gotta go back to Cleveland, I want us to still work, like, maybe you can email me joints and I can work on shit there and I can send shit back. I want to keep the momentum going. I don't want us to stop. We're in a groove."

Dot said, "Oh, for sure, I'm totally down to stay in contact and work."

He was as inspired as I was.

It was three in the morning and I told him, "Yo, man, I do not feel like going all the way back to Staten Island. Can I crash here?"

He told me of course.

So I passed out on his couch, and the next morning he came down and he woke me up, saying, "Hey, my dad wanted to holla at you."

I went up to his dad's bedroom. Dot had told him about my situation and he said he and Dot's mom looked at it this way: If it was their child, what would they want somebody else to do? They felt compelled to help me. He's a man of God and he wanted to do the right thing. He said I could stay with them as long as I wanted until I got on my feet. I couldn't fucking believe it. I thought, *This is the illest blessing. This is monumental. I can stay here. I can work on music with my new partner that I have a crazy synergy with.* Little does Mr. Omishore know how immeasurably responsible he is for the whole Kid Cudi journey. Had he not kept me in New York in that house, everything would have been stifled. Things wouldn't have happened when they happened. Linking me with his son Dot was the biggest, biggest chess move ever. And that's how you know it was written in the stars. A godly man was responsible for it. He felt something; he knew it was the right thing to do. God told him, you have to keep them together. God and the angels were looking out for me that day, man.

Living with Dot was so much fun. It was like the Nigerian *Full House*. And I was the life of the party because I was that American Black boy that came and mixed shit up. They loved me. Dot's mom, Dot's dad— they were great parents. They are great parents. For me, that was the first time I was even in a household with both parents before. So I got a chance to see a dynamic I never saw before. I never knew living with my dad, because my parents divorced when I was three. I only remember living with my mom. That was the first time I actually stayed around a fatherly figure. He was an exceptional role model, this God-fearing, loving man. A preacher too. Many nights, Dot and I would be there making noise, making beats, and their bedroom was right below us. But at no point did they complain. They never tripped because they knew, *Our kid's staying out of trouble when they're making music. They're doing their thing. They're being creative.*

We played video games, I slept on the couch for the first several months, and then his dad renovated the top floor. He owned the house. They had a tenant up there and they moved out, and he turned one of the rooms into Dot's bedroom/studio. He invested all this money into helping Dot get his shit off the ground. We were in there every night cooking up. They turned a closet into the booth. It was legit. His dad cleaned out the space and did construction. He built a control desk for a computer, added soundproofing, put in a mic stand with a state-of-the-art studio microphone, and then put in a little window so Dot could see me in the booth. We were cooking all the fucking time and it was perfect for me because I had that right down the hallway. I could go down there and be like, "Do you want to cook up? Do you want to cook up? Do you want to cook up?" And he was always down. Unless he was doing homework and shit. Eventually, he started living in the dorms and I would only be able to work with him on weekends. I'd be stressed all week long: "Come on, come on! When are you gonna come home?!" Completely distressed, wanting to work.

My first New York girlfriend was Melissa. We met on Myspace, a newish social media platform that allowed you to build and browse multimedia pages, reach out to and connect with people based on their curated profile. I wasn't walking up on anybody to get play, because I did not look the part. I didn't seem like a suitor. Online you could pretend. We exchanged messages for a while before eventually going out to the movies, and before long it seemed as if I was at her house damn near every day. She was super hood. I'm talking about curly hair, tight jeans, and Jordans. A Lower East Side Spanish chick through and through, and I loved it. In Cleveland, wasn't no Spanish chicks. I came to New York and went fucking crazy. I couldn't believe it. All these Spanish women. I thought, *Oh, dear lord.* I was in love. I loved her whole energy. She was so carefree and she supported me and my music. She used to make me these bomb-ass, ghetto-ass nachos with Doritos but oh my god, the shit was hittin'. It was the best. She always used to cook some shit for me.

We'd been together only a little while when I got Melissa pregnant. It was intense, but almost immediately Melissa's mom put her foot down: "You have to abort this." I wasn't worried about having it. I was twenty-one and she was nineteen and I knew that she wasn't gonna keep it because we were just too young. I was some fucking guy from Cleveland with no money. I was like, I can't really argue with that: "Your mom's right." I was just out there. I didn't even have my own place—have my own bed. There was nowhere to raise a kid. I didn't have anything to show for myself. Melissa got an abortion and I was a bit bummed about it because I thought, *Man, it could have been a blessing.* Shortly after, Melissa and I broke up. We weren't meant to be, but we remained friends. Everything happens for a reason. I wasn't ready yet.

After Melissa, I was immediately drawn to this girl I saw just trolling Myspace one day. I thought, *Man, I want to know who this girl is. But what do I say?* And then it hit me.

I type the message: "Hey, you look familiar. Do I know you from somewhere?"

Total lie. She didn't look familiar. But it was the perfect way into a conversation. Little did I know that it was gonna work. Her name was Kerry Lynch, and in time she came over and chilled, and we talked and watched a movie. We started dating shortly after. We were attached at the hip. We fell in love fast. And we got along so well. Homies that ended up dating. She lived in these apartment-style dorms, and she would cook for me. She'd make these big Thanksgiving meals. But mostly I was so broke that we were spending time at my house. It was so funny because Kerry used to be dressed like a hot girl on a club night, in these short skirts, coming all the way to East New York on the last stop on the 3 train in the hood. Niggas used to see this white girl in this skimpy-ass skirt and they'd be like, "What the fuck? You lost?" She was a bold cookie. Came all the way to New Lots to see her man.

Kerry was born and raised in Yonkers. She was and is one of the coolest white girls I've ever met. One hundred percent Irish. She loved old-school R&B like Ginuwine and neo soul. I didn't have much money, so she would bring me food, or we would go get food—Crown fried chicken, which was the hood chicken spot that had the best burgers and chicken. I still miss that shit, but I be eating too much fancy food now. That shit would probably turn my stomach inside out, give me Montezuma's revenge. I didn't have a bed, just a room with a couch and a small little TV on the floor, and we'd hang there, killing time. We were young and having a lot of fun together.

I quickly became part of the family living with Dot, so much so that they put me on the chore schedule. I did chores a little bit when I was a kid, but then I got to a certain age and my mom just stopped asking. At Dot's house, there wasn't a choice. Everybody did them—whether it was sweeping and mopping the hallway, upstairs, downstairs, the steps; taking out the garbage; cleaning the downstairs bathroom. Could be any of those things. I was always dodging my chores. I'd be out, Friday night, doing my thing, kickin' it, when I'd get a call from Dot: "Yo, remember, you gotta take out the trash tonight."

I said, "Man, can you take it out for me?"

"Man, I took out the trash for you last time."

"Come on, man, please, man, I'm not gonna be home tonight. Like, I got a situation," *whoop, whoop, whoop, whoop, whoop.*

Finally, he gave in and was just like, "Aight."

So he would look after me sometimes. But sometimes he couldn't, and I would just be fucked. Then I would have to deal with some type of consequence. If we all didn't do our chores, or one of us didn't do our chores, his dad, Mr. Omishore, would say, "Oh, you didn't do your chores? I got something for you." Every time that man said, "I have something for you," you knew something crazy was coming. *Aww shit, what this nigga got?* He designed this house so he had the circuit breaker downstairs with full control over the lights for the whole building. And he would go down to the basement and cut off our power upstairs. We'd be up there, in the dark, begging Dot's sisters to charge our phones and have them sneak them back up to us in the room. It's funny now when I think about it. After being booted out of two different spots for different reasons, it was a relief to be able to settle somewhere I could feel comfortable.

A few weeks into living with Dot, I came to him with an idea, the same idea I used to sing with Richie. At that point, I was feeding joints that Dot and I would make to Plain Pat. He would always champion it. I came up to Dot one night and I said, "Yo, Dot, I have an idea. I've been sitting on it for months. But I think it's really good."

The song was in my head for so long that I had written the lyrics in there. I knew exactly how I was gonna deliver it and everything.

Dot said, "Let me hear it."

So I hummed it, and he said, "All right, let me try to find some sounds for it."

He sat at the keyboard and went through a bunch of sounds. We found the synth. Then we added drums. Then a couple other elements. Dot programmed everything—from the melodies to drums. He was using a Triton keyboard. It was the first keyboard his dad got him when he decided to produce, so he had it on deck. Dot also had an MV-8000, a drum machine he got intentionally in place of an MPC. Everybody was using the MPC and he wanted to do something different. He did the drums for the song there and then he brought everything into Pro Tools. The session was very chill. No rush to record. It was just about getting the beat down. It didn't take long. At that time, everything was very instinctual. We just did what sounded good right away.

While he was making the beat, I was finalizing the hook and my verses. By the time he finished I had it fully written. We sat there, went through sounds; he added flavor to it that I didn't even hear in my mind and brought this song to life. That was Dot da Genius—the first clear example of Dot da Genius. And it was me. The honesty—in my solitude, weed was a means of getting out of my own head and freeing myself from all my deep-seated anguish. Despite life's distresses, a blunt could carry you off toward your next frontier. It established who I was and established Dot as well. Two unknown artists with a song that sounds like that. The song ended up being "Day 'n' Nite."

The melody had been stuck in my head for months before I got in the studio. That never happened to me ever again. I truly believe that the angels, that God, brought it to me to set everything in motion. Their mission was to go to earth and infect my brain with this melody, and to make sure I never forget it, so I could do that record.

Lyrically, I was writing from the perspective of an outsider chasing highs as relief from a misunderstanding world: I'm not just going to say I'm smoking weed and getting fucked up and not tell you why. I figured hip-hop had enough of that. I wanted to bring people into the mind of a stoner. I knew people would connect with it because it was a song about underdogs, those staying out of the way, focused on their mission. Space represented both isolation and escape to me. Feeling far off from earth can be both freeing and alienating.

We worked on the song for two nights, recording it, tweaking vocals, mixing, getting it just right. So much rap of the mid-2000s was about maximalism, but "Day 'n' Nite" was minimalist, strobing and hallucinogenic as if it were beaming in from far away. There was something floating and weightless about it. The sound was completely at odds with the on-the-ground, in-your-face energy of everything else. When we backed away from it after it was done, we were listening back after I finished the vocals, and we sat there in silence for a beat.

I told Dot, "This is going to be a number one song, in some country, somewhere."

Dot was skeptical: "Number one song? I don't know."

"Bro, I'm telling you, if not number one, it's still going to be a huge, huge song."

"All right," he replied. "If that's what you feel."

Dot was always riding with me, always my soldier ready to go wherever I was going. "We 'bout to do this," I told him.

"Shit," he said, "then let's lock in."

During that time I'd been making stuff with Jerz—nothing was hittin'—and I was getting discouraged. Pat was also giving me beats. We started working on stuff, and at the same time Dot and I were going into working on more music, finding the sound, seeking out things that were spacey and otherworldly.

When we worked on "Day 'n' Nite," Dot was helpful with the actual vocal performance. Initially I was trying to push the vocals and Dot told me, "Man, maybe you shouldn't sing it. Maybe you should just kind of, like, say it in a melodic way."

I said, "Uhhh, OK."

He always used to tell me to go smoke a cigarette before I did my vocals because he thought it gave me an extra coating to my tone. So I would go out, smoke a Newport, come back, then lay it down. He was the musical ear that I needed, both unofficial vocal coach and conductor-composer. He knew if I wasn't hitting the notes right, and he knew how to tinker with sounds until they fit the ambiance. He wasn't just a beatmaker. He produced me, from the ground up. And I needed that because I was not (and am still not) trained. I was never any good at playing instruments. I can't read sheet music. I just do this shit with my ears, inside my own head. So it was nice to have his guidance to formally execute my vision.

That was my brother from the jump. He was only one year younger than me, and we got close. He was more student than producer at the time, trying to get his footing just like I was. He was also producing some of his friends, these four other guys who never panned out, and I'd see them at his house, but eventually they stopped coming, and it ended up being just me around. At the time, he was feeling some type of way about it, but I was telling him, "Man, don't even trip. We 'bout to get it on." I was always building him up, letting him know that he was the illest and that what we had was something special. I was so excited about "Day 'n' Nite" that I knew it needed to be my first single. I wanted this to be the first time people heard me. My uncle Kalil had passed away from cancer, and I felt miserable because we never got to squash our issues before he died. But it stoked my resolve because now the trip had to pay off big. Now that he was gone, it couldn't be for nothing. So I called Plain Pat, sent him the song, and he fucking loved it. He agreed it needed to be the first single. I told him we had to get Jerz on board. He told me to hit him up and let him know.

I told Pat, "I need you to come on board and be my manager."

He said, "Ask Jerz if it's gonna be cool."

"It's gotta be cool," I responded. "I want you to do this."

I told Jerz, "Hey, I have this song. I think it's a really big song. And I want it to be my first single."

"OK."

"And I want Plain Pat to come work in management with you. I think it'd be dope."

"OK, send me the record. I'm gonna listen to it and I'm gonna hit you back."

This wasn't how Jerz and I usually operated. I never came to him with a record, saying, "Look, I made something like this. And I want it to be my first single." He calls me back a few minutes later, and he goes, "Aight, well, I listened to the record, and I thought about it, and I think I'm gonna just bow out gracefully and let you and Plain Pat do y'all thing."

I said, "What? You sure?"

He said, "Yeah."

Got off the phone. I hit up Plain Pat, and told him what Jerz said.

Pat said, "Word??"

I said, "Yes!"

I love Jerz. I really do. He believed in me way before anybody else did. He saw something in me, but I realized right then: Jerz made a huge mistake. One of the biggest songs I've ever made in my life he turned down. He heard it before anyone in the world. And he turned it down. I forgive him now, but that hurt me at the time. He was able to just walk away from me. I thought he believed in me as an artist. So it crushed me. I was being driven by two intense fires now. My uncle was gone and Jerz was doubting me. I had to not only honor my family legacy but convert all nonbelievers. There was no other choice: I was about to blow, come hell or high water.

CHAPTER 14

Navigating New York City's creative communities meant knowing the right people. Hang around the right places, the right parties, long enough and you gel together as if by osmosis. As a result, it didn't take very long for me to get cool with the kids in the city's downtown scene. My time working at American Apparel got me connected. And Myspace spread that network of connections even further. There was a group of kids who were like *the kids* to hang out with. They were so cool to me. The most interesting group of misfits, all creative in some way. Where I'm from, there's maybe one creative person in a group. I saw a whole posse of creatives. It was so inspiring. That was what made this city so incredibly unique: It seemed like icons and trendsetters were around every corner.

I'd found another tribe. They all fucked with my music and my energy. They honored me. I busted Dot's balls about the fact that he was born and raised in Brooklyn yet I moved to New York and experienced more shit in three years than Dot had in his life. He never left Brooklyn. I would always tell him, "Yo, bro, you got to explore. You got to see more." He never wanted to leave home.

I was going out a lot at the time, working my way into industry events or going to parties downtown and in Williamsburg. The party promoter Jason Scott was the connector in that world, and he introduced me to Vashtie, who was the queen of the downtown scene. She used to throw these '92 throwback parties at Santos, a major hot spot at the time, where DJs played old-school records and people would wear fresh-ass gear from that era. They were huge. Everybody came out. You were nobody if you ain't know Vashtie and she wasn't inviting you to her party.

Vashtie, to me, was the ultimate cool girl. She was a supercreative multihyphenate director, DJ, model, clothing designer, and all-around tastemaker and scene maker. She was dating this dude named Scott, which used to stress me out. I hated that. It was one of those things where, when Vashtie and I got cool, I realized that we'd just be friends. It wasn't like that with us. I thought she was so hot, but I didn't want to disrespect. She always had a boyfriend when I knew her, but I always had—and I think everybody in that scene had—a thing for Vashtie. She was the downtown sweetheart, the liason to all things cool at a time when so many subcultures were mingling—indie rock, hipster, fashion, art, hip-hop. It was a moment when streetwear brands were putting out rap mixtapes. Vashtie existed at the intersection of so many crucial scenes and movements. She worked at Stüssy, modeled for fashion designer Rachel Roy, and was the first woman to design for the Jordan brand at Nike. When she wore something, everyone else wore it too. When she threw a party, anyone worth knowing was there.

It'd be her; Jason; Dice the God, who was always popping up at every event; Tommy Campos, a staffer at *Complex* magazine; and the singer Bridget Kelly, who became my crew. Bridget and I were mad tight. I would go over to her house and kick it with her. She was another one of those gorgeous girls where the line was clear: We just gon' be brother and sister. When I meet a woman, I always kind of let them lead the energy. I can tell if somebody's feeling me or if they are being friendly. And a lot of times people were being cool. I love having home-girls. That was my shit. And they were all insanely talented, doing their thing in music or photography or something else. Everybody had a bag. It was inspiring just being around them.

Jason was a close homie. He threw his own parties too, and his shit used to rock. I had no money so I would go to his events and he would hook me up with drink tickets all night. I'd be in there broke as fuck drinking their bottles. They were always looking out for me.

Hanging out with those kids was so eye-opening. I'll never forget it. Taking pictures in the subway. Being drunk and dumb. Hanging out in the city until late. Four in the morning, talking shit, smoking weed, just kickin' it. My boy Tommy Campos used to pick me up in his dad's Hummer and we used to go get beers and kill 'em across a bridge before we get to the other side. Tall boys, double deuces of beer. We'd pack the car with the homies and go into the city. I would drive sometimes. (*Don't drink and drive, children!*) I love driving in New York. This might be bad. His dad might find out about this. Sorry in advance, Tommy. But Tommy was my boy and he believed in my music. We used to go to the magazine parties and get fucked up and look at all the celebrities. *Complex* was like the streetwear bible at the time, existing at the intersection of all things rap and youth culture. Over time, they'd become one of my most consistent champions in media.

There was this one *Complex* party where Chris Brown was there.

He might've been sixteen at the time, and I just walked up to him and started battling him. I can't dance, but I started challenging him out of nowhere and I'm talking about me as a no-name nigga. I was not famous at all. Nothing was going on with music. But I came up to him being bold and started doing the dance shit to him and he started laughing and dancing too. Chris and I have been cool throughout the years. He's been a homie and supporter. But that was the only interaction we had that night. I didn't come up to him asking, "Yo, I make music?" or anything like that.

I'd go to these parties with my friends and just get fucked up. At that time, I used to wear my peacoat that I got from Old Navy for the low low, and my fedora. That was my steez. It was around this point that I got close with Babs from *Making the Band*. She was working with Dot in the studio. When she came the first night, it was the first time I was around somebody who was in the light. And she felt like a big sis. When I couldn't feed myself, she would come and pick me up, take me to get some food. She would hit me up and check on me and ask me if I ate, and I would tell her, "Nah, not really," and she'd take me. She was a real friend.

All these kids were gifted. I don't think any of them understand how much they inspired me. I was just a dude from Cleveland. I didn't have this life. Hanging out with them changed everything for me. Such freedom, being young in New York without a care in the world. Knowing that any moment could become your moment, the perfect opportunity seemingly lurking beyond the next corner.

I was still searching for my opportunity when Plain Pat suggested I go to the release party for Kanye's "Stronger" video at Tribeca Cinema in

2007. It was right after my uncle died and I'd just made "Day 'n' Nite." A-Trak, Kanye's road DJ, was working the event. He'd built a rep as a star DJ, having won the DMC World DJ Championship as a teenager. When I got there, I texted Plain Pat, and I told him: "Yo, I think your boy A-Trak is here."

"Yo, get him to play 'Day 'n' Nite,'" he replied.

"I don't know him like that. You think he'll just play this shit?"

"For sure, that's my boy. Just go up to him and tell him who you are. He'll play it."

I was like, "OK."

It was a super-crowded industry party, one of the events where it felt like everybody there was somebody. I was feeling anxious to be there, but at the same time a little shy. To say there were women was an understatement. I looked over to my left and saw this stunning beauty. It was the singer Cassie. I was a bit sheepish because this was a real industry event, so I was looking around nervously and being low-key. Then I saw her and approached her. I was a fan of her music and her style. I chatted her up and we exchanged numbers. After settling back into the flow of the party, I was standing around for a little bit not knowing who else to talk to. I went up to the booth, which was upstairs—a ways up—and hollered, "Yo, A-Trak, my name is Cudi. I'm Plain Pat's artist. I wanted to know if you could play my single."

"Yeah, for sure, man, give it to me."

He put it in, and before I could get back down to the floor, the song came on. I started watching people's reactions. They were bobbing their heads and getting into it. And I thought to myself, *Yeah, people like this. People like this.*

Kanye wasn't there yet, so everybody was chillin'. When he finally arrived, the place was even more packed than before. We watched the screening, came out, and A-Trak was playing music again. We were all congregated in the lobby, and he dropped "Day 'n' Nite" a second time. I stopped in my tracks and trained my eyes on Kanye. I stood there motionless in anticipation. I wanted to see what he would do. As the song played, I could see him bobbing his head from a distance. I thought, *Yooooo! Yoooo! He fucks with this! He fucks with this!* I was watching him vibe to it the whole time, and then I watched other people in the party vibe to it as well. It was so validating.

Once the party started dying down, I went upstairs to say thank you to A-Trak for not only playing the song but running it back. On my way there, Kanye was coming down.

I said, "Yo, what's up, Ye? I'm Cudi. That was my song that A-Trak was playing." I didn't mention our previous interaction at the Virgin Megastore years prior, and it was obvious he didn't remember that run-in.

"Oh, yeah, yeah, yeah, I fuck with you," he replied. "I fuck with a lot of the songs that Plain Pat played." Apparently, Pat had been sharing music I'd been working on with him.

I stood there dumbfounded. I called Pat and told him everything that happened. Maybe a month later, we got a call from A-Trak, who wanted to do a deal to make "Day 'n' Nite" a single on his Fool's Gold label, which had put out singles for blogosphere darlings like the Cool Kids and Kid Sister. Breaking as an artist in those days took a lot. There was no streaming, so artists had to hit the ground level: Radio airplay was still king, but mixtapes could get you onto blogs and onto a label's radar. The internet was evening the playing field—for me and others—but the labels still held most of the keys to getting music out. Fool's Gold would distribute the single, and we'd let it bubble for a while and just see what would happen. It was super legitimizing to know that my song was about to officially be out on a label. It was all starting to happen.

Just as my music was getting some traction, a different door finally opened for another dream job: working at the Bape store. At the time, in 2007, A Bathing Ape was the pacesetter in streetwear. The brand was already among the most hyped imports stateside, especially in rap culture, which had heavily influenced the style. I fucked with it hard, so I jumped at the opportunity. I've had a lot of retail and service jobs, and a lot of them were cool in their own way, but Bape was groundbreaking. The store brought eye-popping, flamboyant color to SoHo. Hands down. I've had some other cool jobs too—the movie theater, that was probably my second favorite job—but I'd been waiting to get the call from the Bape store. This was maybe my third time applying, and I needed the job too.

I didn't even have any Bape prior to working there; that shit was just too expensive (a T-shirt was like $120), so I pretty much wore my uniform around that they gave me for free. One uniform every fucking day: a brown T-shirt that said "A Bathing Ape" on it, some dark blue denims with the tassel with the cowboy rope logo on the back, and then some yellow Roadsters. I wore that for the first couple weeks until I could get some money and buy more clothes from around SoHo. My friends at the store were holding me down. The manager Danny, a man of few words, would always let me borrow some shit. Danny was a cool muthafucka. Also Eric, who I nicknamed Zolee, a gentle giant, but he was from a tough upbringing. Just a straight-up real nigga.

That was my fam that I met at Bape. We would always have a dream of the brand's founder, the designer and DJ Nigo, coming to the store. Bape was growing into streetwear lore. Founded in 1993, it brought Japanese flair to hip-hop style. The Clipse and Lil Wayne were early adopters stateside, and the unique pieces included colorful hoodies that zipped all the way to the top.

I started to do research and discovered who Nigo was. I just wanted to be a part of the brand. He was a giant, a mysterious figure that had this huge, self-made empire. It was so inspiring to see something he started in Japan have such a big impact worldwide. Only when I started working at the store did I truly understand the fandom. There would be lines waiting before we opened the store. The brand was reaching Supreme levels of cult impact and demand, for hype beasts before Hypebeast.

Everybody would go, "Yo, Nigo might come in today, Nigo might come in today," and everybody would be on their tip-top behavior but he wouldn't show. One day he came with Teriyaki Boyz, his rap group, and I was starstruck. I talked to the crew member Verbal and told him that I made music and that was what I did outside of work. That moment, seeing the guys get out of the car service, seeing them walk through SoHo, just living their lives, spending money, and balling. It was inspiring.

As I was working there, Pat came to meet me in the city. He pulled up to the store in his BMW and called me out to his car. When I got in, he told me he had some new Kanye shit and asked if I wanted to hear it. The answer, as before, was obvious. The first few seconds were so magical. When the drums started kicking in, I lost my shit. Then the stabby synths hit. *What the fuck? How am I going to compete with this? What kind of music am I making? I have to create my thing that exists in the same world with this shit?* The song was "Flashing Lights," and would end up on *Graduation*, the latest in a long line of Kanye albums shifting the culture forward with daring sonic leaps. I would always get discouraged when I would hear Kanye stuff because it was just too good. At some point, I told Pat to stop playing me his shit.

We were still figuring out the deal with Fool's Gold. During my day job, I was going back and forth with the label's cofounder and art director Dust La Rock on the artwork for the single's cover. A-Trak had connected us, and I quickly found out he was a legend. It was an honor to have him do my first cover: this dope cartoon of me in an astronaut costume in space with the planets all around me. I told him that the Moon Man was my character, inspired by the Andy Kaufman movie, and I needed something spacey.

I didn't give him any specific ideas, because I didn't want to restrict him. I told him the things that I liked. I was having to sneak out of view of the store's security camera to see new edits of the artwork, give approval while I was at work, and text real quick and then go back on the floor. I was approving designs for my first single while I was on the clock at Bape.

Celebrities used to come into Bape all the time, and when rappers would show I would disappear into the basement. I didn't want no rapper to be able to use it against me, and go, "Nigga, you sold me clothes." So I would hide so they wouldn't see me.

"Day 'n' Nite" came out on iTunes digital download first on February 5, 2008, and it was also released on twelve-inch vinyl with "Dat New 'New'" on the B side. There was a little DIY release party for that in this shitty little hole-in-the-wall spot you wouldn't expect something to be happening in. I'll never forget when they gave me the vinyl for the first time. It felt like holding a piece of art. That's why I always tried to take it somewhere with my album covers. I was thinking about the kids who might be taken by them and get them framed. I was riding that high for a little bit and then I shot music videos. All of this while I was still working at the Bape store. It was a mindfuck, because people were starting to come into the store and recognize me.

Someone would come up and say, "Man, Cudi, I fuck with your shit."

Then say, "Can I get this in a large?"

I flat-out refused to be the guy grabbing sizes out of the back forever. I told Plain Pat, "You gotta make a mixtape for me."

He had already made this groundbreaking tape for Kanye called *Can't Tell Me Nothing*, and I knew he could make some shit like that for me but in the Cudi flavor. So he brought in Emile Haynie to help produce some of the stuff and cohost the mixtape.

Emile was a fan of "Day 'n' Nite," and we connected immediately. It was the same way I connected with Pat. Emile became another big bro that looked out for me and actually cared. He believed in what we were doing. And it was a different world sonically from what he knew of rap. He was coming from a hard-hitting hip-hop realm, having worked with rappers like Ice Cube, Raekwon, Cormega, and AZ, and he was stepping into something a little bit more whimsical. He switched gears and dove right into shit he might not have if I weren't in that room.

The three of us were in the studio Monday through Sunday. We were meeting up at this place on Broadway, just south of Houston. There was a little lounge room, a control space, and then the booth off to the left, which was packed in. We could be there as long as we wanted, as loud as we wanted. A lot of it was throwing out ideas of what songs we could make. Pat and I would shoot songs back and forth—I sent him the André 3000 song "Pink and Blue," saying, "Nobody's touched this." I told him I wanted to rap on the "Chonkyfire" beat from OutKast. We wanted to find the best songs that weren't obvious. I could take them and re-create them and make them my own. I wanted to approach them as if they were original beats. It was my own version of jackin' for beats, only I wouldn't just rap for twenty-four bars straight with no hook. We would spend hours listening to records, and then I'd discover a loop I liked and tell Emile to flip it. Before he could even put drums on beats, I'd be ready to go.

We all inspired each other. We all pushed each other. They were both more established than I was—older and more successful. They were making money on records they did already, and I was yearning to reach that level. If we went more than three days without studio time, I'd be blowing up their lines. And anytime I got discouraged, the encouragement was always there from them.

When I saw the Cool Kids at MTV Spring Break and I was still working at the Bape store, I was bugging out: *How these niggas get on here?! My music is way iller than theirs!* I was hating, full-on jealous. The Cool Kids made great music. I had trouble accepting my situation. But Emile and Pat had a way of pulling me out of my funk. It was a great brotherly experience working with them crafting that mixtape, piecing that bad boy together. We worked on *A Kid Named Cudi* for about eight months. Dot wasn't heavily involved with the mixtape, but we still were working on shit and I put a couple joints that we did on there. I kind of let Plain Pat and Emile take over and helm that whole project.

I had this idea to start the mixtape with people sitting in an audience waiting for a movie to start, as if to say that this would be the start of my entire career. Listeners would hear it and from there on out they would be watching the same movie. Forty years from now it'd be the same film. That was how I wanted to start this.

My homegirl Jen the Pen, who was the first person that I met when I was in New York, had her ear to the street. She knew what was going on with all of the latest mixtapes and the rappers breaking out because of them. I was excited to tell her about my plans to start one, because she knew I came from Cleveland to do this shit for real. She was a supporter, so I had to hit her. "I'm doing this mixtape," I said.

She asked, "Who's gonna be on it?"

"Nobody, just me," I told her.

At that time, I wasn't even thinking about putting anybody on it. The tape was all me.

She said, "Yo, Scott, nobody's going to listen to your mixtape unless you have a credible artist on it to make noise."

I said, "I disagree. If this shit is hot, it's gonna make noise and people can find it. And I'll be good."

We went back and forth and ended it with her disagreeing with me. It was a bummer because Jen was my homie. When I visited New York the first time, I met her on the ferry. I thought she looked good, so I asked her for some gum to start a conversation, and we became tight. I was checking for her to support me, but she didn't see the vision. When I became successful, I ran into Jen, and she apologized, saying that she'd learned a lesson: Never doubt nobody. You don't know who anybody's gonna be. I thought that was cool—that she was able to see that and apologize. Over the years I would see her around because she started dating the GOOD Music rapper Consequence. It would always be love. She was so proud of me. She saw me from nothing. I didn't have shit. Literally before anybody in that city witnessed Scott Mescudi, she saw it. What she didn't recognize was just how radical and perceptive my methods were, and how the rules of the old industry no longer applied. On the internet, I could carve out whatever space I wanted.

So much of that space was online. At first, Myspace was just a way to connect with friends. I would see artists had music pages, but you had to be on a label to have one. The shit that changed everything was when the site made music pages accessible to everyone, including up-and-coming independent artists. So I made my page, and I started putting my music on there, and it started to take off. The response to the music I put on the platform was always positive. It gave me a lot of confidence as an artist: *Look, I'm nobody, and these strangers are giving me honest opinions, and they're saying they fuck with this shit.* I put "Day 'n' Nite" on there, and the song got so big that it became like The Myspace Song. You would go on a P2P file sharer like Kazaa and sometimes it would be labeled that way. Myspace let people build their own pages and then add songs to the profile. It was a huge part of why I blew up—how other people found me, how execs found me. It was the real start of the independent music movement online. And you could do shows and get promoters hitting you up directly. It gave an artist the means to push their music straight to an audience without a label in the mix.

In 2008, I had built up enough buzz to take my online songs out into the world and I went on tour with Hollywood Holt and Mano. We had a little twelve-seater van or some shit and we slept in that muthafucka. Sometimes we would get a hotel and sometimes we would have to sleep on the road. It was fucked up. I got bronchitis bad on that tour. I gave up Newports and that was the first time I quit. Holt told me, "You've gotta stop smoking them cancer sticks, man." We were in LA at the time and my temperature was about 105 degrees. I was performing and almost passed out. After every song, I kept coming to the DJ booth and Pat, who was my DJ on the road, was asking me, "Yo, you good? You good?" I'd just say, "I'm cool; play the record," and come right back exhausted, destroyed. That was intense. But when you at that level in the game you do what you got to do. The show must go on.

Dennis, my oldest friend, officially came onto the team that year. I didn't need him to be a manager or anything like that. I already had a road manager and Pat. So I was like, "Look, man, you can just be my assistant." And he was holding it down for a couple years.

Kerry and I were still going strong, but we were having issues. I would always go and visit her dorm and hang out with her. But I knew that it was bad and we were better off as friends. So we broke it off. We tried to stay close for a little bit at first, and I think we did, but of course it gets weird when you start seeing other people.

I was out partying one night in 2008 with Vashtie, Pat, Pat's girlfriend Mimi, and some other kids, and Vashtie said she needed to go to the Gansevoort hotel in the Meatpacking District to pick up her boyfriend. I stood outside while Vashtie went to get him from the club and I saw a girl standing by herself. I went over to talk to her, and before I approached her I thought, *All right, man, Scott, don't be scared to go up to her and talk to her.* So I got the courage, walked up to her, and asked her name. "Jamie," she told me, asked mine, I told her, and we hit it off. At the time, Jamie was my dream girl, but I was really wrapped up in making it.

That summer was all about working on the mixtape, trying to make the illest shit possible. A lot of the songs and ideas came from Plain Pat. The goal for the mixtape for me was to make a project that showed every color of the Kid Cudi spectrum. I wanted to show all my different gears—rapping, songwriting, song structure, melody—and no matter where I wanted to go, I wanted people to be ready. It was a perfect introduction to the world. It came out on July 17, 2008—on Dot's birthday. It was mega. The tape was released by the streetwear brand 10 Deep, and it built upon the momentum of "Day 'n' Nite," establishing me as more than a flash in the pan.

CHAPTER 15

When the mixtape dropped, I felt validated. I wasn't crazy after all: *I do deserve to be here. There is a clear role that I can play.* Things started to happen almost immediately, and I was getting booked to do shows, which was putting my music in front of more people. A week later, I was performing at SummerStage pushing songs from the mixtape.

We did the listening party and the release event at Red Bull Space in New York City on 40 Thompson Street. Before I got there, Plain Pat texted me that Kanye was coming. *No fucking way.* This was the first time I'd heard from Kanye since the "Stronger" premiere. I would always hear Pat say, "I gotta go work with Kanye, gotta do something; I gotta go run off and do this," but I never asked him, "Yo, he ever say anything about me?" or anything. I felt that when it was time he would reach out. So when he hit me up to tell me he was coming to my listening event, I was so geeked. Then I wound back my enthusiasm: *Nah, he probably won't come, man. He's probably just saying that.* But that muthafucka came.

He was there wearing these super big shades with the whole crew: the GOOD Music exec Don C; his barber, Ibn Jasper; all kinds of people. It was a monumental moment, man. I felt so good to have support. It was a packed party. Super dope. And I had my fedora on. That was my look back then: fedora, shades, and a leather jacket.

I took that look on the road for my first-ever tour: Kanye's Glow in the Dark tour. This show was not designed for me to shine at all. I had to perform on a stage that was like three feet. I couldn't do much. There was very little room to move around. I appreciated the opportunity, so I went out there and gave it everything I had. But I was out there like, *Fuck, this kind of sucks. I can't wait to do my own tour so I can actually fucking have a stage design and do all the things.*

Being out there was worth it for the tour experience. I loved being on the road. Hanging out with Don C made it unforgettable. He would let me wear his Jesus piece, and he kept telling me, "Oh, you gon' get one soon?"

I'd be like, "For real?!"

One time, I slept with it on because I was so geeked about it and I forgot to give it to him. When I gave it back the next day and apologized, he said, "I knew you had it. I just let you get that off."

A couple months later, Kanye gave me my own chain. I was in a studio session and he walked in, just handed it to me, and tried to walk out. I'm like, "Wait a minute, wait a minute! Holy shit!!" That was a huge moment: the Chaining Day. I felt like I had arrived. It was nice to feel like I was part of a family.

The "Day 'n' Nite" single was out and it was public online. It was taking off. This amazing French director, So Me, came through and gave me the illest video ever. In it, I'm walking around Los Angeles, doing everyday shit—grabbing a slice of pizza, going grocery shopping, visiting a bar—but the scenes are overlaid with colorful pop art graphics that seem to remake the world as I envisioned it, and seem to project my creative future into existence. Kanye paid for it. I didn't have my deal yet. It was around $400,000, and he covered it. I don't even know how that happened, just that he said he'd pay for it and it was paid for. I was so thankful.

Mid-summer 2008, shortly after I had dropped *A Kid Named Cudi*, I was at the club Santos, where Vashtie used to throw parties, and this was one of her nights. The shit was rocking. One of the illest parties in New York City. I was in there walking around by myself. I don't know what the fuck I was doing. I was drunk. I don't know if I was looking for some trim or if I was walking around aimlessly, but this tall white guy came up to me.

He said, "Hey, yo, Kid Cudi. My name is Ian. I'm a big fan. I loved your mixtape."

I was like, "Oh man, thank you, thank you."

He asked, "Yo, man, have you ever thought about acting?"

At this point in my mission, I was so heavily focused on music that acting was not something I was even remotely thinking about.

So my response was, "Yeah, I have, but I'm kind of, like, focused on music right now," or whatever. I'm like a one-dream-at-a-time kind of guy.

He was like, "I asked because I have this TV show that I created at HBO and I wanted you to read the script and have you audition for this part if you liked it."

"Uhhh, OK?"

"Let me just get your email. I'll send you the script. You let me know what you think about it and we'll go from there."

In my head I was thinking, *Man, worse come to worst, he ain't gonna hit me up and it's cap or I can give my email and he hits me up and it's a real thing.* So I decided to give my email. I said, "Let's take a shot." Two days later, he sent me the script. The show was called *How to Make It in America.* I read it and fell in love. *How to Make It* was about young entrepreneurs trying to hustle their way into the fashion scene, using their streetwise mentalities to navigate a cutthroat city and its industry. It was so New York. It was perfect.

I hit him back and asked him what role he wanted me to read for. He said the role of Cam. Anybody who has seen the show knows Cam was super-Dominican, and, though I am Black and Mexican, when you look at me, the first thing that pops into mind is a nigga. Some people think I'm Dominican; some people, sometimes, some places, think I'm Haitian—when I was in New York, I used to get a lot of that. But I immediately had reservations. I was like, *Yo, I'm not gonna get this. I'm not Spanish enough. I don't even know how to speak Spanish.* So part of me felt like I was so wrong for the role. But I went to the first audition, did it, and got a callback. I couldn't believe it.

I did that callback and they liked that too. In a follow-up chemistry-reading workshop I worked with different pairs of actors; I worked on the scenes, and every time I popped up, the show's main director and producer, Julian Farino, would always say, "The Kid stays in the picture," in his British voice. It was so funny. He was a champion of Scott; little did I know. Every time I saw him, he was happy to see that I was still in the running. Seeing that support had me geeked.

I finally got a call to do a last chemistry test at HBO headquarters, but it was at the worst time. I had bronchitis, but there was no way I could not show up for this audition. So, sick as fuck, I went. I was so sick that I passed out in the lobby. Didn't even hear them call my name. Every time I went in the room, I kind of snapped out of it. It was tense when I walked in. Everybody was quiet. The other actor that was with me was quiet. I was like, *Why is everybody so nervous and quiet in here? Man, it's like a funeral.* So I took it upon myself to liven it up in that muthafucka. I was like, "What's up! What's up!" and every time I came in the room they'd be pumped to see me. I just brought my energy—I brought Scott Mescudi to the table, that Scotty charm that gets them every time.

Because I didn't know how to read a script or study a character at all, I was looking at it like this: I was told that this show's a comedy, and I needed to make this funny. So I took the lines and spruced them up a bit and made them a little more comedic. In these chemistry reads, you're not supposed to see any type of reaction from the people in the room. But I genuinely had people laughing out loud when they weren't supposed to. I left that audition feeling good, but I was curious to see how this shit was gonna pan out, because I knew I did well in the audition, and that they liked me, but I still knew I wasn't Dominican enough.

Two days later, I got a call from Ian Edelman: "OK, I got some good news, and I got some bad news."

So, to me, I'm thinking, *OK, the bad news is I didn't get the role, which I knew I didn't get, and the good news is maybe they want me to do the theme song or some shit like that.*

"All right, tell me the bad news first," I said.

"The bad news is: You didn't get the role of Cam."

I knew it.

"But the good news is: They loved what you did in the audition so much that they want to create a new character based on that, and let you name him and style him."

I couldn't fucking believe what I was hearing. Things like this would happen in my life and it was almost like it didn't feel real. I just got an offer to star in an HBO show—*in an HBO fucking show*—based on an audition gone wrong. And I got to create my own character.

A couple weeks went by and I got this other offer from a promoter on Myspace to tour Australia for two weeks for three grand and I thought, *Holy shit, I have to do this.* To me, it was a once-in-a-lifetime opportunity that I had to take. I wasn't stop-on-the-street famous, but I was a little bit internet famous because of "Day 'n' Nite."

I asked Bape if I could take off for three weeks to do the Australia tour and they wouldn't let me. I was faced with a dilemma: Do I keep the job at Bape or do I go out and do this once-in-a-lifetime opportunity, make a little money, and see Australia? I thought, *Fuck yeah, I'm doing this*, and Dot and I got on the plane and flew there. I quit the Bape store and went on my trip.

We were out there on our own in Australia. Seeing people in a whole 'nother country know my shit, knowing the mixtape stuff, it was wild. The power of the internet—right at the time when it was becoming a thing to find music online—and the mixtape took off.

I was very shy offstage, but when I got up there and the mic was on it was a whole other person. That's why I started getting a lot of show offers, because the word was getting around that I was a strong performer. We didn't have any money for a rehearsal space, so I never rehearsed beforehand. We came up with the set list and went, and when the lights came up, it was on. That's half the battle: You can get in the studio and make a bunch of cool shit, but if you can't perform it, that's not a good look. In some shows, it'd be twenty people there. Some shows there would be more. But I rocked every single one of them, thinking, *Fuck it.* Even if it was only a few people: That's what I had to do. It's about paying dues. I never bitched or complained. I had twenty muthafuckas in there? Guess what? Twenty muthafuckas 'bout to be rocking tonight.

I went to this place called Magnetic Island, which required a ferry ride, and I was on the boat, listening to my iPod—to Coldplay's "Viva la Vida"—looking at the ocean, looking at the sun, on a beautiful blue day. All that I could picture in my mind was Jamie: her face, her smile, her voice, her gentleness. I told myself that when I got back to the States I was going to make Jamie my girlfriend. I made the decision right there while I was listening to "Viva la Vida." That became my hero's anthem to make Jamie my girl. The part at 1:30 will always remind me of Jamie. That musical moment conjured thoughts, magical thoughts, of Jamie and me, hanging out, laughing, at peace. We hadn't had sex yet. We hadn't even kissed. It was all puppy love. I was crushing on her. And I was constantly thinking, *I'm gonna tell her how I feel.*

So I got back, and I met up with her.

I said, "Hey, I want to tell you something."

"Yeah, Cud. What's up?" she replied, using her nickname for me. I loved that.

Then I told her, "I really like you a lot."

She was like, "I like you too, Cud."

"For real?" I couldn't believe it.

She said, "Yeah! What do you mean, 'for real?' You can't tell?"

And I felt like a fool, because when I thought about it, of course she liked me, but I couldn't see it. We started to hang out a little bit more after that and it was the best feeling when I was with that girl. She was proud of me, and I thought she was perfect.

When I got back from Australia, I had no job. I was home for two days and I was stressed because I needed work. I didn't know what the fuck I was gonna do for money. The three grand I got for the performances, I spent all that on food, clothes, and just kickin' it. So I had nothing to show for the trip. But on the second day, Plain Pat called me and said, "Yo, Kanye needs you out in Hawaii. You gotta get there."

"For real?" I asked.

"Yes, he wants you to come work on some shit. You gotta get out here. We out here right now. Can you get out here?"

I said, ". . . Yeah!"

I don't know how I got the flight. I think I got a buddy pass from one of my friends who worked at the airport. Pretty much flew over Hawaii coming from Australia and ended up having to fly right back. It was wild. The whole time I was not knowing what I was going to walk into. Super scary, but I was ready to rise to the occasion regardless.

When I pulled up to this huge swanky hotel, Kanye was outside talking to somebody on his team. I got out and I greeted him. He said, "Hey, we all about to go play basketball. You play basketball?"

Me being the least athletic person you'll ever meet, I explained to him that I did not play sports, but if he wanted me to keep score, I could. He laughed and said he'd come see me after. So I said, "Cool."

Later that night, we met up at the studio. Right when I got there he came up to me and said, "Yo, I got some beats for you. I want you to come up with some ideas. I'm working on Jay-Z's album, *The Blueprint 3*, and we need some hooks." He was telling me he had some joints he wanted me to work on. The stunning, massive studio we were working in, Avex, was on the water and had a little patio on the back. The studio was super futuristic and had this very modern style that was like some type of space headquarters. But the entire thing was set against the natural backdrop of this serene island. I found that relaxing, so I went onto the back patio, took my laptop, listened to the music, and just vibed.

Kanye came right back out and asked, "Yo, so you got anything?"

In my head I thought, *What the fuck, man, I've only been out here for ten minutes.* "I only got one idea." He told me to hum it.

"Oh, they want me to fall, fall from the top . . ."

He said, "Get in the booth and record that right now."

I got up, got in the booth. Lots of people were in the room. They played the record. The bass came in. I recorded. Pandemonium in the control room. I just see niggas going crazy, losing their shit. I thought, *Oh my god. They like it! Holy shit, they like it.* I recorded it maybe two more times. I came out and they were all going crazy. Kanye loved it. That was the real beginning of our relationship. Creating banger after banger after banger. Our creative energy melding together was polar synchronicity—a lonely stoner and a Louis Vuitton don, both college dropouts, in a glorious counterbalance of maximalist ego and psychedelic wonder.

As soon as I finished "Already Home," I knew I had to write more immediately, so there was no time to celebrate. The sessions were focused on Jay, but Kanye was also collecting songs for his next album. I thought, *All right, let's get it on.*

I came up with another hook for a song that was initially called "Cooking Up in the Kitchen." The hook went:

Cooking up in the kitchen
Young boy had this vision
I gotta get with it
ooooh, whoo, ooooh whoo, oooooh whoooo
Cooking up in the kitchen
Young boy had that vision
I had to get with it
oooh, whoo, ooooh whoo, oooooh whoooo

Everyone was going crazy over that shit. It felt like a huge anthem. I could see the hood singing that shit at stadiums. But out of all the songs that we came up with, that was one of the songs that Jay didn't fuck with. So when we were working on *808s & Heartbreak*, we took that song, revamped the lyrics, and it became "Welcome to Heartbreak":

And my head keeps spinning
Can't stop having these visions . . .

It was just one of those things, man. I was happy Ye got to keep that one. It was perfect for *808s*. It's the perfect introduction to the sound. The album was moody and electronic, synth-forward, auto-tuned, and minimal. It felt both like a throwback and innovative. And "Welcome to Heartbreak" seemed to tease out all of the album's lofty sonic and emotional objectives.

Working on *808s* was overwhelming because there were always a lot of people in the room. I hated being in a crowd throwing out lines to try to make the cut. That was a disaster for me. I could not handle feeling like I was in competition with other artists. I would sit there sometimes, to write and be in the mix, but a lot of the time I would go to the side or off into another room, record my bits and my ideas, and submit them later. I wasn't an industry songwriter, fishing for placements on other people's hits. If I were, I would have loved the dynamic and process going on in the room. But I was just starting out; I didn't even have my debut out. I'm an artist, you know? I was kind of only doing it to help out my friend. That wasn't what I wanted to do. In the back of my mind, I was thinking that I needed to focus on my album. I hadn't found my groove yet. There was a little bit of anxiousness. I felt I needed to be focused on developing my own sound. Still, the whole thing was a net positive experience—to just sharpen my pen and learn more about collaboration, working with different people. It was a boot camp.

The English singer-songwriter Mr Hudson, who had recently entered the GOOD Music orbit, was there. He was always with his guitar, coming up with salient, original ideas. Damn near everything he turned in Kanye was fucking with. Mr Hudson was a secret weapon for *808s & Heartbreak*.

Plain Pat was with me the eight weeks I was out there, and when I went back periodically over the next year to record. I don't think all that was happening had sunk in for us. We were being heavily courted by labels. One of the people who was fucking with me at Shady/Aftermath was Paul Rosenberg, who had signed and managed Eminem. Paul got it. Eminem, to me, was a god, so making that connection felt like closing the loop on my teenage admiration. There was clearly interest, but they hadn't put a deal in front of me.

I didn't know what I wanted to do just yet. A lot of shit was happening. We also had this man named Nigil Mack that worked at Universal Motown checking for us. He was on my ass, bro; this muthafucka was hell-bent on signing me. Sylvia Rhone, who was running the label, sent that muthafucka to seal the deal. I liked Nigil because he was chill. He understood what I was trying to do as an artist, but I still felt undecided. The situation escalated into a bidding war, but Motown had a leg up. Pat and Emile represented me as my managers, and I had two entertainment attorneys, Renee Karalian and Michael Guido, as my wolves.

In the midst of all the other labels, Kanye wanted to sign me to GOOD Music, which, having put out records for Common and John Legend, was looking to become a next-wave juggernaut. It's interesting: When I think about it now, I'm proud of myself for not being caught up in the hype, the fact that Ye wanted to work with me. I wasn't a child star. I was twenty-four years old. I was comfortable in my own skin. I knew who Scott was. I wasn't confused about that. And I knew I didn't want to live in nobody's shadow. I'm not nobody's sidekick. I'm a lone cowboy. That's how I always looked at my shit. I was fighting against that possibility with all my might. I wanted people to like me for me, not because I'm standing next to somebody else. So I was conflicted for a while with the GOOD Music shit.

Months went by and I was just in my own head. I was finally getting what I was asking for—the opportunity to live making art—but I was hung up on choosing the right situation. I didn't want to sell my soul. The money was good, well into the millions. One day it was $1.2 to $1.3 million. One day it's $1.4 million. Some of the labels wouldn't go higher than $1.1 million. Motown pretty much said "fuck this" and went to $1.5 million. I definitely wasn't trying to make the decision based on who had the most money. I went to Motown because I was going with a Black woman—an impressive, successful Black woman that understood me 100 percent.

When I met Sylvia Rhone for the first time, it just felt right. She felt like my auntie, and I knew she wasn't bullshitting me. I was still green at this time; muthafuckas would smile in my face and I thought they were genuine when they weren't. But, in hindsight, I always knew that Sylvia was a straight shooter. She was a champion for Scott Mescudi. She saw this long and beautiful career for me before I even saw it for myself. So I ended up signing with Motown in a joint venture with GOOD Music (which was an imprint distributed by Def Jam), and I was able to own half my masters. It was a relief, man. Once I had Motown locked in, shit, we hit the ground running.

At the end of 2008, I got my deal, which was for five albums, and we started recording my debut. I got an advance of $200,000, as an investment into me as an artist. I hit my accountant, Phil Sarna, and told him I wanted to see all of my money in my bank account. Put the whole advance in there. I'd never had a bank account before this. I was using my mom's National City Bank debit card when I worked at Bape, because they only did direct deposits. I walked over to the Bank of America on Broadway, which was close to where we recorded, I got to the ATM, looked left and right, making sure nobody was in my business, and put in my PIN, and checked my balance: $200,000. *Oh my god: I'm rich.* I took out $200 and thought, *Holy shit, I'm gonna be good. I don't have to worry about money no more.* I had a new pep in my step. When I was leaving the ATM, somebody recognized me. I took a picture with them and went, *This is your new life, Scott. Old Scott is gone and he's never coming back.*

I had all these ideas that I had been sitting on for years—ways of framing an album as a story that I always said I wanted to do if I ever had the opportunity to make a debut. I was heavily influenced by Pink Floyd's *The Wall* and *The Dark Side of the Moon*. Those two albums changed my whole shit. I discovered them digging, searching for weird and trippy bands. Kids talked about Pink Floyd when I was in high school, but I never got into it. So I took a deep dive and was so struck by *The Dark Side of the Moon* that I wanted to form my entire sonic universe around that energy. Something cinematic. I was in awe of the sound design, the way the music transported you to another universe. That's the energy I wanted my music to have, like you were being shifted out of your reality, into my mind. That record changed the way I thought about creating.

The *Man on the Moon* concept was inspired by the movie of the same name, starring Jim Carrey as Andy Kaufman. My affinity for *The Dark Side of the Moon* was just a coincidence. Kaufman's comedy operated where the line of the joke and discomfort crossed. Even though he was controversial, he was skilled at challenging conformity. I wanted to have that same effect with my shit. In music. I wanted to make people uncomfortable. I wanted to challenge the listener. I wanted to do all the things that we weren't getting in hip-hop in 2009, breaking from convention, blurring the lines of genre, singing and rapping, looking inward with my lyrics. You were not getting shit like that—creative, inventive, emotive shit—and I wanted to arrive with something new, original, fresh. So I leaned into it.

I came at the writing of *Man on the Moon: The End of Day* like it was a film score. The album needed to tell a story. Everything had to fit into the broader narrative arc. When I made the song "In My Dreams," I knew I wanted it to be the intro. Emile made this dramatic, twinkling beat that called to mind a conductor guiding a symphony just beyond the horizon. I thought it was the perfect raising of the curtain. That's

why I named it the "Cudder Anthem." That song was me opening a secret door in my brain and letting the world get into my thoughts.

When we made the beat for "Solo Dolo," I was super hype. We were
flipping through some records one day at the studio on Broadway and
Emile was playing samples. One of them stopped everything in the
room: "The Traitor," by the funk group Menahan Street Band. I had him
play that shit back, told him to pitch it, slow it down, and loop it up, and
then started writing. *Oh my god, this was so eerie and dreamy.* I just tap-
danced all through that muthafucka. I love my tone on that bitch. You
gotta think about it, man: 2009, a song like "Solo Dolo" was so unorth-
odox. There's still no record quite like it. A lot of my music is that way.

I worked on "Heart of a Lion" in Hawaii with the engineer Anthony
Kilhoffer. Free School produced it. My boy Jean Baptiste, who I met
around that time, hooked me up with some beats. He and his partner
Mike McHenry made this beautiful-ass production, and I wanted this to
be my theme music. This was me being the superhero that I was always
meant to be, fighting my demons. I was recording and I started fucking
around and doing the "*No no no no no no no, yeah!*" part, which was a
joke at first. I was totally fucking around, but then Kilhoffer said it actually sounded good and that's the only reason I kept it in there. After
I listened to it back, when we did all of the stacks and shit, I thought,
*Whoa, this is actually fire! This joke turned into something that we can
actually use.*

When I was working on "Sky Might Fall," we did it during one of Big
Sean's sessions at Jim Henson Studios in Hollywood. I kind of deeboed
my way into the session. Kanye was working with Big Sean and I got in
the room and finagled a beat out of that man. I had a melody that I had
been sitting on. I hummed it to him, and he said, "Let's lay it down."
"Sky Might Fall" was a fucking smash. I knew it immediately. Those

chords, the synth, it's an unforgettable feeling. Kanye had the producer Jeff Bhasker with him, who worked on *808s* with us. We met in Hawaii and hit it off, but this was my first time getting to know him. He was this wavy white multi-instrumentalist with the fingers of a magician. Everything he played felt like wizardry.

There was this time at Avex in Hawaii when I asked Jeff to go downstairs and grab my blunts and he said no. I got agitated, and Pat pulled me to the side and said, "Jeff is a musician; he is not your assistant." I had to apologize to him. New fame was rushing to my head and I was thinking people were at my beck and call. But I had too much respect for Jeff to be rude. We used to smoke weed out of fruit. We made apple bongs. Then we would go out by the ocean near the studio and try to see who could throw the apple the farthest in the water.

We were so in tune with each other creatively. We did a lot of shit together on *808s* too. He was just a Zen dude to have around, a musical hippie Yoda. We used to smoke a ton of weed and make music in Hawaii, so it was great to have him on board cooking with us. I eventually let Jeff feature on my album. He asked me and I told him, "No problem. You're going to be Billy Craven. We ain't gon' say shit. We ain't gon' tell nobody about it." I don't think people to this day know that Billy Craven is Jeff Bhasker.

For all the collaborators I connected with in New York, one key part of my network hailed from back home in Cleveland. I met Chip Tha Ripper for the first time in Chicago once at a show, and we hit it off on the spot. He was my type of nigga. Chip had a special sense of humor. He could make anybody in the room laugh. It just seemed infectious. He was a good spirit to have with me. I needed that brotherhood at the time. I had it with Dot. I had it with Dennis. I had it with Plain Pat and Emile, but it was nice to have another brother from my hometown, somebody I could represent with. Putting Chip on the album was me representing for my city. I almost felt I had to. Chip was the hometown hero at that time. He blew up in Cleveland before me. He got popular while I was gone, but I got word about him having a presence. So it was only right. And he could rap his ass off too.

The album was starting to come together into something cohesive with a bigger conceptual story to tell. It was feeling like its own modern masterpiece, something that would usher in a new musical moment. I was becoming more and more sure of myself as an artist. The painting was becoming full. I was seeing everything, track by track. My first album was such a big deal because I didn't know if I was ever gonna get another one. I thought, *I'm gonna make this muthafucka the album I want to make, no matter how weird and trippy it is. This is what I want to create and that's all that matters.*

CHAPTER 16

Paths to both music and acting were emerging for me, and each presented opportunities to work with some amazing artists and establish collaborative relationships, some that would last a lifetime. It was all building to the big debut.

As we were putting the finishing touches on *Man on the Moon*, I had to fulfill one of my creative dreams: working with Ratatat. I was obsessed with the band, which featured the guitarists Evan Mast and Mike Stroud. I listened to their music religiously in my bedroom. Their trippy instrumental music was the soundtrack to my early twenties, straight up. I would sit in the dark for hours listening to them. When it came time to do my album, I knew the producers I wanted to work with, and they were at the top of my list—before Pharrell, before Kanye, before anybody, it was Ratatat.

The label reached out to Evan, and he gave me his number so we could meet up. I called him from my BlackBerry on my way to his spot in Crown Heights to tell him I was on my way, and his phone went to voicemail. He had this dope-ass beat on there. I thought, *Damn, this shit hard.* I left him the message: "Hey, man, I'm on the way."

I got there and one of the first beats he played me was the beat for "Alive," and I was in there vibing. I came up with the hook and everything instantaneously.

We finished the song, but I had that other beat on my mind. I had to let him know: "Man, there was a joint on your voicemail that was dope. What was that?"

Evan said, "Oh, that was some shit I just made and put on there."

I told him, "Yo, play that for me."

He played it, and it blew my fucking mind. "Send me that! Send me that too."

I got beats from Evan and sat with them to record in my sessions. I just followed my impulses on the melody and the lyrics. First idea, best idea. It's all feeling. *This is how it came to me and this is how it should be.* I don't let my head dictate shit. Writing the lyrics only took one night. I was sitting in the room thinking about how I could come up with the perfect expression of debauchery. I wanted to bring a moment of wild youthfulness to life.

"Pursuit of Happiness" was labeled "Nightmare." It was meant to be a fucked-up song from my perspective. I was trying to write about the recklessness of being young and looking for happiness in drugs and alcohol. When I wrote the song, it wasn't really supposed to be a party anthem. I was twenty-four thinking about all of the bad decisions a kid can make in the hunt for joy. When the remix came out, it turned into something else. People were celebrating and getting fucked up to it.

That was not what I wanted. I wanted people to take heed to what I was saying and learn from it. I thought the message got misconstrued: *I'm going to be fine once I get it.* That was really the lesson of it: to just shed a light on the lost. The ones that are just out here trying to maintain. Those who seek happiness but can't acquire it because there's so much pain. The remix took it to another level. I was standoffish at first because it was meant to be a warning, but over time I embraced it because I saw that the song brought so many people joy. That helped me make peace with it. I recognized that we had done something powerful that had helped people. It became an anthem for kids all around the world.

A beat that Evan didn't even play me, that I just heard on his voice-mail, became *the* song.

I opened for Ratatat at Terminal 5 in April 2009, and when I got there I heard the actor Josh Hartnett would be in attendance. I was dead set on meeting him. After the show, I came up to the top of the VIP area where he was and I approached him. He told me he loved the show, and we exchanged numbers so we could kick it. I didn't know what I was in for. One time, he took me to The Box, which is this erotic burlesque show that combines music and theater. It starts late, goes until morning, and is very intense. There was shit going on on that stage that I was not prepared for. I looked over at Josh like, *Where the fuck did you bring me?* He just laughed.

Having these wild nights with him, just hanging out, drinking, kickin' it, was such a blast. As famous as he was, I didn't get a pretentious energy from him. He was just Josh. I knew when I met him, I had to keep him close. There aren't many people like that in this industry.

He was talking to me about how he produces, and we just decided to do the "Pursuit of Happiness" video together. He set it up with his homeboy Brody Baker, who directed it, and Drake came through to support and made a cameo.

Shooting that video, I kept telling Josh, "We're making something really fucking ill, dawg."

He said, "I know. I can feel it."

I think everybody on set could sense just how monumental that production was. It was an epic thing that we were doing.

That year, I reached out to Jay-Z and told him I had music for Willow Smith. I was really inspired. "I can produce for her. That would be cool." He told me he would connect me with Omarr Rambert, who was her brother Jaden's producer, mentor, and creative partner. Omarr was like, "Yo, you got something for Jaden? I need you to work with him. He could really use it." So I met up with him and his little friends, and they were so full of energy and life. Such cool kids. He was eleven or twelve. I had picked up cigarettes again at the time, but I would make sure I was smoking far, far away from where they were, so he didn't see me doing it. I was super protective of Jaden. I'd always wanted a little brother, and he looked up to me. He was my little homie. He grew up listening to my music with his older brother. That was how they bonded. So he and I were locked in from day one.

Music was connecting me with a lot of new people. I went with my buddy Jean Baptiste to the video shoot for the Black Eyed Peas' "I Gotta Feeling," and when I was there Jean said, "I need you to meet this guy. He wants to meet you. His name is David Guetta. He's one of the hottest dance producers out there."

David was a fan and he wanted to work. He had something on his laptop that he wanted to play me right then. Between takes, sitting outside by the pool, he's playing me this beat, and I gravitated toward it instantly. We got in the studio a couple days later and recorded it. I'll never forget how quickly it came about. Building that track with him, working on song structure, was so enriching. Trying to figure out what pieces we needed led us to the catchiest moments. I knew it was going to be one of those songs that are gonna be around forever, it's just too fucking undeniable. The message in it. So many nights, I had the feeling expressed in "Memories."

Sometimes it felt like all I was doing was making memories. I did this show in Cleveland, my first real show post–Kid Cudi, at a House of Blues, and my sister, Maisha, came backstage. She was crying, and I was like, "What's wrong?"

She said, "Man, I don't know. I can't deal with this. All these people screaming at you. All these fans you got. It's so weird to me. You my brother!"

She couldn't wrap her head around it. She was stressed out about it. I think it was like that for all of my siblings: *This is happening? My brother is famous?!* To see how kids reacted to me and the energy, it just fucked her up a little bit.

I felt like I was only just getting started. The next big milestone was launching my debut without a hitch. I was with Kanye finalizing the mix for the whole album in Hawaii at the Avex studio, listening to a song we were calling "I Poke Her Face," when he turned to me and said, "This is going to be your first single." I was sitting there and he was looking at me because I wasn't responding enthusiastically. I told him, "I don't know if I want something so vulgar to be my first single. I got a mom. I got a sister. My first single is a song called 'I Poke Her Face'?"

He said, "Bro, this is a hit. This has to be your first single."

But that was not the first impression I was trying to make. I liked the song, don't get me wrong, but I made a bunch of songs for that album and that was one I wanted to cut. We ended up changing the name to "Make Her Say" and pushing it as a follow-up to "Day 'n' Nite." When you hear that first album, it's the only song that's a little out of place. We could have led with a stronger first single. We could've led with "Pursuit of Happiness." "Make Her Say" didn't even chart like that, despite having big "we need a single" energy. About a year after the album was released, Kanye told me, "You were right about 'Make Her Say'; always follow your heart."

I had a checklist as we were mixing the album, and I didn't think I was missing anything, but there was one group that I still wanted to fuck with: MGMT. The first time I heard MGMT, I didn't know it was of that time. I thought it was some shit from the past I'd never heard. We were filming a video with these dudes BBGUN for "Day 'n' Nite"—the first real video for "Day 'n' Nite." They were playing music while we were setting up for the next shot—playing "Electric Feel"—and I said, "Yo, what the fuck is this?"

"Oh, this is MGMT," someone told me.

I said, "When did this come out? The seventies or something?"

"Nah, man, this is now. It just came out."

What the fuck? I was hearing that shit in complete amazement. My brain melted. I knew MGMT was the last piece to make the album complete. The two dudes who were in the group, Andrew VanWyngarden and Benjamin Goldwasser, were psychedelic masterminds. Their music seemed both of a different generation and ahead of its time.

I linked up with them in a studio at Electric Lady the day that Michael Jackson died. When I left my apartment, Michael was in the hospital in a coma. Andrew broke the news to me right when I got in the studio. I stood there for about two minutes in shock and just mourned. Michael's music was everything to me, since I was a kid. In the immediate wake of that, it was time for us to start the session. That cast a dark cloud over the vibes. That, and also I had liquor and weed and I got MGMT too drunk and high. They were giggling at the sounds on the synth. They would hit a note and then start chuckling to themselves. They did it over and over again for a while, and I was looking at them having a good time, but, at the same time, I was thinking to myself, *Holy shit, man, we ain't got no song.* We'd been there for six hours and we didn't have a song. *What the fuck?*

Early on in the session MGMT asked me to play them some songs so that they could catch a vibe of the album. "Pursuit of Happiness" was one that caught their ears, so we listened to it a couple times.

I said, "Hey, guys, I know we couldn't come up with something, but y'all seemed to like the joint a lot. Why don't y'all fuck with this hook?"

And they said, "Cool, yeah, we'll try it."

They went in the booth, they both did their layers, came out, we listened to it, and we knew we had something special. It was indisputable for me. I just knew.

When we finished "Pursuit of Happiness," I couldn't believe what we had made. I thought, *This is a perfect song.* Sonically, it was so new. As I was playing it for people, before the album came out, they would ask me, "What's that synth in there? What's that sound?" They were curious about how it came together.

It happened quickly. A lot of the songs on that album did. I had a lot of ideas and things to say. On my mixtape I was making a bunch of songs that would showcase my abilities as a rapper and a songwriter, but the album was meant to dive a little bit deeper into my psyche and show people who I really was. "Pursuit" was the essence of that. It's a little time capsule of what I was going through and where my head was at. A lot of kids still deal with those same things, and they will be forever and ever. The mid-twenties are confusing for so many people. It's a song of hope, one that will endure until the end of time. I knew we had accomplished something great. I had Ratatat. I had MGMT. I had a funky-ass guitar solo. It was my dream record.

After MGMT left, my engineer and I were mixing until five in the morning at Electric Lady. I was in the studio. It was late, I was tired, and I was in this place in my life where I was looking for something else to get me to the next high in my life—to numb me up—because things were happening so fast and the weed wasn't enough.

I was in the studio with my homeboy Martin and he had some coke. I had been curious, so I asked him if I could have some. He was hesitant at first. Martin was my big bro and he was looking out for me at the time. But I felt a part of him was thinking, *Hey, if you doing this shit, I'd much rather you do it with me, and not out here in the streets with some random muthafuckas giving you some sketchy drugs*, you know?

We did it, and it was the most thrilling experience ever. I felt so alive. I thought, *Yes! This is it! This is what I needed!* I wrote in the song "Soundtrack 2 My Life": "I'm prolly this close to goin' and tryin' some coke," because that was where I was. It turned out to be a premonition.

The danger of it was intriguing. I liked to live on the edge at the time. It was a fun drug, but it meant death if you misused it. That was part of the allure. I don't think, in the moment, I was thinking my fame-fueled lifestyle was happening too fast. I was thinking it wasn't happening fast enough. When you're doing what you've always dreamed of doing, you're not thinking, *Oh, I'm doing this too much*, or, *I need to take a step back and breathe. I need time for myself. I need to think things through.* It's, *Yes, let's go. I want to do more.*

Once I became Kid Cudi, there was suddenly a lot of pressure to deliver. As soon as that first album is complete, the label's checking for the second one, and they want the second one to come out next year, and I didn't have any ideas yet. For me, the first album held all the ideas I'd been sitting on since I was a kid. It captured an entire life of experiences and emotions. *Man on the Moon II: The Legend of Mr. Rager* was the first album that I had to make from scratch. Coke got me into the studio, working, and confident. I would do it just to get out of the house. Instead of taking a car service, I would walk so people could see me and recognize me. Coke made me way more comfortable being around strangers. It gave me superpowers.

What I really wanted to do was create a cinematic album that you could put on and just let rock from beginning to end. I had the idea to have this story kind of play through it with these different acts, like chapters, going through my life's journey from my younger years to entering adulthood. It was like a review of everything I'd been through.

Part of the reason *Man on the Moon: The End of Day* sounded the way it sounded was the sample choices. The songs we chose were different from anything else people were doing in hip-hop. Sonically, I wanted to push the genre. I was eager to work with an orchestra, and Larry Gold understood exactly what I was trying to do. We would finish the records and then send them to him; I had ideas in my head for what I wanted to create and Larry would build on them.

As I was working, I wrote the interludes, which I decided would feature Common. He was already a part of GOOD Music and I liked his voice, so I just thought it would be dope to have one of the OGs narrate the album. I would take the interludes and send them to Larry Gold, telling him what I was looking for, and he would just embellish and make them fully realized ideas. It was fairly simple. I had it all mapped out. The album kind of pieced together. When you're working on one, you do all these records, and then eventually it all makes sense. When I was making a track listing, everything just fell into place. It was really a way to just take the listener on a ride. My mixtape was my introduction to the world and now I wanted to display my purpose as an artist. What I stood for and what I went through. How I became the man I was. Honesty was key. I never wanted to tell fables. I really wanted to speak from a true place.

Beyond that, I needed to show the world there was a different perspective in this space. We had a few artists, like André 3000 and Kanye and Pharrell, that were doing their own thing, but, for the most part, like 99.9 percent of hip-hop was all street shit. I felt early on that the only way I was gonna make a name for myself was to be unique.

I did an interview at the radio station Hot 97 with Angie Martinez and DJ Enuff where I said that *Man on the Moon: The End of Day* would be the most magnificent album ever made, and they were looking at me like, *Yeah, right, nigga.* They were really trying to clown me on everything else but the music. I mean, we spent like thirty minutes talking about my skinny jeans, and then finally, at the end, Angie asked me why I felt the album would be so great. I broke it down: I said, "Hey, it's broken into acts; it's really cinematic; it's different." They really didn't fucking get it. It fucked them up. But I knew they'd see eventually. I understood how weird it was. The adjustment would take some time.

My reference points were so far away from the Hot 97 norm. In 2009, I went to this Band of Horses show at Carnegie Hall and I saw the lead singer, Ben Bridwell, come out in a flannel, some jeans, and some dusty-ass sneakers. And he sounded amazing. I thought, *Look at this dude, coming to this show like he just woke up and threw anything on, and he sounds like this.* From that point on, I told myself that was gonna be my vibe: no superstar jewelry, just very casual.

The tour with Asher Roth and B.o.B. that summer was a monumental tour for me—my first real tour front and center. They were the chillest guys and we all had a camaraderie. We didn't hang out that much. But when we did, it was like homies, because we knew each other beforehand. We were all in the same *XXL* Freshman Class, in the same blog-rap circles. That was the first time I really took homies on the road with me. We were all at the same place in our careers, and were all trying to take rap to new places, albeit differently. That's what made it such a cool thing: We were literally all on our own frequencies, but we fit.

The day before the album came out, I was stressing, like, *I think I made a mistake. "Pursuit of Happiness" is such a weird song. People are going to think this shit is so weird, like, oh my god, what have I done?* I was second-guessing myself the whole time, wondering if I made the right decision.

I told the label I wanted to do a trailer and have it play in movie theaters across the country. It was a little teaser—the shot travels through space, going all the way to the moon's surface, then I pop out; you see my face and the date of the album. It ran for a couple weeks. I did *106 & Park*, BET's music video show, with Kanye, leading up to the release, and I did my first late-night performance on *Letterman*.

On the day of the actual release, I went with my *How to Make It* costars Bryan Greenberg and Victor Rasuk to Times Square to hand out CDs. We were out on the town, blasting the album, cruising around. It was such a moment, man. They were happy for me, and I was on a high. I couldn't even fathom what was happening. My debut album, in the world. Unreal.

Man on the Moon: The End of Day entered on September 15, 2009, and boom: It was a massive success. One hundred and four thousand copies sold in the first week, just behind Jay-Z's *The Blueprint 3*, Whitney Houston's *I Look to You*, and Muse's *The Resistance*. This is in a time when people actually had to get up and go to the stores and buy an album. You had to get in a car, drive to the record store, and buy that album. That was a helluva strong number for a debut. It turned out I'd been worried for nothing. After that first album, there wasn't anywhere I could go without security. I had one guy attending me at all of my public appearances.

In the fall of 2009, we started filming the first season of *How to Make It in America*. The pilot was my first time acting ever in my life, and I had to prove myself. I didn't have a talent manager or an agency. Amid label talks with Shady, we knew that Paul Rosenberg was an attorney, so we asked him if he could represent me in the deal as a favor. He recommended somebody at an agency, a guy who went to school with me, whose sister I had classes with. So I felt comfortable with him speaking on my behalf. But Paul set it all up and was very helpful. The show's vision of the American Dream was running parallel to the one I was living.

When I started to get the rundown for the episodes for the season, I was seeing that I had more and more shit to do, and I thought, *Hey, I gotta be toe-to-toe with Bryan and Victor in scenes.* Eddie Kaye Thomas came into the fold. I was a huge fan of his and of *American Pie*. I geeked when I was working with him. He was my favorite. He made me laugh all the time. Eddie is a golden gem to the world. He and everybody on that set, everybody on that crew, everybody on that cast, they all embraced me. Nobody treated me like just some rapper-actor that was just there. Everybody honored me.

During one scene, it finally hit me. While I was delivering my lines, in my head I was thinking, *You're doing it.* I didn't forget what I was there to do, I still did my thing, but I had this out-of-body experience watching myself at the same time: *Whoa, I'm doing this shit professionally on an HBO show.* It was unreal.

I was nervous at first; I'd never taken acting lessons, but after the first couple days I could feel it getting easier. I was way more comfortable. Everybody was so cool, and my character was meant to be the comic relief, so there were a lot of jokes. I was clowning around on set, having fun. Playing Domingo, I was just being myself. The character didn't even exist before the showrunners saw me, so they gave me a lot of freedom to embody my vision for him.

Acting was so different from making music. With acting, I was playing a small part in a big production. It's not my thing. I'm playing my position. Music is all me. The packaging, the beat selection, the mixing, and the lyrics—it's all coming from my mind. The beauty of acting was I could simply play this part and I didn't have to feel the pressures of having to create something. When I was acting, I felt like I was taking a break. I was used to shouldering more of the load. I was coming from Pat, Emile, Dot, and me sitting in one room by ourselves; the walls could start to feel like they were closing in on us given the demands. With a movie or a TV show, you have a whole crew. You got all this camaraderie, all these people to befriend—costars, the crew, the director, producers. It's like we're all working together to make some cool shit. I took a load off when I was acting.

The deeper I got into abusing drugs, the harder it was for Jamie and me to stay in sync. It was off and on a little bit. We were off when I was in Chicago for Lollapalooza in 2009, and I hit up Jackie from my Applebee's days. Jamie and I were talking, but we weren't together yet.

Hanging out with Jackie felt amazing, and I was happy to see her. We had stayed good friends even after the breakup, and we were able to maintain this bond over the years. It was something I cherished. I performed at Lollapalooza, Jackie came, and it was an epic show. It was my first time performing there, at one of the biggest festivals in the world, and I was on cloud nine. We hooked up that day. Weeks later, she texted me and told me she was pregnant.

Once I realized it was happening, I got excited about the idea of being a parent. When I came back from a European promo run, I went to Jamie's house that night and told her. She was hurt and upset. Her words at the time were: "You ruined everything." I stayed with her that night and we worked through it. She didn't want to leave me. It was the realest shit ever.

That fall I spent a lot of time with Jamie. In between meet-ups I was touring with Lady Gaga. It was so cool going on the road with a real rock star. She didn't give a flying fuck, and I resonated with that. I didn't give a fuck what anyone was talking about either. I was just doing my thing. We would perform "Make Her Say" together every night with her playing the piano. I didn't see her much otherwise, but when I did, it was always love. Or at least it was initially.

Following shows on the tour, I would often do other little aftershows at a smaller venue in whatever city we were in. While I was performing at one, this fan threw a wallet at me onstage. I was upset, and asked those muthafuckas, "Who threw this? I should come down and steal on you right now." Somebody raised their hand, and I was like, "Look, I'm gonna give you this back. Don't throw it back up here." I handed it to them, and then they threw it back. I jumped in the crowd and just swung on the first kid I saw, thinking it was him. It wasn't. I punched this random kid multiple times in the face. Gaga found out about it. It was all over the news, and she kicked me off the tour.

I was so butt hurt, and I was mad at Gaga for a little bit, because I was like, *Man, she's judging me. She don't know about what happened.* But soon I found out that the kid was trying to get in contact with me. He didn't want to press charges or anything like that. I invited him and his friends to a couple shows as an apology, and afterward we sat in my hotel room, ordered pizza, talked, and listened to music. In a weird way, the incident gave me an opportunity to meaningfully engage with a supportive fan.

After leaving the tour I went and spent Christmas with Jamie's family. Her brother Jimmy, who I connected with, got me a Darth Maul lightsaber as a gift. He knew I was a *Star Wars* fan, he was a *Star Wars* fan, and we hit it off. We used to play *Gears of War* together every time I would come over his mom's house when they would have family gatherings. He was a good kid. I liked being around him and the rest of Jamie's family. It was when I was away from people that I was suffering.

I only ever did cocaine alone. I was drawn to it in isolation. I wasn't doing it that often at first—just here and there. I'd go every day for like a week, then stop for a month, start again for another couple weeks, quit for a week, start again. It all depended on what I had to do. When I traveled I didn't do it. I never did it when I had a show, because I was worried I would do it and perform and my heart would burst. I would only do it when no one was paying attention. But my time by myself was increasing. I'd become reclusive, and I felt cut off from anything real.

The fame was getting intense. I was suddenly managing press obligations for TV and radio and print. I was being asked to festivals and doing my own gigs. My music was still making the rounds on blogs, and now it was getting reviewed too. And as social media platforms were growing in size, my profile was inflating at a similar rate. People noticing me was starting to affect me; I struggled with being watched 24/7. I never set out to be famous. All I wanted was a meaningful music career, and for my music to reach people. But it was a package deal. Getting paid was obviously an incentive too, because I wanted to look after those I loved. I just figured my success would be simpler: I'd release cool albums to critical acclaim, like Mos Def, but I'd still be out and about, not mobbed by kids thinking they were entitled to have access to me.

People started to see me a lot of places. My name was out there, and gauging what the people around me were after was tough. And I never knew who they thought they were meeting. It was hard to be sure what all the recognition was for, whether or not those around me actually liked who I was or saw me as a GOOD Music sideman. The enthusiasm would often seem hollow, as if conditional. It bothered me that for a long time I was just some guy, going mostly ignored, and then overnight I'm a public figure.

It was disorienting. Nearly everyone around me was so pumped to see me, and yet it was performative; many were simply there for the rush that came with the lifestyle. So many people were pretending. And I could tell. But calling them all out meant being left by myself, alone with my thoughts.

■ ■ ■

On Halloween 2009, I met my manager for my acting career, Peter Sussman, at this party at the Roosevelt in LA. Earlier in the day, this girl gave me some Xanax. She told me they were weak. I'd never taken Xanax before. I took two: *OK, let's see the vibes. Mellow me out. Whatever.* Nobody briefed me on Xanax and how to handle it and what not to do on it. At the party, Pete gave me a shot. I met some people. He gave me another shot. I met some people. I blacked out.

I woke up the next day in my bed fully clothed, lying on top of blankets like a corpse. I thought maybe I'd lain down and taken a nap without telling anybody. I called my buddy Cage because I was supposed to meet up with him that night so I could meet Shia LaBeouf for the first time.

I called and Cage picked up, and I said, "Yo, bro, I'm such a bad friend, bro. I'm so sorry I didn't come pick you up from the airport."

He was confused: "Yo, what are you talking about? I saw you last night. I picked you up from the Roosevelt."

"What?"

"Bro, I saw you."

I was like, "Aw, man. Well, at least tell Shia sorry we couldn't get up, but I'm definitely trying to get up with him."

He said, "We met Shia. We went to Shia's house. You were fucked up, bro."

". . . Did I embarrass myself?"

"Nah, you good," he told me.

I said, "Nah, bro, I know I was fucking wild'n'."

I jumped in the car and went over to Shia's house right then and there. He was happy to meet me sober, telling me how I was on his couch just laid out. His dog kept licking my face and I didn't wake up.

We'd only met the night before—a night I couldn't even remember—and Shia said he thought I was gonna die on his couch. He was super scared and tried to wake me up a bunch of times. That was a gnarly night. But it became clear that Shia and I were kindred spirits.

I turned twenty-six in 2010 and my birthday was that Saturday, so I made everybody go out the five days leading up to the thirtieth: Virgil Abloh; Hit-Boy; Ricky Anderson, Kanye's cousin. I called it the Five Days of Rage. It was a fucking blizzard outside and I told Virgil we were doing this and he told me he was coming every night. I hadn't had a Saturday birthday in years, so I had been waiting for my weekend celebration.

I met Virgil when he was working with Kanye during the sessions for *My Beautiful Dark Twisted Fantasy*. I would come around and see him in the room on his computer, focused. I'd ask him what he was up to and he'd show me. He was always working. An architecture student turned Fendi intern turned creative director, Virgil was a gateway between street and luxury sensibilities, rap and high fashion. He'd be doing album cover designs or sketching out clothing for Kanye. That was one of the reasons why I wanted him to come out that week for my birthday, because I figured, *This dude is in this room like a little soldier in front of this fucking computer all day and night. We need to get out of this hotel and go experience some shit.*

One of those nights, we had a snowball fight in the city. I must've just met Hit-Boy a week before. We were on the street, and there were mounds of snow on the curbs where they had plowed. Hit-Boy was standing there throwing snow at people and I clocked him across the way. I ran full speed, screaming, and I speared this nigga as hard as I could. He's laughing. I'm laughing. Everybody else is laughing. He literally could've gotten up and said, "What the fuck is wrong with you?!" I didn't know him that long, but I guess he thought, *Yo, that's fucking crazy. Kid Cudi just speared me!* I felt like I could see it in his soul that he was a good dude. I wanted him to be there to support.

It was great to celebrate surrounded by my people with so much going right for me, but there was darkness under the surface. I was getting deeper and deeper into cocaine. I was an expert at keeping it away from Jamie. I never wanted her to see me do it. I never wanted to even be on it around her. I was making sure that it wasn't out around the house when she was over, and I went out of my way to be sober when I saw her. But eventually, despite my best efforts, she started to see. When you're fucking with drugs, it's fucking up your head. Your mood swings. I'd do coke on Monday and Tuesday, go somewhere with Jamie Wednesday and Thursday and be clean, but I'd still be fucked in the head from those two nights before.

I started working on my second album around that time. When I was making it, drugs were the fuel, and they plunged me into a grisly headspace. To be honest, it was as if the demons had me in their clutches. I had to capture my volatility, all the gloom. Initially, it was just bumps. But soon I was all in. Each day—every day—I would do lines one after the other, most as fat as a cig for a single nostril. Once I started descending the rabbit hole, there was no stopping. When I had Cage come through to do "Maniac," before we started doing the record, I escorted him to the bathroom and I had two lines laid out for us. Cocaine wasn't his thing, but he didn't want to leave me in there to do the shit by myself, so he did it with me because he was my boy. I felt bad about that later on—forcing him to do cocaine. I was a madman. Drugs got me through *MoTM II*, and they saturated that album's sound. There was no way I would have finished without some substance driving me.

One time, Emile came to my house when I was doing coke. I was doing lines on the counter, and when he came in he told me he had to talk to me. He broke down crying, telling me he was worried about me. I felt really bad, but I was so on coke, so crazy out of my mind, that I went up to him, touched him on the shoulder, and told him not to worry, that it was going to be fine. I was trying to calm him down, but I was so high it didn't reach my soul like it should have. The reality was it should have woke me up right then and there, because I could have died.

Around this time, things were starting to take off, and all I could think about was the people that I was leaving behind. I had lost touch with so many people and I never felt like I would talk to them ever again. That sense of disconnection left me searching for something. I didn't know what was missing, and drugs could only fill the void temporarily.

Managing stress and anxiety often led me to harder drugs, which felt like a way to take some of the edge off. I was struggling to reckon with my demons. My career was going at warp speed. During these times, I turned to people like Jim Morrison and Kurt Cobain to try to understand my turmoil. I discovered Kurt because my dude Cage put me on. I knew about Nirvana, and I knew he killed himself, but I didn't know the story of how he got to that point. Learning more about him, seeing what he went through, I started to connect to his music. I immediately started loving his style and adopted it: vintage tees, oversized clothes. I found out that Kurt used to wear baggy clothes because he was so skinny, and I hated how skinny I was at the time, so I did the same thing. There was a vintage tinge to my fits. I could relate to his struggle, but there wasn't an answer there. I needed a miracle, but I couldn't have imagined the form my miracle would take.

My daughter, Vada, was born a month premature, on March 26, 2010, so I wasn't in Chicago when it happened. I got there the next day. My mom was there already. On the phone she told me, "You spit this baby out."

I couldn't believe it. "For real?!" So geeked.

I got to the hospital. I saw Vada. I held her, and I felt peace. Make no mistake: That was my baby. She was so tiny. As big as my forearm. A little angel—something so perfect. I knew right then and there that there would never be an album I would make as perfect; nothing I would ever make in life would be as perfect. Part of me felt she wouldn't need me or something. The circumstances being what they were—me not being with Jackie, me living all the way where I lived in New York and her living in Chicago—I just couldn't see it. I was paranoid.

We took Vada home the first night, and she had this little glow blanket that she had to wear because she was a little jaundiced. As soon as I left that night, I missed her. I thought about her all the way home. When I got back to New York, the love and the light from being around Vada was gone. Becoming a dad had been a centering force, but without her near me, I began to spiral again.

FREE
Acrylic on Canvas
40" × 40"

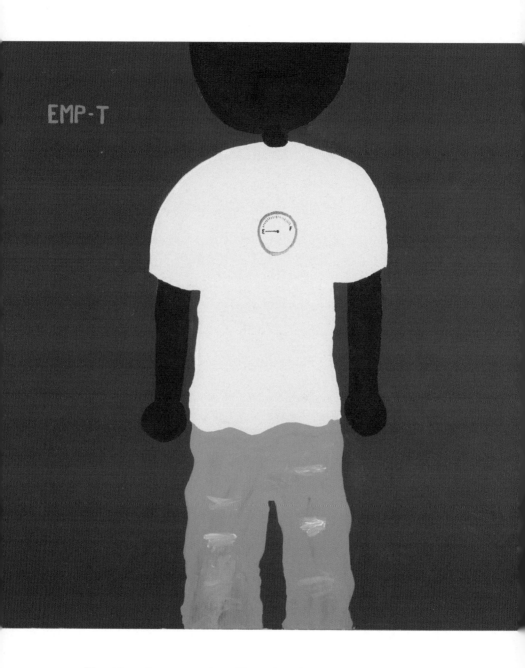

EMP-T

Acrylic on Canvas
40" × 40"

THROUGH HELL

Acrylic on Canvas
40" × 40"

WHEN THE LIGHT DIES

Acrylic and Oil Pastels on Canvas
40" × 40"

THE WATCHER

Acrylic on Canvas
24" × 30"

SABOTAGE #2: VERSUS

Acrylic on Canvas
24" × 30"

My dad, Lindberg Skiles Mescudi, in the US Air Force in his twenties (1940s).

My mom, the queen, Elsie Mescudi, in the 1990s.

Me looking cute. I know.
I was a couple months
old here. 1984.

This is me at my first birthday, and that's my mom dressed as a scary fucking
clown. As you can see, I was not amused. I cried shortly after this picture was
taken, so I'm told. I love my mom for even trying, though (ha ha).

My sister's graduation from Shaker Heights High, in 1994. That's my mom, baby Quinton (my uncle Bey's son), and me, jealous because my sister got to hold the baby.

This was common around the house. Me, messing with Maisha. That's my big bro Dean in the red.

Family photo from around 1989. My sister, Maisha; my mom; my big brothers, Dean and Domingo; and me (in front in the middle). I was about four.

Me at three years
old being a little
rascal. Love the fit.

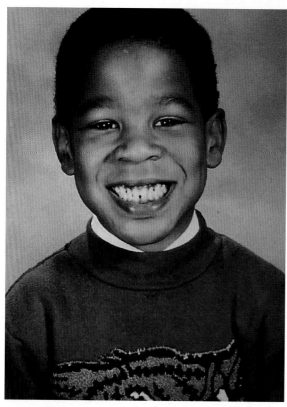

I believe this was
second grade, when I
just smiled really hard
in school pictures.

Me at my crib on Chelton Road, Shaker Heights, Ohio. I think I was eleven here. 1995.

At the crib, doing some homework and tearing up some McDonald's fries. That polo is hard as hell. I think this is in 1997.

Vada and Daddy, 2010.

Back at my mom's house for the holidays. This was 2010. That's my brother Dean; my mom, Elsie; my niece Zuri; and my sister, Maisha.

This was a fun day. I took Lola to New York for her birthday week and planned some things for us to do. It was all a surprise. One of my surprises was seeing *The Lion King*. This is backstage before the show. We ended up getting a tour backstage, too. It was unreal. I always wanted to go and she had never been, so I decided to take her with a couple of our good friends from Paris, Emma and Victor. It was def one of the best times I've had in the twenty years I've lived in New York.

My beautiful queen, Lola, and me at the Yves Saint Laurent show in Paris, 2025.

This is from a shoot I had my good friend Pamela Littky do for me at my house back in 2020. Vada and her mom were in town, so I decided to get some pics of us. Vada also wanted to color her hair, so I had my homie Dani Moon come by and hook me and her up. Vada was ten here. My little angel baby.

CHAPTER 17

Away from the anchor of my newborn child, cocaine was laying waste to my personal and artistic worlds. I was in Los Angeles when I wrote the song "Mr. Rager," recording at the Sunset Marquis. There was a beat that Emile had made that rocked my soul. But working on it, I couldn't hit the notes because of the lines I was doing. It was fucking with my pipes. I couldn't sing the song I was meant to sing. I thought, *OK, I guess I'll just write this for someone and it'll be that one song that I never finish.*

The coke was also making me erratic and unstable, and Jamie and I were arguing more frequently. There was a time when we broke up for a couple weeks and I didn't talk to her. I don't know what we were fighting about, but I guarantee it was something about me being temperamental, or moody, or just not nice. There was a lot of anger inside me that came from the Kid Cudi experience not aligning with the vision in my mind. I'd always imagined success as a magic bullet for all my problems. When you grow up without money, you think money will fix everything and that the new life it brings comes with a clean slate. Becoming Kid Cudi was supposed to overhaul the entire world Scott had known. But there was no clean slate. No reboot. The euphoria of my rise had dissipated. So few people around me were real. I struggled to accept that the thing I envisioned for myself could be fool's gold.

I went to this event that Spike Lee was throwing for an Absolut vodka launch in Brooklyn and I was high out of my mind. I never just did cocaine and nothing else, I did this thing called the trifecta. It was my special little way of doing coke. I would have some with a Corona and a blunt. When I did all three it kept me in rotation, kept me on a level, kept me at a place where I wasn't looking like I was tweaking out of my mind.

Spike was a god to me. I got to the party and said, "What's up?" I could tell that he could tell that I was on something. I made a shitty impression. I never talked to Spike Lee again. I fucked that up.

All I could think about was Jamie at the time. I did some more cocaine and got the nerve to just go to her house. I thought, *I'm just gonna go there and talk to her.* I wanted to fix it, whatever it was. My intentions were in the right place. But cocaine was in the equation, so there was no way this wasn't going to be a disaster.

I was buying a few vials a week, thinking they wouldn't last forever. I never went out and got an eight ball. It was always smaller quantities. I would have died for sure with an eight ball in my possession. I was trying to keep at least one little hurdle between me and using. Sometimes I couldn't even get it that way. I had one guy that I used to hit up for it because I didn't want everyone on the scene knowing: Kid Cudi did drugs. My connect was cool, I could count on him having some good shit, and, most importantly, I could trust that he wasn't going to tell anybody.

I got to her house in Chelsea, and I always used to forget what buzzer was hers. I don't know why; I'd been to her house so many times. I'd end up buzzing her neighbor and this guy would come out and be like, *What the fuck!* So just like any other night, I went to that apartment and I buzzed this guy's apartment door. He came out, and I said, "Sorry! Sorry!" He looked so annoyed. It was maybe eleven o'clock at night or something. Jamie buzzed me in. We started talking and my energy was off because I was off the rails, and I asked her why I hadn't heard from her in two weeks. She tried her best to explain all this shit and it was going through one ear and out the other. I was not even soaking any ounce of it up. She was making all the sense in the world, but I was so riled up on drugs that I didn't want to find any truth in it. I saw her phone on her bed, and I picked it up, and it was a conversation with this dude open. He was flirting with her, and she was responding back to it.

I said, "Who is this?"

"It's one of my friends."

"You're flirting with him? You're flirting with him?"

"Cud, we haven't talked in two weeks. I haven't heard from you."

"What the fuck. So you're going to talk to somebody else? You done with me?"

I took the phone and threw it against the wall, shattering it in pieces. I stormed out of the apartment. She closed the door behind me. I almost made my way outside before I stopped: *No, no, fuck that. I want answers.* So I went back to the front door. I knocked on the door. I told her to let me in. She wouldn't. She wouldn't even talk to me. I knocked on the door. She still wouldn't let me in. I literally started ramming the door with my shoulder—ramming the door, screaming, telling her to let me in, on and on. I go to the other end of the hallway and run full speed down the hall, ramming the door and knocking it off the hinges little by little.

The top right-hand corner of the door was bending. I was smashing the shit in—this huge metal door, in a New York apartment that's been there for fucking forever—and I was crying hysterically. I just wanted her to talk to me. I fell to the floor against the wall, and I was lying on the ground crying. The neighbor saw me there and he told me, "Go home, Cudi."

I said, "No, I'm not going anywhere. And I know you hate me. I know you hate me. And I'm sorry I keep ringing your doorbell. But I need to talk to her. I'm not going nowhere until she talks to me."

He said, "If you don't leave right now, I'm calling the police."

I said, "You can call the police, you can do what you want, I'm not leaving."

He looked at me, gave me one of those *OK* looks, went back in the apartment, and closed the door. I was still out there on the floor when she eventually opened up, letting me in. I went in and she calmed me down. We were talking, getting through it. One of the things I will say is that Jamie understood me, man. She knew I wasn't a bad man. She knew I was dealing with so much.

The police eventually came, knocked on the door, and I went out there to talk to them in the hallway. It was a Black lady cop, kind of short.

She went, "There seems to be a problem here?"

I told her, "I'm sorry; me and my girlfriend were having an argument. We worked it out and everything's cool now."

She looked at the door, which was half bent off the fucking hinges, and she said, "Sir, did you do this to this door?"

"Yeah—"

She pulled out her cuffs so quick. She told me, "Sir, you're under arrest. Anything you say can and will be used against you in a court of law."

I was like, *Oh shit.*

They frisked me. Took me outside and I stood on the sidewalk with this other cop, a Spanish dude. I guess they were waiting for the lieutenant to come by and talk to Jamie.

He turned to me and said, "Kid Cudi, what you doing, man?"

"I had a little argument with my girl, you know?"

He told me, "Yeah, man, but you can't be fucking up like this. C'mon, man."

I said, "You right."

It was in that moment that I noticed I had a vial of cocaine in my fifth pocket in my jeans—the lady cop didn't catch it when she frisked me. I had a decision to make: I could, without this other cop looking, take it out of my pocket and throw it on the ground, or keep it in my pocket and hope he doesn't frisk me again.

I didn't have time to decide because, just then, the lieutenant came outside.

He came up to me: "Hey, so no guns, no weapons on you? No drugs?"

I said, "Nope."

"If I search you I'm not going to find nothing, right?"

"Nope."

He went through my pockets, felt the vial, took it out, and saw a little bit of cocaine in there. First thing I said when he pulled it out: "How much I'ma get for that?"

I wanted to know how much time. I was just so green to this shit. I thought to myself, *Man, I'm going under the jail. They about to take me away right now.*

"This all you got?" he asked.

I told him yes.

He said, "Oh, you'll be fine."

I thought, *Holy shit.*

That night was wild, man. They took me to jail and the cops that were taking me were friendly with me. They said, "What are you doing? Why are you getting into trouble? Come on, that's not your vibe."

At the time I'd been doing all this cool shit with Jay-Z and Kanye, and I was well loved. I was at the beginning of the stardom.

When I walked out to get my picture taken, it was a line of niggas there, and the last one saw me and said, "Ohhh shit! They got Cudi too?" and I thought, *Fuck, I'm in here with the riffraff. These niggas done spotted me. They know what time it is.*

So I went in and took my photo, and when I was on my way in, the security guard took out his camera and took a picture of me walking by. I clocked it. I went in, took my mug shot, came back out, and dude had his camera out to take a picture again.

I turned to him quick and said, "What the fuck, you taking a picture of me, nigga?" and he put his camera away real quick. "You're filming me right now. Delete that shit. He's filming right now."

Everybody told me to calm down. I said, "Nah, fuck this guy."

"Fuck you, dude!" he yelled back.

"Fuck you. You filming me. You filming me. I saw you filming me."

We broke it up. I was still in handcuffs, so there was no way I could do anything. We got to the end of the hallway and the dude said, "Yo, bro, I feel you, but just keep your head down, stay out of trouble, and it'll get you out of here a lot quicker."

So I went in. They put me in the cell. It was just me and this other older white man in there. This muthafucka was talking shit to himself, and then he tried to talk to me.

I said, "Yo, man, don't talk to me."

"Oop, sorry," he replied.

I didn't want to talk to nobody. I didn't want any friends in the muthafuckin' jailhouse. At least not like this nigga. Hours went by. I was trying to go to sleep but I couldn't. I was just up in that bitch. It was freezing. It was a good thing I had this KAWS/OriginalFake hoodie that KAWS had given me, which saved my life.

These two homies got in the room and I heard them talking about their situation, enough that I felt their pain. They were security guards at a club and they were breaking up a fight and they ended up getting arrested. We started making conversation after a while because I connected with them. This other dude was handing out peanut butter and jelly sandwiches, and so I went to go get one. I guess it was a nigga that was in jail but was working. I went to grab the PB and J from him, and he said, "Yo, Cudi, if you need any weed, I gotchu."

I was like, "Bro . . . we're in jail!"

He said, "My bad, my bad," and walked away. I thought, *What the fuck was that?* Eventually, I met with an attorney, who apparently helped Wayne with his shit. She pretty much worked on cases for all the rappers. In court they let me off with a warning and gave me community service. I thought I was gonna do some time or some probation. But then again, the last thing on my police record was from when I was nineteen years old. I hadn't done shit. I was twenty-six. I was not somebody that got in trouble. And I haven't been arrested since.

When I was leaving the courtroom, there was a paparazzo there trying to take my photo and I hid behind my security. I jumped over these steps and ran all the way to the car. The dude did not get the shot. I was so excited. He was pissed. I had a show that night at Bonnaroo. Everybody on my team was nervous; they didn't know if I was gonna make it. I took the money that I was gonna make from the festival and used it all on a jet to make it there on time. I ended up arriving with an hour to spare. Aziz Ansari was there and I asked him if he could intro me. He did and it felt like such a festive crossover moment. I wore this gray charcoal T-shirt that Jamie made that said HIGHLY ENDANGERED on the front in white letters in honor of her.

I talked to her later and we worked it out and got back together again. I quit cocaine cold turkey. Got clean and got out of my coke-buzz haze in my mind. I'd been scared straight. I got arrested and now everybody knew my secret. It was not cool anymore. I'd almost fucked up my life. I had a three-month-old baby. It was a wake-up call.

I started to focus on my daughter, my career, and finishing my second album, which I had started earlier in the year. People were waiting on it. I had to do it right.

To start fresh, I needed a clean slate. In 2010, I was in Cleveland for a show and I was like, *You know what? I'ma go back to my old high school and just squash it with my principal. I'm successful now. I made something of myself. I just want to show her that I did good.* So I went up there. I walked in and asked for Ms. Short, and they told me she'd be in the office soon. As I was seated there, so many kids were recognizing me from the hallway and freaking out. It was so cute.

About five minutes later, Ms. Short walked in, and she went, "Kid Cudi! What?!" And I was so happy, because I was like, *Oh man, she knows who I am. She knows about what I've done, and she's obviously proud of me.* I had a chance to apologize to her about what I said before I got expelled. It gave me some closure. I liked Ms. Short when I went to school. I didn't have any real issues with her. What I did was super fucked up. Threatening to hit her, and she's a woman. That shit was not cool. So I had to let her know. Even if it was all those years later, I had to tell her to her face that I was sorry. I had to make peace with her to close that chapter.

I was finishing an album that I started high on coke. Now I was newly sober, but I was still in the fog of that moodiness. I only had a few more songs that I needed. A dream collab that I always wanted was with Mary J. Blige, but I was not sure if she would even be interested in doing a record with me. I reached out to see, and she responded. She came to the studio one day, and I had this kind of backyard barbecue song, family reunion vibes, and she liked it. She asked to hear anything else that I had on the album so she could get a vibe. I told her I had this one unfinished song I thought she'd be dope on. So I played it for her, and when it was over she told me, "I want to get on something like that."

I was a bit surprised. "For real?"

She said yeah.

I told her, "All right, well, you could touch this."

She got in the booth, did her one-two, knocked that shit out. I was sitting there in amazement, man: *Yo, I got Mary J. Blige on my song sounding like classic Mary. Killing it on my shit.* It was the most powerful shit ever. She got out of the booth, and it was like, "What else you got?" I played "These Worries" and she went in there and knocked that out too. It was crazy: back-to-back, two Mary J. features, just like that.

Before I finished the album, the one thing that I wanted to try again was "Mr. Rager." That song was about feeling like I was going to overdose. There was that day I did so much coke, I collapsed and couldn't get up. Immobilized, I was stuck there, sprawled out on my back, staring at the ceiling. I thought, *This is it; you're going to die.*

I wasn't scared. I closed my eyes. When I opened them again, I was in the same spot on the floor to a bright day, but I couldn't hear any traffic. I lived right by the West Side Highway, so I used to always hear it, but now there was nothing. I thought I had died. It took me a while to realize that I hadn't. I wanted to sing about that out-of-body experience.

I went to the studio, drank some tea, sang my soul out, and that's what you hear on the final record. I had my voice back and I was able to deliver it exactly how I heard it in my mind. When *Man on the Moon II: The Legend of Mr. Rager* came out, it was such a relief for two reasons: I was able to beat the sophomore slump, and I knew that the album was, if not better than, as good as the first. I knew I delivered, and I didn't know if I was ever going to finish it when I was making it, and I did. It was a fucking miracle. The album did well commercially: sold 169,000 copies in the first week—better than the original. It debuted at number three in the U.S., number one in R&B, and number one in rap. I did better than the last time in every way. Charted higher and sold more records. It was a big year for me, but also a big year for another rising rapper I'd met at one of Vashtie's parties: Drake.

Throughout my rise, Drake had always been a supporter. He'd come to my shows; he appeared in the "Pursuit of Happiness" video; we saw each other here and there and showed love. We weren't hanging out at each other's houses, but we were good industry friends. If I was in Toronto doing a show, or he was in LA or in New York, we usually linked up. We stayed in touch, texting each other after important milestones. But I hadn't heard from him at all since I'd been arrested outside of Jamie's. A few months after my arrest, I was at this after-hours spot in the upstairs of this restaurant. All these people in the industry were there.

Jamie came by. Everybody was just chillin', and Drake showed up. He came up to me and tried to talk to me.

I just said, "Yo, nigga, don't talk to me. I ain't heard from you. You ain't check in on me. You not a real friend."

He just looked at me. He couldn't say anything and was stuck. I just walked away, and he did too. That's when we started being at odds. I thought he was phony. In my time of greatest need, when I actually needed comfort, he was nowhere to be found.

Other industry friendships were evolving, both personally and professionally. Shia had an idea to do a short film for the song "Maniac." I told him I wanted to do something in horror, and he had an idea to do something in homage to *Man Bites Dog*, the Belgian film, following the same theme of a film crew shadowing murderers on a rampage.

When Shia gave me the storyboards, he said, "And at the end, you shoot me in the face and my head blows up."

I told him, "Dude . . . I'm not shooting you in the face. I'm not doing that. Maybe I shoot you in the shoulder or something, but I'm not shooting you in the face."

He said, "All right, all right, all right, we'll figure it out."

But Shia came up with the whole story himself. He's a brilliant muthafucka. Reading that first draft, I thought, *Holy shit, this is gonna be next level*. When you see *Maniac* right now, it holds up. That muthafucka is damn good. We shot that over four or five days in Detroit, in the freezing winter. A blizzard was actually happening in the middle of filming. It was the wildest shit, but it was the dopest experience. Playing that role was so much fun. It was almost disturbing how much fun it was, knowing I had to do some dark shit. But it was scratching that itch that I had as an actor. I was mostly known for playing the funny guy, but that was the type of shit I wanted to get into—something that was so different from me. I craved it and fucking with Shia allowed me to do that on my own terms. Instead of spending money on some cars, we went half on a short film. We put in $250,000 apiece.

When the *Maniac* short film came out, we were all at the Mercer Hotel. Jay-Z was there and I was telling him about it and he said, "Yo, put it on, put it on." Kanye was there; Hype Williams was there; everybody was there. I was nervous to have Hype watching. He was one of the defining video directors of the nineties, a visionary who released the cult classic film *Belly* with Nas and DMX in 1998. *He's probably going to think I'm a crazy-ass muthafucka.* I thought a lot of people in there would feel some type of way. We watched it, and when it was over, it was silent.

Out of nowhere, Hype said, "All right, I'ma get ready to go, man. Good seeing y'all," and just left. Then everybody else left and nobody said anything. Except Jay-Z—he said he loved it. Later on that night, Kanye took me to the side.

He said, "Yo, I'm worried about you."

"What do you mean?" I replied.

"I'm worried what people will say about you after they see this."

I said, "Whatchu mean?"

"I'm just saying. I don't think you should put this out."

It's so funny to think about it now knowing that this was Kanye West telling me that he was afraid of what people would think about a decision that I made making a horror movie short. *You're worried about me, bro?* Knowing what he would get up to, you can honestly tell it was a different time in his life. He was a much different man.

At first I was a little bummed out that Hype didn't seem into it, but then I thought about it being punk rock. Making something that Hype didn't like was kind of cool. It was the juxtaposition of those two things: *You think I give a fuck what Hype Williams thinks? Jay-Z loves it.*

When Kanye was working on *My Beautiful Dark Twisted Fantasy* at the Mercer, I was the one who brought Jameson to the crew. Nobody was drinking it except me, and they would make sure that there was always a bottle in the studio for me. (I had kicked coke but would still drink.) As I'm sitting there writing, somebody came out of nowhere: Noah Goldstein, Kanye's engineer of several years, who, in addition to being a genius who can accommodate the recording methods of any artist, is the most awesome guy you'll ever meet; if you know him, you're a lucky person. He's a sweet man—but he took the bottle of Jameson.

Noah was getting ready to walk out with it and I said, "Hey, what are you doing?"

"Jay and Bey want some," he told me.

"Give me the bottle," I said.

I took the bottle and some glasses and I went over there and kicked it myself. Whenever I see Beyoncé, it's always been love. She's always been a supporter of mine. So I'm happy to see her.

And Jay asked, "Yo, can you put on the short film?"

So I put on *Maniac*, and I was nervous because I was thinking to myself, *Beyoncé is watching now; this is crazy! Beyoncé is gonna be truly disturbed, oh my god.*

When we finished, she turned to me: "I just only have one question: Why?"

I replied, "Um, that's the question, right? It's kind of senseless, you know? That's the scary part of the whole thing: They're just doing this as a game."

But she was like, *Oh my god, no, what the fuck did I just watch?*

I got closer with my brother Dean over the years. Back in Cleveland, our relationship wasn't as tight as I wanted, but as we got older, I think we both learned that family is the most important thing, and you gotta stay close. Dean visited me in New York in 2010, and we were hanging out in the room at the Mercer with Kanye and Jay as they were making *Watch the Throne*. All four of us were just chillin' in room talkin', and Dean ordered room service. When the food came in they thought it was for Hov, but he grabbed the tray and set it up in front of my brother for him. Jay is so fuckin' cool. It was so crazy to see my worlds collide.

I did another short film around that time for "Mr. Rager" that was less provocative. I rehearsed for a few days on the choreography. I wanted to fight a bunch of dudes, like an action sequence. That was always one of my childhood passions: I wanted to be an action hero, since my days shooting little imagined movies with G.I. Joes and Ninja Turtles. I wanted to be John Wick before John Wick existed. That was my take on the genre: me taking on eighty dudes, no gunplay, all fighting, hand-to-hand combat. That whole thing was about me being overcome by darkness. I didn't feel like I was gonna make it at all. I felt like the devil was on my ass and he wouldn't stop until he had my soul. I'd been off cocaine for a while, but I was still depressed. And now that I was off the drug there wasn't anything to keep me out of my funk. I had to face it and the weed could only camouflage the shit.

The *Maniac* process sparked something in Shia and me. Darkness can be attractive, especially to someone else experiencing their own darkness. We would spend a lot of days at his house, watching movies and talking and smoking weed. He showed me books in his library that he was reading. He was a really smart and thoughtful dude, immensely talented. He would show me love as an actor, saying that he wanted to direct me, and I put him on a pedestal.

I had worked with Jaden Smith a couple times, and Omarr Rambert told me that Will wanted to meet me and asked if I would come down to the *Men in Black 3* set to talk with him. They were shooting on Long Island on the beach. Somebody was escorting me around the set and they let me watch filming. I'll never forget seeing Will act. And then as soon as the take ended, he came under the tent where I was: "Kid Cudi!" He was like, "Sit right here in Agent Jay's chair," and I was thrilled because I'd never been so up close and personal with the studio experience before.

Then Will said, "Yo, so my kids talk about you all the time, and they love you. And I was just like, 'Let me meet this guy. I have to meet him.'"

I told him, "Man, I really appreciate you letting me work with your kids and you being so open to that."

My reputation wasn't the best; I was pretty fucking rock and roll and reckless. So I was grateful to him for giving me a shot. He took me to his trailer, a massive eighteen-wheeler that was like a mini apartment, and I was telling him how I just fired Dennis from being my assistant, all the things that Dennis did wrong, and then he goes, "Let me ask you something: Did you tell Dennis what you liked and what you didn't like?"

"No," I said.

"So you never trained him and gave him a list of what to do and what not to do?"

"No."

He's like, "First thing as a boss you have to remember is that everything is your fault. You didn't give Dennis the tools he needed to succeed."

I was like, "Oh, fuck, you're right."

I got home and I immediately hired Dennis back.

It all made sense. It was a powerful moment. Anybody who's ever had the chance to hear Will talk or give game knows he's a really wise man. It was priceless as a young Black man to just receive his guidance.

Guidance was something I desperately needed. On my twenty-seventh birthday, I was miserable. I couldn't see my daughter as much as I wanted, and I felt like I was descending the path of previous brilliant, tortured artists. I thought for sure I was gonna die that year. It seemed as if the road I was traveling had only one destination. Was going to jail an omen? Was the *Maniac* short film a premonition? All I kept thinking about was being in the 27 Club. I was the textbook artist for it: tormented, dark, emotionally in pain. I was the poster child for fucked-up kids. All 2011, I was shook. It was as if the Grim Reaper himself was hanging over me, biding his time.

CHAPTER 18

would go to Chicago to visit Vada whenever I could. Jackie wouldn't let me get overnight visitation, as much as I wanted it. I thought she was just hating on me, but I *had* just been arrested for cocaine the year before. Imagine you get pregnant by this rapper and he gets thrown in jail a few months after the baby is born and now he's talking about he wants to get visitation. She was in the right to be cautious, but at the time I thought it was absurd: I would never do drugs around my daughter. I would never have her around any negative energy. But admittedly there was a disconnect between the parent I knew I wanted to be and the realities of where I was in life.

Jackie would only give me and Vada five hours at a time, and that was starting to take its toll on me. The realization that I couldn't be with my child the way that I wanted to be was painful. I'd fly to Chicago for a couple days to hang out with my daughter for five hours a day. I was trying to stay positive, but I wasn't sure if things were going to swing my way or not. Being away from her fed a lot of my depression at the time.

The first time I visited, we did the visitation at the hotel. Jackie dropped Vada off, putting her in my arms, and when I went to walk away Vada started crying all the way up to the room. Every time I did visitation, my mom was with me, because that was the only way my mom was going to see her granddaughter. Vada wouldn't stop crying, and I was telling my mom, "She don't fuck with me."

My mom told me, "Give it some time. You just gotta be around her."

After a while, she stopped crying and fell asleep on my chest.

I was like, "Ma, look, she's 'sleep!"

My mom said, "Told you."

Every time I saw her, Vada got better and better: from crying a little bit to barely crying to not crying at all. She was finally getting comfortable. The more time we spent together, the more we got connected. My mom would remind me that this was all a gift. "You will be in your daughter's life," she'd say. "Vada will know you. Just believe that everything will work out."

I was holding on to this idea that things would not be like this forever.

Financially, I was more than stable. I was sitting on millions. I was still on my first contract with the label, which was already paying out royalties for the *Man on the Moon* albums, but the show money was the best money, and I was in demand, doing venues that held from eight thousand to seventy-two thousand people. I'd been helping Jackie financially, giving her thousands of dollars every month—so she could take care of Vada. She wasn't happy with the amount, but I thought it was sufficient.

On my daughter's first birthday, Jackie hosted a party at her house in Chicago. Jackie's whole family was over there—her cousins, her nieces, her sister, her dad and mom—and my mom was there with me. I was on the floor playing with the kids, letting them play with Vada's toys, watching Vada enjoy being around her cousins. They always had a good bond. I was taking it all in when Jackie came up to me.

She went, "Can I talk to you for a second in the hallway?"

I got up and went with her. She closed the door.

"What's up?" I asked.

"I just want to talk to you for a minute, just away from the family," she said.

"Yeah, what's going on?"

I looked over to my right and there was a dude walking down the hallway with a folder.

He went, "Are you Scott Mescudi?"

"Uh, yeah?"

"You've been served."

I grabbed the envelope. "What the fuck is this? You served me with papers?"

Jackie and I walked back in the room. "Well, she served me with papers. Nice! On my daughter's first birthday." I asked, "Is this about money, Jackie? Is this about money? I've been giving you money."

She said, "I told you I wanted to talk to you about all of that."

"All right, that's cool, that's cool. You know what? We out."

Her mom interjected, "No, no no no."

"Nah, look, I'm out," I said.

I kissed Vada good-bye; then my mom and I bounced.

I was crushed, man. I couldn't even spend my daughter's first birthday with her. During what should have been an incredibly special moment I got served with a summons for court in pursuit of an increase in child support and Jackie's sole custody of our daughter. But it was a blessing in disguise because it allowed me to fight for my rights, my visitation, all that—what I wasn't getting, what I should have been getting. No one should have been policing my time with my daughter. I'm not an irresponsible person.

I lawyered up fast and my attorney was a shark—young, focused, and hungry. And she was hell-bent on me getting justice. I was in court all year long. I was nervous every time I went because it was open for the public to come in and listen to it. Anybody could have come up in that bitch and got my whole tea. I was in there for months having to go through everything I'd been through since I knew Jackie: how we met, how we stayed in touch all these years. Jackie didn't want me to have visitation. She wanted me to have supervised visits if I did, and she didn't want my mom to do the supervision because she said my mom was an enabler and she would do anything that I told her to do. The judge actually read this in court. My mom was appalled.

The judge said, "I doubt that this woman right here would just let her son run all over her like that. She's an educator. I don't see that happening."

I didn't know how things were going to turn out. The litigation took a long time. It wasn't until we got to the part of the trial where I had to take a drug test and it came back negative that I finally started to see the light at the end of the tunnel. I quit weed several months before. The judge knew I was in there fighting for my baby. I wanted nothing more than to be in my baby's life. That's all I dreamed of. And that judge got it. I ended up with guaranteed visitation. Jackie and I divvied up birthdays and Christmases and summer breaks, but whenever I'm in Chicago now I have a right to see Vada. If there's a weekend where I want to fly her out, I can. There are no restrictions. Jackie was not happy, but I walked out of that courtroom with my head high and a smile on my face. I won the battle, fair and square, and I could finally be the kind of parent I wanted to be without anyone on my back. This whole episode had been holding me down for over a year and a half. I felt an enormous sense of relief, vindication, and, most of all, joy about being able to be a part of Vada's life.

That year Jamie and I broke up, because part of me didn't know if Jamie was in it for me. I had a hard time believing it was true. Not that she was a gold digger or acted any type of way.

That wasn't the vibe. It was my insecurities that made me feel that way. Fame had made me paranoid about what people in my life really wanted from me. I didn't know what they were after: love or clout, proximity to celebrity or true companionship. Those insecurities kept pushing her away. And I was always fucking with some other chicks because I didn't want to be alone.

I did a session earlier that year with Cassie. She had a record she wanted me to work on and we vibed—purely friendship; homies, nothing intense. Then in November, around Thanksgiving, she called me and told me about the abuse Puff was subjecting her to. I was stunned and disgusted. To me, in that moment, she needed somebody to listen. So that's what I did, and for months I was this sounding board.

We gained an emotional intimacy during our talks, and next thing I knew, we were physical. She and I were attracted to each other like magnets. We were a great combination, and the sex was magical. We spent a good amount of time together in 2011, hanging out almost every day.

I was also working on my rock album, *WZRD*, at the time with my boy Dot. After *Man on the Moon II*, I wanted to make a band, explore more as an artist, and differentiate myself from all the other artists. Being compared to my contemporaries was tiring; I was bringing something completely different to the table. Starting a band was a way to create that separation.

Dot was not a big rock aficionado—he's from East New York, born to immigrant parents from Nigeria—but he took it as a research project. I showed him all the bands I was fans of, and he showed me bands that managed to make their way to him. I was into Nirvana, Black Sabbath, the Red Hot Chili Peppers, the Pixies. And then Dot would have heard about songs like "Where Is My Mind" through cultural diffusion, from watching *Fight Club*. Dot was the drummer and the bassist. I was the guitarist. The process was simple: We picked up the instruments and made it a point of duty to try and write licks that I could sing to. Then we'd supplement that with bass, keys, and drums.

Dot stayed at the Roosevelt for half a year and we worked out of the basement of my house in the Hollywood Hills; in the downstairs area was a little space for us to just record and jam out. I had moved to LA that year and I was living off Laurel Canyon in a $2.3 million modernist crib just past Lookout Mountain. It was a way better thing for me, being in Los Angeles, more like back home. I could drive, and there was wide-open space. But I was lonely. Dot was a temporary resident, and none of my other homies lived out there yet.

Dot and I were working on the album heavy and I wanted a new look so I decided to get a perm. It was a great choice. The rock album was my way of releasing myself from the hell that I went through with *Man on the Moon II*. I wanted to let go of that dark image and do something brighter. I wanted to play in this rock space because I felt I fucked up my hip-hop energy so much that I needed to rinse and refresh. I had to cleanse the palate. I just knew where I was gonna go next. I was gonna get back on the rapper shit, and, when I did, I wanted it to be a complete 180 from what people heard on *Man on the Moon II*.

Working with Dot was part of the restorative process. Having my friend with me uplifted me, made me feel safe and confident about doing music again. Making the record was a huge adjustment for us. We had never worked on anything like it before. But we are used to holding each other's hands and going into the unknown together. We're explorers, adventurers in sound.

I was done with getting so fucked up and thinking that getting high was fueling the cool shit about my creativity, in this very rock star way. That's part of why I chose to do this album without smoking weed and drinking way less. I sipped some whiskey every once in a while, but I wasn't getting drunk. I'd taken a step back from touring because I wanted to see what direction called to me. I love that album so much. For me, some of my most brilliant work as a songwriter and producer is in those songs.

With *WZRD*, I was looking for a sound that felt free from the darkness. I wanted positivity, uplifting songs, songs with a spirit, one with religious undertones. When we were doing *WZRD*, I couldn't think of who I wanted to do the cover art and then it hit me: *Oh shit, this man Virgil can do this shit no problem.* So I hit him up and I said, "Hey, man, I want to do something real simple, I want to do some block letters, but I want it to feel kind of old-school with borders with different colors and with the sky in the background." And he basically was able to take my vision and bring it to life. That was early on in Virgil's career, but he had already done some ill shit by 2011. He owned his own gallery in Chicago and would throw parties, and as Kanye's art director, he had input on all kinds of projects. You just had to know. He was the chosen one. The shit was brewing. He was breaking off into becoming his own person.

I recorded "Teleport 2 Me, Jamie" for Jamie; we weren't together, but I wanted to make a song that celebrated her and showed her how much she meant to me. I don't know how much that song meant to her. I don't know if it meant much at all. That's the sad thing about it, truthfully. It's the first song I wrote about any girl, and I meant every word in it. I think she thought it was some manipulative way of me trying to get her back.

She sent me a picture showing me that she bought seven albums. I thought, *Oh hell naw.* It was so dope, seeing her support. In the credits, I dedicated that album to her and my mom and my daughter—the three most important ladies in my life at the time.

CHAPTER 19

Toward the end of 2011, while I was gearing up to figure out what my post-*WZRD* music would sound like, a storm was brewing. Cassie and I were spending a lot of time together. I got a call from her during the holiday season around five in the morning. She was breathless.

"Puff found out. He knows."

I'm confused. "Knows what? What are you talking about?"

"He knows we've been kickin' it."

And I'm like, "So?"

"He's pissed. Can you come pick me up?"

"OK."

I got in my car and picked her up. She seemed nervous and stressed, so I took her to the Sunset Marquis to lie low. She was sitting there, we were hanging out, and she got a call from her homegirl

Capricorn. She was frantic and on the verge of tears in the backseat of Puff's car, saying that Puff and his guys were in my house.

I was pissed.

I said, "Yo, Cassie, stay right here. I will go over there and handle this shit."

I got in my car, drove over, and called that muthafucka on the way. He answered: "Hello."

"Yo, muthafucka, you at my house?"

"Yo, wassup, man?"

"Are you in my house, muthafucka?!"

"I'm just trying to talk to you."

"Yo, muthafucka, we ain't gotta talk. I'm coming to you right now."

Puff said, "I'm over here waiting on you."

Puff was a huge figure in rap and beyond. The man behind Biggie. The Bad Boy mogul.

I got to the house and I was ready to fight him. I was so angry. I couldn't believe this muthafucka was in my shit. He wasn't there when I got there, so I left my house to look for him. I think I passed him on Laurel Canyon. I called him and I asked him where he was, and he said he would be right back.

As I was zooming over there, I took a moment: *Hold on. I hear so much shit about this nigga Puff just being a grimy muthafucka.* So many people would talk about how this nigga got Pac killed. Everybody in the industry knows this conspiracy. I thought, *Look, man, this nigga is not about to get the drop on me. He in my house. Ain't no telling what he's on. I ain't got no weapon on me. I'm out here and I can't call my nigga to get no pistol. I'm fucked.*

So I called the police and I told them I had a break-in. As I was on the line they said someone had already called and a squad car was already there. They asked me if I knew who was in my house, and I told them, "I don't know. I think I know who it is, but I'm not sure." I said this knowing in my head it was Puff, but I didn't want to say anything over the phone.

By the time I got over there, the police were already there. I walked up and my cameras outside were turned the opposite way. I got in the house and like a fucking idiot I'd left my fucking front door unlocked, and that's how they got in. There's a puddle of piss in the bathroom where they'd locked my dog, Freshie. It was crazy.

I met up with Cassie and we were talking about this shit. They had been together since 2007, and she had been dealing with Puff's terrorizing like this for years. *Yo, this muthafucka is crazy. We've gotta get the fuck out of here because who knows what he'll do next.*

She said, "I need to go to Connecticut to see my family. Can you come with me?"

And I was like, "OK, I'll go to be there with you, and we'll just lay low, and I'll have my security," because she kept saying, "He knows where I live! He might come by the house."

I told her, "Look, I'ma have my security outside the whole time. It's gonna be cool. Ain't nobody gonna come to the house. It's gonna be straight."

So we went to Connecticut and I stayed at her house with her family. I kicked it with her mom and her dad and her brother, spending time and making sure she was safe, making sure she was comfortable, making sure she was not tripping. The situation was so stressful. It was my job to keep her cool and make sure she was all right, and that was what I was doing.

He was texting me the whole time: "Yo, man, I just want to talk."

I just texted him back: "Nigga, I don't want to talk to you. You broke in my fucking house. What the fuck are you talking about? There's nothing to talk about."

When he broke into my house, he had ripped open these gifts I bought my mom and my sister that had mad shit from Chanel. It was all wrapped up and he went through them all thinking they were for Cassie.

I told him, "Fuck you, man. I'm not talking to you. I'll let you know when I'm ready."

I came back to LA and it was all cool for a while. I thought things were chill. But they weren't.

Shortly after that, I was at Jamie's sister's house one morning hanging out—we reconnected and I had stayed over—when I got a call from my dog sitter saying that my Porsche was on fire.

I said, "What?"

"Your Porsche is on fire. You have to get home now."

I looked at Jamie, and because I didn't want to alert her, I calmly said, "OK."

I got off the phone and sat down on the bed. In my head I was thinking, *Scott, you have to tell her. There's no way you can dodge this. You have to tell her about this.* So I let it all out. I told her about Cassie and me—I told her everything. She couldn't believe it. She wasn't mad at me. Not like *mad*, because Jamie could get mad and it'd be the end of all things. I mean, we had been broken up and we weren't together. She was a little upset, but I was being honest. I was desperately hoping to fix things with her at some point. I was kickin' it with Cassie because it was good company. But Cassie had so much going on that a long-term, committed relationship never felt possible. That was never my goal. I was still madly in love with Jamie.

Cassie and I were friends that ended up getting close. The circumstance was the circumstance. With all the drama that was unfolding, I thought, *OK, I need to talk to this muthafucka. This is something serious.*

I got to my house and saw that the canvas fabric of my Porsche's drop-top was ripped open. Inside the car sitting in my driver's seat was a burnt-up Molotov cocktail. Some of the interior had melted and the roof of the car had a hole in it from where they'd dropped the bottle. Whoever the person was that tried to firebomb my car obviously didn't know how to use a Molotov cocktail. Thank God.

That whole area in the Hills where I lived was all trees and wooden houses. If my car had fully exploded it would have burned down the whole fucking Hollywood Hills. He didn't give a fuck. I filed a police report. It disappeared. I called them. They didn't return my calls. The case was gone.

I'd had it. The situation was at a point where I needed to see this dude face-to-face. *All right, I gotta meet this muthafucka.* We met up at Soho House in early 2012. This was when they used to have private meeting rooms, before they built the restaurant on the second floor. I went up there with my security. We walked in and his security greeted us. The guard was all cool, showing love. Then he guided me to the room. I went by myself. This muthafucka is staring out the window with his hands clasped behind his back, looking like a villain. I thought, *He's so ridiculous. He's so ridiculous!*

I sat down. He sat down. He asked how I was doing. He asked me if I wanted some water. I told him, "No," because I don't know what he put in it. And also, him being pleasant was unnerving. He was doing it on purpose, trying to intimidate me.

I told him the story of how Cassie and I linked up. His whole thing was that I knew that that was his girl. I'm telling him, "Hey, she told me y'all weren't together."

I'm not gonna follow behind her and make sure that's factual. Because, in my head, I was thinking, *I got this hot babe in my face saying she wants me and she's single—I'm not double-checking that.* I was trying to tell this nigga I wasn't trying to steal his girl; that wasn't my motive. We were hanging out and things got intense between us: There was a connection and we couldn't deny that. She wanted a real nigga and I was that for her. I pleased her—not simply sexually; I'm talking about as a friend. She was facing unspeakable abuse at the hands of a tyrant with immense influence, and I did my best to try to provide some refuge.

When I got up, he extended his hand for a handshake. I went to shake it, and while I had his hand, I looked him dead in the eyes.

"What we gonna do about my Porsche, though?" I said.

He looked back with a cold stare. "I don't know what you're talking about," he said.

I simply replied, "Oh," and I took my hand away.

"What? I thought everything was cool," he said.

"You said that's your word, right? You didn't set my car on fire? That's your word?"

"No."

I said, "OK, cool."

I knew right then: I won. *Man, you can't even be a G and just say, "Yeah, I did that shit. Do something."* I would have respected that. I would've been like, *Damn, OK.* But he was being smart. If he had told me he did it, I would've had the evidence. I thought, *Fuck this dude, I lost a car, but I got a chance to have a special moment with a special young lady and be there for her while she was struggling and dealing with some severe pain*, and that made me feel good. Me being with her bruised his ego, and that also made me feel good, because I was the underdog in the industry at that time. I was all skinny and shit and wasn't working out. I was still the style god, but I wasn't to my full potential, and he was crushed. This whole situation is probably the wildest shit that happened to me. I was pissed at Cassie for going back to him, but over time I realized she was a prisoner. I just prayed one day she would be free.

CHAPTER 20

With my next album, *Indicud*, I was hell-bent on returning to form. I had fired Plain Pat and Emile as my managers before *WZRD*. They weren't necessarily managers by trade. They served a crucial purpose when I needed them to, but at the end of the day they were producers. They believed in me when others didn't, and stood by me. But once I started to get it going, things needed to be handled, and I needed certain things they didn't have the bandwidth for. They were upset, but I had to do what I felt was right for me.

I wanted to prove to the world, and to them, that I had the ability to produce an entire album front to back by myself. The one thing I hadn't done was show them that I'd be OK on my own—that I am in this position because I am the core of all this. I am the common denominator. They discovered me; they nurtured me; we made two great albums together. But I was feeling that these guys might think that they had made me who I was. I had to show them I made myself. So every day I was in the studio with Ian Finley, my engineer—still my engineer to this day, a great kid from Cleveland. We banged out joint after joint.

My friend and fellow hometown rapper Chip had gotten me a Maschine for my birthday and told me I should start making beats. So I got in the studio with Ian and got to work. I was coming up with so much shit. Ian helped me set up my whole situation and get drums and synths. I was in there cooking every day, making beats for hours. He helped me work in these different textures and use sounds that other people weren't using.

I sampled the Father John Misty song "Hollywood Forever Cemetery Sings" for the album, and I even had Josh Tillman come to the studio—but I forgot that he was coming; I had done 'shrooms and was fully tripping balls.

"You know Father John Misty is coming today, right?" Ian said.

I was completely caught off guard. "No way."

Next thing I knew, Josh walked in the room. I turned around: "Yooo!"

He said, "Hey, what's going on, man?"

I told him, "I just want to let you know I'm tripping on 'shrooms right now."

He said, "Oh, then you need one of these then," and just gave me a hug.

He recorded extra bits on "Young Lady," background vocals and other little accents in the song to build it up and make it whole. I wrote that song about Emma Watson. I had a crush on her, and the lyrics wondered what I'd say if I met her, what it would be like. It was a harmless fantasy: "Wish it wasn't my imagination running away with a dream."

Working on *Indicud*, I had to prove something to myself too. I had to prove that I wasn't a fluke, that I was meant to be here, that I had the abilities. Nobody got me here. Nobody made me. I made myself. With everybody that produced for me, I had my hand working in all of those songs. I helped conjure up all this shit with these niggas. It's not as if I left, they made beats, and I came back hours later and rapped on the beat and that was that. I had my hand in everything. This was my way of proving that. If it wasn't true, there was no way I could produce this whole album by myself front to back, as cinematic as that album sounds. You hear how *Indicud* came out. That shit is a masterpiece—the way the songs go into each other and there's no breaks—that was all designed on purpose. You play that shit end to end and it's like one long song.

The album was my first break from the Moon Man mythology, but I meant for it to be the uplifting yang side to the yin of what I was doing with *Man on the Moon*. My production style is super strange, so I was leaning into that a lot. I think this is the record where people realized that I was a creative force. Not many of my peers can get in the studio by themselves and make an album from scratch. I wasn't known as a producer. It could've been a disaster, because I'd never produced by myself. But I needed to embrace that challenge.

While I was doing the movie *Goodbye World*, I played some of the album for Mark Webber in the car while we were taking a break. I would go to the car in between scenes and smoke, listen to music, and vibe out, and he would come by and listen to music with me.

He was telling me, "Oh, this is crazy!"

He was one of the first people to hear that music. I didn't play it for that many people, and he was giving me my first real reactions. I was feeling more confident seeing him react to it. He said, "I can't believe you made this beat."

I wasn't the only Mescudi with something to prove. My brother Domingo was homeless, living on the streets, and trying to get his life together; he lived with my mom for a bit and that didn't last long. Domingo had been in rehab and in 2013 he left and came to LA with my mom to get away. I took them up to Big Sur and we hung out there for a while. They loved it. They didn't love the drive up the coast, though—the cliff, that shit, had them freaked out—but they enjoyed just being up there, out the way. Big Sur was always my getaway, and I knew they'd feel it too. That was one of the last good times that I had with my brother. It was one of the rare times we had some normalcy. We got in a Jacuzzi together and just talked.

Shortly after that, he got into it with my mom and returned to North Carolina to be back in his bullshit. My brother had two kids, including a three-year-old who was born before my daughter. He was the smoothest homeless man I'd ever seen. He still had women—one of them didn't even know he was homeless. He had her fooled for years. He's got a mouthpiece on him, boy. He can talk his way into anything. A master manipulator. I couldn't have imagined then that it would only be a matter of time before I would be experiencing rehab myself.

In the short term, things were going well for me to start the year creatively. That April *Indicud* came out, and I directed my first video that year: "Just What I Am." I wanted to do a party video where people just saw me having fun. I reached out to noted partiers I knew. Firstly, Mac Miller. I was always a fan of his, and I wanted to meet him and hang out. Before I lived in LA, I used to come to town and party. Steve Aoki was always in the center of it. I thought it would be dope to bring him and let people see that connection. I meant for it to look like a great fucking time. "Just What I Am" was a huge song; when me and Chip did it, it was as if we knew that it was glorious. I put Chip first because I wanted to hear him, and he killed his verse. He has the most memorable moment in that song. Any record I throw at Chip he rises to the occasion.

The video was a glimpse of something I was searching for. I eventually found LA to be phony, but at this point I didn't care because I wanted to be around people. My homies still weren't in town yet—not Dot, not Dennis. I found myself occupying my time with people that I shouldn't have been with, people chasing the highs of being in proximity to fame.

The same month, I started working on the movie *Need for Speed* with Aaron Paul. That was a huge experience because I was chasing that role. The character called for humor, and they knew I could deliver. Scott Waugh, the director, allowed me to be myself.

He told me, "Just do your thing. Just be as goofy as you want to be and have fun with it." He was only the second director to champion that—that just wanted the Scott energy. I had a ball, man. It was crazy. I'm afraid of heights and they had me in these small-ass planes flying around. They showed me the plane in the hangar and I'm thinking they're showing what I'm going to be sitting in for the green screen.

They told me, "No, we're going up tomorrow. We're doing a test flight."

So I had to get over my fear of flying small planes, dealing with turbulence, and all that shit. I had to become a master pilot in the scenes. The director couldn't fit in the planes during the majority of the shooting so every day was me riffing, clowning, and trying different things. He would get the dailies and check them out and use what he needed. I would give him so much material that he had so much to choose from.

I was filming in the helicopter doing an aerial stunt and had decided that I would smoke weed before to see how it would be. We went up earlier that morning when I was sober and it was fun as fuck, so I told myself, *Let me smoke and see what happens.* As soon as we got up there, we were in Detroit hovering over buildings. The action was in between buildings and I literally thought we were going to crash into one. It was the scariest shit. Don't smoke weed and get in a helicopter.

Things were less up in the air with regard to my future. My life was going just how I envisioned it. I was coming off *How to Make It in America* at the time and I did maybe two indie movies, but they were small movies. But then I booked *Need for Speed* and they eventually put a huge billboard on Sunset. And when I saw it, I thought, *Wow, I've arrived.*

In an effort to keep fulfilling my childhood aspirations, I wanted to get more into TV, particularly in a way that could satisfy my cartoonist ambitions. I had an idea to do an animated TV show about my high school experience. I wanted Shia to write and develop with me. We were supposed to meet and talk about the script and flesh it out, because he set up a meeting with Cartoon Network. He wrote some shit that I didn't even see, and this was supposed to be a story about my life. I never told him to start putting pen to paper. I wanted to do that with him. We were sitting in the meeting, and he mentioned that he wrote a bit of a script. He pulled it out, but I took it out of his hand before he could pass it along. "We're not ready to submit this yet. Let's just wait and hold off," I said. Shia was upset about that, and walked off without saying bye. We didn't talk again for five years.

Jaden reconnected us. Shia was still trying to deal with his stuff and figure it out, but when he came back into my life it wasn't the same self-destructive Shia that I knew. He was sober, doing the work to get better. He was running for so long, leaving a trail of madness in his wake. He had to look in the mirror and make some changes. Everybody I know that's dealt with some shit has had to do that in order to get to the light. Shia was a broken man for a long time, and I know what that feels like. It was part of what bonded us. I know what it's like to hurt people. I know what it's like to make mistakes. I just connected with him in such a profound way. None of us are perfect, but we must learn, and that's the biggest thing. Can we learn from our mistakes?

In 2013, I went off on the Cud Life Tour and took Logic, Big Sean, and Tyler, the Creator with me. I had this idea to bring people into the world of the Moon Man. I wanted to have a space suit, and I wanted the stage to look like my headquarters on the moon. So I drew this sketch and we re-created it. For the suit, the costume designer Jose Fernandez took a prop that was going to be used for Jamie Foxx in *The Amazing Spider-Man 2* and altered it. That was my first real moment in arenas doing a full show and bringing people into the world.

On tour in Montreal, I got a call that there was a young up-and-coming actor who was a big fan who was going to be in town. He wanted to meet me. I said to have him come through and bring his friends. We hung out and he was stressing about work. The kid had just worked on the Christopher Nolan film *Interstellar* and a lot of his

SCOTT MESCUDI

scenes were cut. He was bummed about it. He was only seventeen at the time, and I made sure to give him some advice because I saw that he needed it. I didn't think I was ever gonna see him again. He would probably go on to do great things, but I thought this would be our last conversation. In the moment, though, this kid was looking for guidance. He was saying he didn't know if he felt like he could still go on; he must have kind of given up on getting his big break. I said, "Hey, man, is this the only thing you can think about? Do you obsess over it all the time?"

He was like, "Yeah."

"Then this is your destiny. You gonna be fine, bro. Everything is gonna work out."

I just told him that and didn't think anything of it. His name was Timothée Chalamet.

A couple years after *Man on the Moon: The End of Day* had been out for a while, after people had lived with it and absorbed it, I started to get stories about how the record saved people's lives. This one kid told me at a show that I got him off heroin after several years, and it just fucked me up. I felt really low about it. I was happy that I helped him, he was saying he was suicidal, that he wanted to kill himself, and it's heavy when you hear that out of nowhere. It would throw me off a little bit because people would say things like that to me all the time, and I'd think, *Well, who's gonna save my life? I'm fucked right now. I'm not in any way, shape, or form a role model.* I didn't feel that way for years. I was still trying to figure it out, and people were looking up to me in that way. I just couldn't embrace it.

It didn't happen until later in my career, when I realized, like, *Man, I'm a beacon of hope and I need to embrace that and become the chosen one.* I was meant to come and bring an understanding to the youth,

220

someone that could bring to life your darkest, innermost emotions through song. That's so fucking dope that my music was able to be a warm blanket for them.

My old music was still resonating with younger fans like Timothée, but I needed to do something new. I did the surprise album *Satellite Flight: The Journey to Mother Moon* because I wanted to make a project that was out of the blue and unexpected. But I also wanted to lean back into the Moon Man mythology. Over the years, I had transitioned from writing verses to freestyling them. Freestyling my verses and hooks allowed me to tap into a more spontaneous energy. Sitting in a room and dwelling on one line for ten minutes was a far less instinctual process. It couldn't provide the charge I was chasing.

Freestyling was improv: *This is what's coming out of me.* This is what I'm feeling, rather than sitting there with a pen and paper, trying to think of the hardest line and melody. It was so much more freeing.

I was still dealing with the weight of trauma as I was recording the album. It was heavy and I was trying to push through. I was thinking, *I'm nearing thirty and I'm still not fully healed internally.* I hadn't reckoned with everything I lost when I was young, or how forsaken I felt. On the heels of *Indicud*, I didn't have a clear direction musically, and so *Satellite Flight* was the only album of my career that wasn't fully mapped out. I wanted to kind of come up with this theme where the Moon Man goes to the moon to find some type of answer to all of his problems.

That summer was when things took a turn. The previous year, I'd met this girl named Rocky throwing these Monday-night parties at this spot called La Descarga. We started seeing each other, but we didn't start dating for several months. Our relationship was always on and off. Once I was in the car with Rocky, and we got into an argument. I was so frantic that I put a blunt out on my palm. That was what I used to do whenever I was stressed out. The first time I did that was in that car. There are still spots on my palm from the burn marks. She tried to take it out of my hand, but I just kept it there. She was disturbed. That was a tough relationship. I was definitely not nice to Rocky. I was a bitter maniac. I shouldn't have been with anyone during this time.

But I was still a caring person. Once I was coming down the intersection of Sunset and La Cienega in West Hollywood, and I saw this skinny greyhound-looking dog in the street limping. Then all of a sudden another car just ran over him and kept going. My mom was with me and I turned to her and said, "Stay in the car; I'll be right back." I hopped out without even thinking, ran in the middle of the street, and stopped traffic trying to help the dog get out of the intersection. He was so scared that he was backing up from me, but it was good because it was getting him out of the street. I could've gotten creamed, but I kept waving people down. This dog was fucked up and I was so mad at this driver who just left him there. I got out of my car because nobody else was doing anything. People kept driving by. *Why am I the only one in the street right now?* Eventually, another guy came, we called animal rescue, and I let him wait for them to arrive. Jumping into hero action shit out of nowhere, risking my life—that's the type of nigga I am. If somebody needs something, I'm definitely going to help.

When the director Josh Mond sent me the script for a film he was putting together called *James White*, it resonated with me. I felt the pain that James was going through in the film. The movie was about an unemployed, self-destructive New Yorker in his twenties taking care of his terminally ill mother. I had such a strong relationship with my mom, and I kept thinking, *This is something every person has to deal with, losing a parent.*

I took the part of Nick and immediately was taken with the character. James is straight and Nick is gay, but it wasn't a problem for James. He didn't judge him. He was super accepting of his friend. It felt like a rare thing, in movies and real life: this camaraderie, this true friendship, where there was no judgment. Even when James is having the hardest time, Nick doesn't judge him, and he's right there by his side. He could be hard on him at times, but he was always looking out for him.

Josh Mond wrote the script from his own experiences. He lost his mom to cancer. I thought he did a phenomenal job telling the story and bringing it to life, making people feel the pain. I'll always champion him because that must have been hard for him to write and shoot, dredging up memories for him. But the result was this movie that felt really powerful. That was the first film I did that really pushed me into territory that I hadn't been before. It's one of my favorite movies I've ever done, and I did the score too. I was able to give Josh what he was looking for, to tap into what James was going through emotionally in each scene.

There was still so much I needed to work on and even more I needed to work through. It was seeping into the music I was making. After *Satellite Flight*, I knew I wanted to do a grunge album, and I wanted to produce it all by myself like *Indicud*. I started to fuck around with a guitar. I went to London with Plain Pat and we vibed out trying to build. Every time I work with Pat, it's easy. We tend to figure it out. Toward the middle of it, though, I started to feel the darkest I'd been in a long time. I was starting to think I'd never find the solution to whatever was plaguing me, the nagging sense that I would never have a true confidant. Me and Rocky didn't work out and I was bitter. Mad at her. Mad at myself. Mad at the world. I was seething at the thought that we had been unable to make our relationship work, and how that might just mean nothing ever would.

Satellite Flight didn't perform as well commercially as I wanted. I was letting it get to me. I was like, *Fuck, I suck. People don't want to hear me anymore.* I was discouraged, but I also thought, *Fuck it, this is what I need to do now.* It wasn't about making hit records; it was about, *This is what I'm feeling, and I'm angry.* I wanted to shred my guitar and yell. During this process, I met the director Brett Morgen and we hit it off. He was working on the documentary *Montage of Heck* about Kurt Cobain, and I was telling him about my project, and he told me he had some unreleased music from Kurt that he recorded before he was famous and he was gonna give it to me and maybe that would inspire me. That shit blew my fucking mind—hearing unreleased Kurt ideas and scratch vocals gave me the whole idea for my album.

Speedin' Bullet 2 Heaven was supposed to be my version of *Montage of Heck*, the mixtape that Kurt made. That's why it felt so mixtape-y, because it was meant to sound like somebody took a tape and dubbed over it a bunch of times and spliced shit. I wanted to create my own version of that. The whole album was recorded analog— all on tape. That's why it sounds so rich and heavy. All of Kurt's shit was tape recordings that he recorded on cassette. In the sixth grade,

I borrowed this Talkboy from my friend and forgot to give it back to him. I still had it after all those years, so I put four AA batteries in it and started doing crazy voices, just having fun creating the texture of the album.

But the fun was only on the surface. I was calling it *Speedin' Bullet 2 Heaven* because I was literally thinking about putting a bullet in my head. The load of all my accumulated damage was finally crushing me. I had the Kid Cudi stuff, but I didn't have anyone in my personal life. My relationship with Rocky had deteriorated, and when I took a step back and looked in the mirror I didn't like what I saw. I was hanging out with women who didn't give a fuck about me—they were there to fuck and leave and tell their friends that they fucked the rock star.

I couldn't find solace in those closest to me, because I didn't want to be a burden to them. Shouldering my pain felt like my responsibility; to shift that onto anyone else seemed unfair to them. And what if they couldn't make sense of what I was going through either? I didn't have the wherewithal to think that my guys would understand and they would give me insight. I didn't want to bring anybody down. But it was written on the music of that album. It was a huge cry for help.

We rented a house in Big Sur and recorded for a couple weeks—me, Anthony Kilhoffer, Plain Pat; I think Dot came through too—and we were cooking. The song "Edge of the Earth" was inspired by that location, this quaint, secluded spot, a house right on this cliff and you could go down the stairs to this private beach. Being in the backyard, looking at the ocean, I felt like I was on the edge of the earth:

"Oh what a beautiful scene/Oh what a beautiful ending to see."

■ ■ ■

I was talking about killing myself and dying on that mountain and just seeing that view. That was my whole thing. When that album came out, in December 2015, for a couple months when I was alone I'd been looking online for ways I could kill myself. I wasn't just imagining it, I was planning it out. I designed *Speedin' Bullet* to be my last album; when I said good-bye toward the end, that was me signing off. Somewhere during that process I was going to commit suicide. I didn't think I would see 2016.

The whole time when I was recording it, I was like, *I'm gonna just be as honest as I can, and let out all my pain and just scream.* It's a perfect example of a man struggling with his demons caught on wax. I think about that album as one of the most important albums of my career.

When it first came out, people hated it, but over the years, it's become a fan favorite. It's kind of similar to when a movie comes out and it doesn't do well at the box office but becomes a cult classic. I knew people would catch on later; it was just so dark and aggressive.

That's the one album that my mom and my sister say they can't listen to. Some of my friends say they don't listen to it either. Even when I listen to that record it can be disturbing. I was like, *I need to be a true artist and tell people what's going on in my life right now, and right now it's pain, pain, pain.*

Loneliness was really getting to me, especially not having a mate. I didn't really go out. I didn't do much. I just sat in the house and smoked weed and fucking felt horrible. I had a lot of time to stew and be in my mind about things. Being alone with my thoughts pulled me deeper into the vortex of hell.

■ ■ ■

When I got an offer to do a TED Talk at my old high school, it felt like another opportunity to channel my depression into something constructive that could potentially help others. I was super nervous, but I was excited to go back and revisit and talk to the kids. I was like, *What the fuck am I possibly going to talk about?* I thought it was a mistake. But I talked to my mom and my friend and we all kind of agreed: I should just tell my story, and that's ultimately what they wanted me to do. They wanted me to get up there and tell the tale of how I came from humble beginnings to make it to where I made it. I didn't write anything down. I went right in and was just winging it. It was so intense. I kept looking over to the side of the stage. They've got this big-ass clock that was counting down and it was like *The Hunger Games*. I thought, *Oh my god, I gotta make sure I wrap it up before the time is over.*

By that point in my career, I truly understood my impact. To be able to go back to my high school and reconnect with old friends, see the new generation of students, and give them some guidance—that's all I ever wanted to do with my music, to be a guide. When I think about it, that is why I'm here.

I did *Arsenio Hall* the year before and I made a statement about how my main mission was to stop kids from feeling alone and stop kids from committing suicide. A simple mission, but a powerful one. That went viral and it was this big thing. I still see it circulating online. That's truly what this is all about, man. It's never been about flashy shit, even though I love some fly shit, but that's not what I stand for. In the core of Scott Mescudi, that's not who I am. Wholeheartedly, I'm someone who cares about helping people. I get a chance to do that through my music.

It's a gift that keeps on giving. All these years later I still have kids who I'm reaching.

Passion, Pain & Demon Slayin' came about by accident. In 2016, when I was at a session with Kanye, I went out of the room for a bit with Mike Dean and some other people and we started cooking up. We made the first two songs—"Swim in the Light" and "Frequency"—and I was on fire after that. The songs kept coming out. I truly feel that when I work on an album I'm possessed by some spirit. That's why every album sounds different and I can't repeat the vibes. Every time I'm possessed by some different being.

I didn't want *Passion, Pain & Demon Slayin'* to be a dark album. I wrote it from a hopeful place. It was all songs talking about what I wish I had with someone. And I felt that kids needed to hear someone authentically and openly dealing with their most toxic baggage.

I reached out to André 3000 to connect for the album. I had always wanted to work with him. I tried to get him on a couple albums before and his fee was around a hundred grand and I didn't have enough money in my budget to get it, but I told myself, *Look, one day I'm gonna have enough money in my budget, I'm gonna set aside a hundred grand and I'm gonna pay for my André feature.*

At this point, I was ready for it. I hit him up and set up studio time. I was with Pharrell, and he always sits you down to ask you what you want. I told him I was looking for something fun, something that felt good, and he knew exactly what I needed. He whipped up "By Design" in fifteen minutes. Fifteen minutes! I watched with my own eyes. It was perfect. He's such a master at what he does, man, so skilled in making the off-kilter pop.

I played it for André and he totally connected with it, but he wanted to see what I'd do with it so he could get inspired off of that and build on it. So I did my part and then he did his part. *This is the André I've been wanting to see*, I thought. That's the thing I don't think people realize—those features on *Passion, Pain & Demon Slayin'*, André didn't sound like that for nobody else. Everybody else wanted him to spit some bars. I had him singing and doing *The Love Below*–type flavor.

I directed two music videos for *Passion, Pain & Demon Slayin'*. The first was "Frequency" and the next one was "Surfin'." We didn't have storyboards. I was just putting the camera places and telling people where the camera goes. It was the smoothest, most fun shit ever. "Frequency" looks so fucking good. It's a sexy-ass video. It was me in this Alice in Wonderland dreamscape. That's the sexiest I've ever looked. I was working out and building my physique and I took my fucking shirt off. The video had these women dancing in the background and there's this gnarly threesome scene between me and these two girls in the bed making out. It's super sensual. But that video was a luminescent fantasy so far away from the nagging torment I was actually experiencing.

I still felt like I wasn't getting any relief, and the last thing to bring me instant relief was cocaine. I had other avenues to solace, but they were slower acting. So I relapsed. It could relieve the pressures of having to be on all the time for people who didn't want to know me, if only momentarily. When I was working on those videos in the editing suite, I would go to the bathroom and do bumps. Six years, no cocaine, then boom. I thought I could go do it a bit and it wouldn't be a big deal. My mindset was that it was medicine, all for the sake of trying to maintain and not lose my balance.

Coke wasn't the only drug I was doing. Once I was smoking a cigarette outside this cafe in Los Feliz when some kid walked up and sparked up a conversation. He was with his girlfriend and he basically said his friend had some acid if I wanted to do some. I was bored, so I said, "Cool, we'll do it at my house."

Didn't know these kids, but I got into my Porsche and told them to have their friend meet us with the 'cid.

We got to my place, I put on some music, and we smoked some weed. The kid's buddy came over with the acid. There were five of us, and we all did some. We listened to music for hours. The shit started kicking in and the high was a super euphoric, magical feeling. It wasn't visually striking, but the music was leading to a rapturous, astral place. I was on the floor with the dude and his girlfriend sitting across from me and we were about six hours into the trip when I looked over at the girl and something seemed off—I don't know if she was fucked up or she just wasn't feeling the trip. The music was mad loud and so I mouthed the words, *You cool?* and she said she was. Then I looked over and the boyfriend was looking at me. Then he looked at her. He thought I was trying to get at her or some shit. It was crazy because I invited these guys to my house trying to be cool. That wasn't what I was trying to do at all. I was trying to make sure this girl wasn't tripping in my house.

But he said, "Yo, you hitting on my girl, man, why you trying to talk to my girl?"

I replied, "Yo, man, come over here, let me talk to you."

I took him to the corner of my living room. "Yo, what the fuck is wrong with you?"

"Nah, man, I was just saying—"

"No, no, no, what the fuck are you talking about? I brought you here to my fucking house. I brought you here."

I was trying to tell him I would not bring him here to disrespect him like that: "I know that's your girl. Ain't nobody trying to hit on your girl, bro."

"Nah, Cudi, you pick us up in this Porsche and you take us to this nice-ass house, you know what I'm saying? And I ain't got all the shit that you got," blah blah blah.

I told him, "See, that's your own insecure shit there, bro. That ain't got nothing to do with me, man. You better get off that fuck shit."

He was like, "All right, all right."

"You cool?" I asked.

"All right, man, all right."

Do you know how hard it is to reprimand somebody on acid? It took every fiber of my body. I had to focus up. So when we went back, the vibes were all fucked up. I called my homegirl to come over and visit us and she was completely sober. I had her come to try and save the vibes. I was trying to show him: *Hey, man, look, I got some chicks already coming over for me. I don't need your girl. These are the chicks I got. It's not that deep.* But the acid was wearing off and the mood was ruined, so everybody left. I thought, *That's what you get, Scott, for being Mr. Random Hippie, having these strangers coming to your house.* I don't know what I was thinking. At the moment, that's just who I was. I was super wavy, man. I would follow my impulses, chasing any high to get me through.

The highs were unsustainable. I started to get suicidal again and started to plan it. I was starting to be scared of myself, and of what I might do. There were days I would get in my car and do 100 mph down Los Feliz Boulevard, zooming at two in the morning when there were no cars out there. Every night when I would come home from the studio, I'd do a buck down the strip. I could've spun off and crashed at any minute. I had a death wish.

My coke usage went on for about two weeks in late September. I woke up one day and started playing some *Grand Theft Auto*, and then

Dennis came over. Since before my debut album, Dennis had been like the glue for everything Kid Cudi. He was a childhood buddy turned assistant turned body man. Whenever any business needed to be handled, or some negotiation, or I needed anything, anything at all, Dennis was the guy. He made sure to take care of me at all times. Even when he wasn't living in LA, he held me down. As he was my best friend, I knew he was gonna be honest with me.

I started thinking about everything I'd been through, thinking about how I'd been fighting for so fucking long, how I was in a cycle, stuck in the same place I was at six years ago. I knew if I didn't get help I was gonna either blow my brains out or drive off my cliff on Mulholland, because I fantasized about that shit all the time.

So as I was playing the game, I told Dennis, "Hey, I think I need to go to rehab."

Dennis went, "Yes."

"What you mean, 'Yes'?"

"I mean 'Yes, you should do that,'" he said.

That meant my friends had been seeing it. Everybody had been seeing it.

We started doing research, found a good place, and went. But before we went, I tried to come up with so many excuses. I kept telling myself, *I'll do it later; I'll start later.* Then finally I said, "Nah, I'll go now. I don't know if there's gonna be a later."

One thing I wanted to do before I went was The Last Hurrah. I went upstairs, did a little bit of cocaine I had left, smoked a blunt, drank a beer, then smoked weed all the way to rehab. I got there fully fucking loaded. They were asking me all these questions. I was so fucked up I was barely answering shit, cracking all sorts of jokes, not taking shit seriously.

Then, at some point, I told the intake nurse, "Miss, I apologize. I'm in here fucked up."

She said, "Don't worry about it. This happens all the time."

"For real?" I couldn't believe it.

"Yeah, you'd be surprised; people come in here high all the time."

"Fuck! Niceee!"

I was so loaded, man. That next month changed my life forever.

Act III

CHAPTER 21

Talking through things was something that I'd never really done. It was time I started. I learned that when I was in there. I was having breakthroughs every fucking day. But the first two weeks I was trying to leave that bitch. It was tough to convince myself I needed to be there.

I never felt addicted, because I was able to quit cold turkey when I got arrested in New York. I never craved cocaine. It was something that I used as an escape, a distraction, a detour. It was a brace. Even though I didn't feel like I had to have it, it had become something I was much more comfortable with than without. Every other day I was trying to find an excuse to get out of rehab, because I thought I was fine. But the suicidal tendencies had been getting stronger, the coke wasn't numbing them anymore, and I was starting to scare myself. I needed to find another way of coping. This sweet lady working there named Nika, who was super loving and nurturing, did not want to give up on me, and did not want to see me give up either. She kept me in there, for sure. At some point, after fighting for so long, I finally embraced it.

Rehab was all about having a schedule. I'd get up and go to a meeting at nine o'clock in the morning. Then have breakfast, lunch, and then another meeting. Maybe there'd be a Reiki session, a meeting with my therapist, and then I was done by like five o'clock. After that, you can do whatever: hang out, play board games or cards. I never did that. I just kind of sat in my room and watched Netflix, listened to music on my phone, and stayed to myself.

There was one album by the Red Hot Chili Peppers that came out that year that I listened to all the fucking time, *The Getaway*. It set the tone for rehab. I just listened to that back-to-back all day long; when I woke up in the morning, when I was in the shower, I had it playing. The songs helped me think about my own journey. One song called "Dark Necessities" helped me on my path to the light. The melody and production drew me in. As I was a man of music, things like that would always get me: sonics first, then lyrics second. It was just a really happy, uplifting album that seemed to exist in the place that I was trying to get to. A place of peace. I was trying to outrun the darkness.

About two weeks into rehab, I'm sitting and watching TV and my vision went double, as if my eyes were crossed. I closed my eyes, rolled my eyes, and opened them, and they were still crossed. I'm freaking out because it's like this for about five minutes. Then ten minutes. I'm panicking and everybody in the place is telling me it's going to be OK, to calm down and have a seat. Eventually, my vision comes back. *What the fuck was that?* Nobody knows, and we're all tripping and confused.

I went to sleep, and when I woke up the next day I noticed my speech and my movement were much slower, and that's when I decided to go to the hospital. They told me I'd had a ministroke. It was a by-product of doing the cocaine. When I started up again, after all those years, I was trying to go as hard as I used to. I was in the hospital for some time. My mom came out to visit. She was with me every day.

I've always had my own personal relationship with God. I don't really go to church, but I do speak with the Lord, and I talk to Him as if He's one of my homies. During some of my darker moments, I don't think I had the wherewithal to ask God for help. I was always dealing with my shit and just being like, *This is what it is.* I wasn't imagining that there was anything that could lift me out of that gloom. But I think rehab was one of the first times where I was like, *God, please help me.*

Throughout rehab, I was definitely praying and asking to come out of this darkness, and asking for Him to help me and guide me. I needed to find my strength, and I called on Him for that.

I always knew that I was touched by God. I knew I was one of His soldiers. He made me sensitive for a reason, and that's part of why fans love me: the fact that I've brought my feelings to the forefront in my music. I definitely feel like my faith has always gotten me through even when I wasn't praying. But my mom was always praying for me. God has always recognized my faith—that I knew how powerful He is. And when I prayed in rehab, my prayer was answered.

Therapy sessions helped me deal with my loneliness and with my father's death. I realized I'd never talked about his death with anyone and had been unable to find closure. I didn't feel anything about my career that got me down and depressed. It was just a lot of internal shit that I had been dealing with behind the scenes. I learned how to manage my mental health better, and it put a lot into perspective for me. So much so that I was able to contact people that I cared about and kind of give them some context to help them understand why I was where I was.

I wasn't supposed to talk to anybody, but I saw Jamie emailed me saying that she had heard I was in rehab and that she was concerned. I was explaining to her what I was dealing with and that I appreciated her reaching out. We went back and forth via email for a couple turns and then I straight hit her with the "Hey, this is what I've learned about what I've been dealing with the past ten years." She was responding to everything and then she didn't respond to that email. A day went by and she didn't respond and I took that as her way of being like "whatever." I hit her back and I said: "You know what, we're not friends. Don't hit me up no more." And that closed the casket on Jamie and me. I did it to myself. She never responded.

I had a show that I had booked before I went to rehab. I was locked in to perform at ComplexCon 2016. There was a whole thing about if I was going to cancel it or not, and we were trying to see if I would get better from the stroke. Not being able to perform at 100 percent made me super nervous about the whole shit. I didn't know what I was gonna bring. I thought that I'd fucking took a giant shit on everything. I thought I let my fans down. That October, I revealed I had checked into rehab on a post to my Facebook page. I felt like such a loser releasing that letter. But I needed to be honest, and in hindsight I'm glad I did it, that I could be real with the world.

I didn't tell anyone about my stroke for years. I was insecure about it. The combination of coke and cigarettes popped a vessel in my brain. That was the moment I realized: *You can never do cocaine ever again. You cannot slip ever again. Or you will die.* And that's how I looked at it. So I made a pact right then and there when I was in rehab that I was never going to fuck with that shit ever again.

While I was in rehab Drake dissed me on a record, taking shots, attacking my whole shit—my character, my career, trying to disrespect. I knew why: I called him out publicly about having writers. He had to do something. But the timing of it—it was fucked up. I was in the middle of rehab, and this nigga was kicking me while I was down. I don't make diss records. If somebody disses me in a record, I'm not gonna put no nigga in my art, especially no nigga I don't like. I'm not going to the studio writing about no nigga for no hour, sitting there angry.

I decided I'm just gonna come to this nigga's doorstep and let him know what time it is. So I tweeted at Drake: "You think it's a game. I wanna see you say it to my face. I'll be out soon. Promise." I don't play the rap games. That's not the type of nigga I am. This is not a joke.

When I said I was going to see him soon, that was a promise that I was ready to keep. I was low. I was having suicidal urges. I didn't give a fuck. If he saw me at that time it would have been over for him. I would've destroyed that boy. Because I was so angry, so mad at the world, that I needed a release. The disrespect was heavy. But I was the first one to say something. He must have thought I was gonna play the game. *I'm not playing a game with you, nigga; I'm gonna come see you.*

After that happened, I had an outpouring of support. Mad people were defending me, attacking Drake for taking shots at me while I was dealing with personal, life-and-death issues. People did not like that. That support revitalized me. To see the response to the tweet—it was a beautiful thing. I don't think I took a second to stop and realize how blessed I was at the time, but when I think about it now I can see it.

■ ■ ■

Talking through pain, how past relationships made me feel like a failure, eventually led me to an epiphany: Things like these are just a moment in time, and it may feel like it's going to be forever, but it's really not. You can overcome these things. You can find ways to handle them differently in the future. I realized I needed to release a lot of pent-up anger. That's what helped me find peace. As soon as I started talking about things, my heart became a little lighter. And by the time I left rehab, I was at a level of peace that I hadn't felt ever in my life.

One of the things they would say was, "Scott, you know, you're gonna have bad days again. It's how you deal with it that makes you who you are." And I've had bad days since, but instead of letting it ruin me for a month, I just deal with it for thirty minutes, and then I get past it. Because I'm like, *OK, I can't let this ruin my day. It's just a brief hiccup. I'll get over it. I'll find a solution. It's all right; let's move on.* I take things as they come, and I don't let them fester and eat me alive.

I got out of rehab on November 4, 2016. I quit cigarettes. I quit smoking weed. I wasn't drinking booze. I was completely sober. That was a great time of my life, facing the day 100 percent clearheaded. The day after I got out, I had the ComplexCon performance. It was my first appearance out and I was seeing people for the first time. Don C came by. Pharrell was there and he came through; he was performing and he wanted to come do "Surfin'" with me. Travis Scott came out and performed with me. I felt the love that night. I needed that. That brought me back.

After my rehab I got tight with the actress Kathryn Hahn. We had met when I was flying to Sundance for the *James White* premiere a year prior. We exchanged numbers and said we would stay in touch and we did. Throughout the years she's been a supporter. Every once in a while, I meet someone in the industry who just becomes family—I lock in with them—and Kathryn is one of those people. She's a good human and she sees me for me. She sees my soul. I've been through hell, but I've always been good. After rehab, I was in a better place and I could be a friend to people and show them my light.

Before rehab I couldn't do that. I was a dark muthafucka. But I was healing. I was taking time to recover through the holidays, and I met up with Ye a couple times.

We had a conversation and he was telling me that he wanted to finally do the album. I thought he was talking shit. Because sometimes Ye will say something and then the moment will pass for him and he'll lose interest. But the next couple months, he kept bringing it up. Eventually, we actually had a session at his house in LA and he, Plain Pat, and I started cooking. We were working in this bedroom: finding samples, making beats, and coming up with song ideas. I didn't know how confident I was in my music coming out of rehab, trying to figure out who Kid Cudi was on the other side of intoxication. Having Kanye to uplift me was what I needed. I told him I was gonna make a super positive, inspiring, uplifting album, and he told me, "Yes, I want the same shit." That made me feel so good—that we were on the same page about the direction we wanted to go. We were in sync. We were both at that place in our lives where we had both come out of some dark shit and we were alive to talk about it.

We worked on *Kids See Ghosts* all of 2017. I was thinking about my life, post-rehab, and I was in a new space. I didn't want to make melancholy music anymore. I wanted to give people something to get through their troubles, and if they weren't in that place yet, hopefully it could help get them there. The hook had come to me as all my hooks do. It was instantaneous. Dot and I have crazy chemistry. We're always on the same page from day one. The songs were a clean slate. I thought, *This is where I am now, and people need to know I'm OK.* The whole idea behind those songs, and that whole album, was that, for the first time, people needed to hear me genuinely happy. I was experiencing true clarity.

We went to China for a little bit and worked on it in a hotel room. Kanye was out there handling stuff with Yeezy, and so I was out there with him going through my laptop and looking for different joints that we could use on the album. I had a song that I did with Dot in a session: "Reborn." Dot and I had worked on the song when I was on tour. We were in Texas and we were recording in another hotel room; we made that song and "Cudi Montage." And when I went to China, I played them both for Ye. I had the hook, but that's all I had. When he heard it, he went crazy for it. His reaction was swift and emphatic.

He said, "That's it. We gotta have that on the album."

At that point, he was even talking about that song being a single. He believed in it.

And so did I. I knew it was a smash. So powerful. From that point on, "Reborn" was one of them ones that we were going to use. I don't think we had anything solidified yet at that time. But that was the first song we really chose to be on the album.

Dot da Genius just fucking killed it. I think that was the special sauce: me working with Dot and then bringing what we made to the table for the album. That's how we came up with "Cudi Montage." I was going through samples and seeing what I could fuck with. I always wanted to do something with "Burn the Rain" from *Montage of Heck* and I finally had an opportunity to do it. I thought, *This is perfect; let's do it for this.* I crossed my fingers and hoped to God that the Cobain estate would approve it. To start it off, the subject matter of the song was super uplifting. I think we did it justice and that Kurt would be happy. My goal was to show that if he was alive now this is the type of shit he would be on. He would be fusing with hip-hop.

The album didn't really get into a rhythm until Wyoming. I was out there for a long fucking time, months on end. We were staying at the Aman in Jackson Hole. Other artists were recording albums there at the same time. We all stayed in these futuristic cabins and we worked out of this one main house where Kanye stayed. Just being there with my bro—hanging out at the house and chillin', eating breakfast together, getting dinner together—it was stimulating. Kanye and I were totally locked in creatively. So much so I could go and work with Dot in another session and bring songs back and he'd be like, "Oh man, this is amazing!"

Jackson Hole itself is really white. It's no Black people, at all. When we went out, locals were looking at us, like, *What the fuck is these niggas doing here?* We would frequently go to this one spot to pick up food and they would be chill. Some people would be excited to see us. They didn't bother us, but they were always staring. Over the course of months, it became common knowledge that we were there working on an album—or, in Kanye's case, albums. I didn't sit in on any other sessions. I was completely focused on *Kids See Ghosts*. I knew what was going on, but I was holed up in the room with Dot and my engineer, Bill Sullivan. We'd be on our own, and Kanye would come down to hear what we were working on. He would send me beats. I would write my part; then I would play it for him. He'd write his part and we'd go back and forth.

On the song "Fire" Kanye wanted me to write his verse. I was like, "Dude, like, you're one of the illest rappers ever. How can I fucking write a verse for you?" I just didn't see it going well. But I wrote something that I thought he would fuck with and thank God he did. I was like,

"For real? You like this shit?" He just went with it and recorded his verse immediately. Cyhi the Prynce, who had been on the GOOD Music roster for years, was in the studio with us and he gave us one line. Everything about those sessions just seemed to click into place.

The *Kids See Ghosts* shit brought people back to liking me because I was standing next to Kanye. That's part of the reason why I agreed to do it: because it was a test. I saw the decline in my sales. From *Satellite Flight* to *Passion, Pain & Demon Slayin'* there was a bit of uninterest, and I was aware of the turn. And I said to myself, *Watch me stand next to this man and people will jump on the Cudi train again.* I was right. It was nearly overnight. People were back. We sold 142,000 copies that first week. We didn't debut at number one, but we got to number two. I hadn't done sales like that in years. I figured, *If my plan goes the way I think it's gonna go, my next albums should do extremely well too.*

But it was never really about the numbers. I think about every album I did, and it's all a fucking moment. Everybody knew about those albums when they came out. It's great to have the peaks and valleys and the ups and downs. I'm being a true artist. That's what counts. That's all that counts. I'm not doing it for sales. I'm not doing it to try to get an award or anything like that. I'm making shit based on what I'm feeling, and if what I'm feeling works, then it works. And if it doesn't, it doesn't. But at the end of the day, when I finally turn in that album, and it's mixed and mastered, I'm 100 percent happy with it. I let the chips fall where they may.

Sometimes albums got pushed back, or one wouldn't come out when it was supposed to come out, because I'd be sitting there making sure that I was 100 percent happy with the product. So when I put it out and it did what it did, I can never have doubts. I don't have any regrets for anything I've ever done. I have one of the illest discographies out of anyone in my league. Not only because, sonically, the shit is always for-ward thinking, but because of the message in it. There is no other artist that has a more powerful message than mine in hip-hop. No other artist that speaks to their fans like I do.

2Pac once said he didn't want to change the world, but he wanted to spark the mind that would, and I took that like he was talking about me. My music opened the door for generations of nonconforming art-ists in hip-hop and beyond. Recognizing that impact left me feeling so fulfilled. I had done something meaningful with my career. I was touch-ing people, and my music will always help people to the end of time. Kids will find these records, fucking absorb them, and they won't feel so alone. I changed the game for the better. I was really reaching out to the lost, the ones that didn't love themselves, or the ones that didn't know where their future was headed. The misfits. When I was adrift, I didn't have a lighthouse to guide me. I wanted to be that for the next generation—and for the generations to come.

On the *Passion, Pain & Demon Slayin'* tour, it was as if I was reintro-ducing myself to the fans. Post-rehab, I saw them waiting for me. It was nice to get back out—twenty-six cities and I could feel the energy and love at each one of them. I think that's when I started to actually feel pure joy. I had a complete 180. I started to appreciate my music more. I started to appreciate my fan base more. Even the element of the live show was refreshing in a way I couldn't have imagined. It helped me re-alize that I had been doing some really amazing shit: *People are always going to be there supporting you. You have really done a great job sup-plying quality music to your fan base, and they're always going to fuck-ing show up. You can get down on yourself and get in your head about things, but you have millions of fans all around the world that love you.* This was kind of like the tour that opened my eyes to that. I was getting a second chance. Not many do, and I was taking my opportunity to see everything with clear eyes. Looking out at those crowds was revitalizing. *There's a reason I'm here—and a reason that I need to stay.*

There wasn't a better time in my life than when I got out of rehab and was completely sober. I felt fresh and brand-new. Detox rejuvenated me. Do you know what it felt like to not have to run to smoke a blunt, not have to run to smoke a cigarette, not have to run to grab a drink? For five months I was sober off of everything, and I felt clear. I wasn't in need. I only started smoking weed again because I thought, *Maybe I can pick it up again. It ain't bad. Let me just see.* I wasn't craving it, but I figured, *I can smoke some weed.* It was my biggest mistake. I wish I never went back. Because that, I can say, is an addiction. I'm addicted to weed. I still smoke blunts back-to-back. I want to quit one day. Hopefully that happens sooner than later, because I don't want to be an older man smoking weed. I want to be clearheaded. I want to be present. I'm even thinking about one day going back to rehab for another month and approaching it differently. I'm not in a dark space anymore, but going in there again would provide another opportunity for detoxing.

In 2017, I got an offer to audition for this play, *Lobby Hero,* that was going to star Michael Cera and Chris Evans. I was excited because I was a huge fan of both those guys, and I felt ready to do some Broadway. This could be my first step into that world. I got the script and it was the most intimidating bit of material I've ever received on any job. I mean, just endless lines and small print, pages and pages, monologue upon monologue.

Poststroke, I didn't even know if my mind was strong enough or if I could handle this shit. It had affected me immediately. I didn't know if I was going to be able to write music the way I did before. Trying to do a play—to commit so many words to memory—felt even more daunting. I asked for about two weeks to study. I studied every day, for hours all day long. I practiced that shit until I knew every page word for word. I had all the emotional beats down. I knew what choices I was gonna make. I knew how to change it up. I had to audition a couple times and I knew the different approaches I could take. I had it all figured out, and when it came time to read I walked into the Theater District in New York.

Michael was a homie I'd known for years. It was nice to see him when I walked in the room. He was excited to read with me, and the director was there with us. I didn't have any script in front of me, but Michael pulled out his script and he was reading from the pages. We read together and I fucking delivered. I sold the fuck out of that shit. I didn't fuck up in following my lines, not once.

The next day I found out I didn't get the role. But they said they would have hired me if they didn't have Chris in the play, because they didn't want two first-time Broadway actors in the main lineup. I didn't have enough experience. I was disappointed, but I felt good knowing that they had faith in me and knew that I could deliver it. It was at that point that I knew my mental strength had returned. If they felt confident enough to even consider me, I could be confident in myself. Any notion of me not being at full capacity was gone.

CHAPTER 22

After rehab, I told myself I was going to take a year off between albums. I wanted to start pacing myself. For years I had been overdoing it. Ever since 2012, I had dropped an album every year. I only took one year off from 2009 to 2016. I was overloaded, not finding time to live my life and relax. It drove me crazy. I almost killed myself. *We ain't going back to that. You gotta find another way.*

In February 2018, I got word that this twenty-two-year-old kid thanked me in a cover story he did for *GQ*. I'm thinking, *Yo, why'd this kid just thank me? Who is this kid?* I couldn't, for the life of me, put it together. Dennis put it together for me: That's Timothée Chalamet, who you met in Montreal five years ago. *No fucking way.* When I met Timmy, he was shorter than me. His face looked different. His hair was different. It looked like a totally different dude. *GQ* had reached out to me because they were hosting a dinner for Timothée. I was like, *I'm coming.* It was the first time that we reconnected since he saw me when he was seventeen. It was so great to talk to him again. He had a problem looking me in the eye before but not anymore.

A couple days later, I told him I wanted to see *Call Me by Your Name*, his breakthrough role, directed by Luca Guadagnino, and he took me. He bought tickets and autographed them. Ever since then it's been our tradition: Every time he has a new movie, we go watch it together. Timothée is just one example of an artist I inspired who has grown to inspire me, someone my music helped draw into my orbit—a blessing that has led me to so many lasting friendships.

A few months later, I went to Paris to connect with another such confidant, walking in Virgil's first Louis Vuitton show. He had asked me to do it, and I was completely blown away because I had hoped he would. I was nervous but excited at the same time, and I was proud of my nigga. He was on the cusp of doing something extraordinary and I was about to be a part of it. Supporting my boy just felt so good. The way he thought about and approached fashion felt revolutionary. Steve Lacy, Dev Hynes of Blood Orange, and Playboi Carti all were there to walk in the show too. Virgil doing what he did with Off-White, and then branching off and doing what he did with LV, taking luxury shit to a fresh place where he was incorporating hip-hop flair, brought the whole culture to the French house's door. He brought worlds together, which in turn created new worlds. The way he synergized culture won't be replicated in our lifetimes.

The first day I went in for a fitting, I saw what I was wearing and all that; Virgil was showing me around, showing me all of the clothes. His office was so cool; he had everything laid out and was going through piece by piece, pointing them out and showing me details and explaining it. He had such a beautiful, beautiful spirit. Being around him was special. He was so open and so caring and gave a lot to his friends. He was just that kind of man.

I was about to get dressed when I saw this short girl, about five-three, in a black dress and sandals, wearing big hoop earings and these circular oversized-framed glasses. She was taking pictures of the models for the board. I wondered to myself, *Who is this girl?* It was something about her; I kept staring at her. She was so focused on her work, so I went and got dressed. I came out, and she asked to take my picture. I didn't say anything to her; I just got into position. She snapped my picture, looked at her camera, snapped a couple more, and that was it. We didn't say anything to each other. But I walked out of that fitting telling myself if I saw that girl again I was gonna get her number.

The show was the next day. I missed rehearsal because it was early in the morning and I had been partying the night before. I was not prepared to get up and go. I figured, *Hey, how hard can it be? We're walking in a straight line. It's easy.* I got dressed and the energy in the place backstage was powerful. Seeing all the models—Black models, beautiful, dark-skinned Black models, in these fresh-ass suits, the colors with the Black skin—it was so epic. It was a moment in Black excellence.

The show started and I felt like I was going to shit myself. I was so nervous. When we walked out, the only thing I was thinking to myself was, *Keep a straight face and look straight.* So that is what I did. Now, my eyes are sensitive to fucking light. When I'm outside and it's sunny, I'm squinting bad. When I have to do a movie and we shoot something in the sun, I dread it every time. It was mad sunny at the show; I'm squinting my eyes and I'm high as shit. You can imagine. I'd just started smoking again that year. I'm walking so fucking slow. I noticed the dude ahead of me was an entire field ahead of me. I went, *Oh shit*, so then I started to walk fast. I'm walking fast, fast, fast, fast, trying to speed walk. I saw Kanye. I saw Takashi Murakami. And I thought, *Keep a straight face. Keep a straight face.* They were cheering for me. I smiled.

When we were working on *Kids See Ghosts*, Ye and I went to Tokyo and we met with Murakami at his studio. We saw all his art and how his shit is made and it was fucking wondrous. Murakami had been one of my favorite artists for a while. To see where he works was inspiring. He knew I made a rock album, so they had a Fender and an amp plugged in waiting for me in the studio so I could play. "This is for you," they said.

Holy shit, I thought. I went up there and I shredded for a little bit and they were into it. And I'm a shit guitarist, but I guess it was the charm. We went up to the room and started working on some designs, talking about cartoons for the album cover and talking about doing this TV show based on animals. We went to the studio for a couple days, working for hours on designs for different things. I'll probably never get to experience anything like that ever again.

The studio was in this ginormous warehouse with these incredibly high ceilings. There were people everywhere working on artwork. Dozens of paintings were being started. It was an intense, meticulous process. Sometimes there would be two or three painters working on a single piece. Despite all the hustle and bustle, it was very quiet. Nobody was to be disturbed. The work in there felt urgent.

When I finished Virgil's show, the first thing that was on my mind was finding the girl with the glasses. I was looking everywhere for this girl. I go out to the courtyard, and I finally see her standing there talking to her friend. I made a beeline straight to her.

I went to her and I said, "Excuse me. Do you have a boyfriend?"

She said no.

I said, "Can I have your number?"

She said yeah and gave it to me. I was so flustered, so focused on the number, that I forgot to ask her name when I approached her. I discovered her name was Lola when she put her number in my phone. I seldom approach women, but when I have it always worked out for me. I can't wait to have my son so I can tell him to be confident: "My young boy, if you like a girl don't be afraid to approach her and let her know. It has always worked out for your pops."

I got fresh for the after-party—I was in the full Tom Ford suit, head to toe, fucking classy in that muthafucka—and Lola and I hung out that night. She was so cool, man. I was hanging out and talking to Kristen, Don C's wife, who'd been with Don since the beginning. So my whole career I saw her around.

She said, "Oh, do you know that Jamie's getting married?"

This news rocked my soul. It shattered my heart into a million pieces. All I could say was, "Oh."

She said, "Oh . . . you didn't know. I thought maybe you would've heard."

"Nah, I didn't know," I replied.

I don't know if Kristen could tell that she made a mistake or not, but I had already excused myself and made a beeline to the bar, and had my first drink in two years. I had been sober off alcohol since rehab and I wasn't touching it. And I went to the bar and got some tequila immediately after I got that news.

That night, I stared in the mirror for twenty minutes straight. It was like watching a heartbreaking scene in a movie where we see the rock star had nobody. The girl that I loved so dearly was getting married. I had to take it in stride: *Hey, this is life. You're getting older. You haven't talked to her since 2016. People you know are gonna get married.*

They're gonna have babies. This is bound to happen. That's what Jamie wanted: a family. She finally had it. I was happy for her, but I was heartbroken because it wasn't me.

I got back to the States and I shook off whatever I was feeling. I was back in a good mood. *Kids See Ghosts* was well received. That November, Kanye and I performed at Camp Flog Gnaw, and he had this idea to perform in a cube that was suspended in the air. It would go up and down and I'm fucking terrified of heights. But hey, *let's fucking get it.* We rehearsed it and I was so freaking nervous. Night of the show came, we were doing the performance. The whole time I was thinking that shit was gonna fall along with me to my death. Kanye was dancing all crazy, hopping all over the place, the shit was shaking, and I thought, *Aw, man, stay still, muthafucka!* But we pulled it off, and the kids loved it. Tyler, the Creator came up afterward and was appreciative. I was glad we did it.

Then, a couple days later, I got a text at five in the morning from Lorde. Now, I ran into Lorde maybe two years prior and we exchanged numbers at the Sunset Tower one day because I was trying to work with her. I loved her music and I loved her vibe. So she had my number all this time and texted me: "Hey, Cudi, what's up? It's Lorde, what's this?" and sent pictures of the Camp Flog Gnaw stage alongside pictures of the stage at one of her shows.

She said: "I did this last year. I'm trying to figure out what's going on."

I got the messages at eight when I woke up and I called her. Didn't answer.

I responded: "Hey, I want to get on the phone and talk to you. I'm pretty sure we can figure this out."

I didn't know what else to say to her.

I told her: "Call me when you get a chance."

She responded: "Hey, phone service is kind of weird where I'm at, but what's up?"

I thought, *This girl does not want to get on the phone and talk to me . . . you've got an issue with me, but you don't want to get on the phone like an adult. You're accusing me of stealing, and I'm appalled.* Because I'm an artist. I don't steal. But then again, this wasn't my idea. This came from somewhere else. So I was trying to figure some shit out and make sure that she knew that what she was claiming had no merit. Kanye and the stage director collabed and came up with the idea, and I went with it. I thought it was original, and then when I looked at her stage and looked at what we did I still thought it was a different take on that concept. So for a while she started trending on Twitter because she was making a big hoopla, talking shit, posting screenshots, and saying that people were stealing from her. I thought, *Look, Lorde, I liked your music. I liked you as an artist, but chill. Ain't nobody trying to copy you.* I took offense to it even more because then she told me she was sorry, she couldn't be on a phone because phone conversations were weird for her, and she promised the conversation would stay between us. When she said that, I thought to myself, *All right, this conversation is definitely not gonna stay between us*, and I just stopped responding.

Es Devlin, who designed the stage that Lorde was claiming we ripped off, made a statement where she pretty much said she admired both and saw no imitation of her work. So once that happened, I thought, *All right, cool.* Because I was wondering if I needed to make a statement and then her own stage designer was denying the connection. Lorde lost that battle. I don't know what she was on that day. I did like her, but that was wild, man: A white woman accusing a Black man of stealing some shit rubbed me the wrong way.

It was time to draw another feud to a close. In 2018, Kanye set up a meeting for me and Drake at the Yeezy office in Calabasas so we could try to patch things up following our squabble while I was in rehab. I came through. Drake, Kanye, and I all talked; Drake and I squashed our beef. It was cool to sit there and have a real one-on-one. Regardless of the diss record that Drake made for me, one of the things that he said was that it didn't feel right. He said he gets into it with these other niggas, but he said with me it just didn't feel right. I agreed with him. It didn't feel right for me either. I don't feed into that angle of hip-hop and I know that he respects me as an artist and that respect has always been intact. That's one thing I learned about us meeting up and talking.

He told me, "Hey, come meet me at The Nice Guy"—this bar on La Cienega Boulevard—"tonight, and have a drink." So I met up with him. We were having a real heart-to-heart. He said to me, "Hey, man, you remember, when we were at that party at that bar. You came down on me for not being a real friend. You was right. I wasn't being a real friend, and I apologize for that."

I said, "Yo, bro, I was just being hard on you, bro."

He countered: "Nah, this is real shit. I should have been there for you. I've been holding on to that for all this time."

I thought that was the realest shit. I took that and it meant so much to me. I was thinking, *Oh man, things are about to get back to normal between us. We're gonna be homies again.*

I saw him when we were making *Kids See Ghosts*, he came out to Wyoming for a little bit, hung out, kickin' it out there, and it was cool. Then he asked me to do the record on his joint a couple years later, "IMY2." I recorded the verse at home, and when I sent it to him he responded with a long voice note telling me how much he loved it.

I haven't heard from him since. I think I texted him once and he didn't respond. He wanted that record, and I guess he got what he wanted. And that's it. I'm too old to be having beef with niggas again. I was beefing with this nigga for over ten years. I had anger in my heart. But if we don't match up now, that's just what it is. We grew past our moment, and we're just not there anymore. And that's OK. I don't have beef with him. He was able to apologize to me about some shit I guess I've always wanted an apology for.

Being out of rehab, on the other side of a successful collaboration with Kanye and a beef with Drake, I was feeling reenergized, and I was starting to figure out my new life. I was enjoying living for a change. I used to dread waking up in the morning, but now I welcomed the sun.

At the top of 2019, I was kind of thinking about my next project, and I wanted to do something different—something that I'd never done before. I started throwing around ideas and I always wanted to do a visual album, but that had already been done, and I didn't want to do something that people had already seen. My whole thing is all about how I can get people new experiences.

So I sat and thought about it. My original idea was a series of short vignettes by different filmmakers organized by a theme. One of the segments was going to be animated, and the theme would be "love" or something along those lines. Every story would have that through line. I started talking about the idea a little bit more with Karina Manashil, the president of my production company, Mad Solar Productions. She helped me figure it out and she wrote down all my ideas. It was something we kept on the back burner.

A friend connected me to showrunner Kenya Barris, known for TV hits like *Black-ish* and *Grown-ish*, who had recently signed a deal with

Netflix, because he wanted to talk to me about speaking at his daughter's school. Me, I'm always down to talk with the kids, so I got on the phone with him to figure it out, and in the middle of the conversation he asked me flat out, "Yo, so what are you working on? What are you doing? What's up?" And I proceeded to tell him about this idea that I had been sitting on for a couple months. He said that it sounded dope, and he wanted to hear more about it. So we met at his office, and talked it through, and he went back and talked to Netflix.

In the Netflix meeting, they were not into it being live-action, because the market was flooded with scripts and they weren't into the concept at all. Mike Moon, who was the head of animation at the time and was in the meeting, told Kenya, "If you think about making this animated, that could be really great," and so when Kenya pitched it to me things came full circle. I love animation. I'd always wanted to be involved in it. This was the opportunity.

I came up with the concept and I decided to turn the whole show into a love-themed story centered around two young people that find each other randomly. And I knew I wanted it to be a Black love story, something that we don't get a chance to see that often. As soon as I told Kenya I was down to make it animated, we had Mike Moon, Elizabeth Porter, and Mike Penketh from Netflix come to the studio to hear the pitch and some music. I played "Willing to Trust," "Do What I Want," and "Angel," but I didn't have the lyrics yet. I gave them the whole rundown, the concept of the show, certain beats when things were going to happen, the cast we were thinking about having.

I was pitching this shit like I was trying to save my fucking life. I had never pitched anything but I was just going off like someone who had done a thousand pitches before. I knew this idea. It was mine. I knew it was gonna work. I believed in it. And the music was so powerful. There was no way those people were going to walk out of that studio after hearing that music and not want to buy that show.

In the next couple days I heard they were on board, so we started to get it going. We got animators. It took us a while to find a director. Maurice Williams, who'd worked with Kenya, came on board to write with Ian Edelman, who I reached out to from my *How to Make It* days, and I made Ian my showrunner.

We all got together and started talking about the concept and got a director, Fletcher Moules. I knew he was the right guy for the job. I knew he would be able to help execute the vision. He understood exactly what I wanted to do. It was a blessing that we found Fletcher because we went through two animators before we hired him. I knew exactly what style I was looking for. I wanted it to be a new take. I needed it to feel real but still be an animated space. I was having that conversation with different animators, and the only one that had a take was Fletch. We were stressing about who to work with. And it was a "third time's a charm" type thing. He was perfect.

He was doing some rendering, showing me stuff, and I was giving him notes to get the look right for the characters. I told him I wanted all the characters to look like the voice actors. We went back and forth for months on the character designs. When I saw some of the earlier art-work of the city, some of the backdrops, the apartment, I thought, *Oh man, this is exactly what I was thinking*. It started to feel like we were on to something remarkable and if it was executed we could fuck around and fuck up the culture.

Once we started getting everything going and we had a director, we started to figure out casting, and Timmy Chalamet was somebody that I knew I wanted to be in it. I told him about it when I first started conjuring up the idea and he told me he was down to be in it.

Ty Dolla $ign came in, when we came up with the character Ky; I thought, *Man, I think Ty's look fits the animation so well, his voice is perfect, and I feel like he could play this character and kill it and bring the comedy.* I never saw him do it before; it was just a hunch, and when I have hunches I always go with my feeling. The casting director, Carmen Cuba, wanted to meet him and get a feel for him to see if he could do it, and he fucking killed it. He showed up and blew Carmen away, and I thought, *Yeah, I knew my boy was gonna kill it.* In situations like this, my friends are like Pokémon that I throw into battle. I know they gonna come out victorious.

When it came to the character Meadow, I was telling Carmen that I wanted a beautiful, dark-skinned woman. I didn't want anybody confused about what this story was. I wanted it to be a Black love story through and through. When she brought up Jessica Williams, I thought, *That's her.* Her face was warm. I felt as if I could fall in love with this woman if I met her on the street, and that was what I wanted my character, Jabari, to have—that feeling about whoever the person was going to be.

We got the cast together—we got Macaulay Culkin, which I was so excited about. I got a chance to talk to him on Zoom and broke it down, gave him some rough storyline, and he was excited to come and play. I wanted the wardrobe in the show to be the illest shit. On some animated shows you don't see the freshness. There's only a few animated shows that fuck with the fashion element, and I wanted to do that with this show. The only person I knew that could do that and execute it was Virgil. I hit him up and told him about it and he was all in, no hesitation. He was getting asked to do a bunch of shit, but I guarantee he had never been asked to do no shit like that. So I was giving him an opportunity to touch new ground in his list of many accomplishments. He killed it, as he always did.

When I was putting together *Entergalactic*, I thought about adding my sister, and there was no one that could play her better than she could. I told the heads of Netflix, and they were all supportive of it. I knew my sister was gonna show up, and she did. She already told me that she had the passion to do voice acting. I gave her an opportunity and she delivered one of the most memorable lines in the whole show. I was so proud of her and my mom was too. When I showed my mom the movie for the first time, she leaned up in her seat when my sister came on-screen. As the pride welled up in her eyes, I sensed I'd crossed a pivotal threshold. With this new creative horizon, I'd brought people I loved from different worlds to create something daring and new. In reaching this new frontier, so many of my childhood ambitions were realized.

CHAPTER 23

was looking to take on new challenges, and, in the summer of 2019, another one presented itself. I got an offer to do this HBO show with Luca Guadagnino. I was a huge fan from *Call Me by Your Name*, and I couldn't believe that the man wanted to work with me. He set up a Zoom and they sent me the script. I read the first two episodes and I loved them. I met with him and the first thing he said was, "Oh my god, you're so beautiful."

I was bashful. I replied, "Oh my god, thank you so much."

He was the sweetest Italian man. I loved him the moment he signed on to the Zoom. The compliment got me. He had my heart from the jump. We talked; he explained the role to me, then asked me if I wanted to come join him in filming. I said, "Hell yeah."

From August to October we filmed in Padua, Italy. The series was a coming-of-age drama set on a military base in a fictional Italian city.

It starred Chloë Sevigny as Sarah Wilson, an army colonel who had moved from New York City with her wife, Maggie Teixeira (played by Alice Braga), and their son, Fraser (played by Jack Dylan Grazer). I got there early to train. In the show, I played a lieutenant colonel in the military. I had to learn how to salute, how to march, all that.

We trained for about two weeks and then I left and came back for another two weeks. We started shooting and I had a lot of fun with the hair and makeup department. That trailer was always a good time, mainly because of these two Black women named Nikki and Kai, who were the realest muthafuckas on that set. It felt good to be around my people all the way out in fucking Italy. Shooting the show was a ball, but some of the more intense scenes were a heavy lift. It was a great learning experience, but it took its toll emotionally.

When the cameras weren't rolling, it was different. We would all party. I had a villa that I was renting for the time I was out there, and I would have them all over. They'd come hang out all the time. We'd have dinner. I had my private chef, Johnny, out there, and he'd throw it down. The camaraderie with the cast was great. Alice Braga, who I was a fan of for a while, was a very delightful human being. So sweet. I thought she was beautiful. So elegant. So cool. Man, I feel like in another life she was my wife or something. We had a connection.

Me and Faith Alabi, another gorgeous Black woman, who played my wife in the show, hit it off too. I got lucky with this role. I met some great people and I had a lot of support from everybody. There was this club we used to go to—we'd get a table, get some bottles, and just fucking party party party. That was our thing: get fucked up and just enjoy ourselves. The kids would be with us. It was a good time. I haven't had any dark moments with liquor post-rehab. I realized I'm much more of a smoker than a drinker anyway.

I'd never done anything quite like *We Are Who We Are*, so it was a first, but everybody knew I could show up and do it. When we did our first table read, I had to get to my scene where I spoke some Italian, and I worked with the dialect coach to try to figure out how to do that because, even though we were probably about a month away from film-ing that scene, I still didn't want to be in a table reading sounding as if I didn't know what the fuck I was doing. So I polished up on the line and got it together. At the table read, when it came time for me to do the line, everybody started clapping when I finished. Luca was impressed and I felt good.

There was one scene, where Jordan Seamón, the girl who played my daughter, felt like she was my daughter. She was such a special girl with such ability. Strikingly beautiful—on camera and in real life—and a down-to-earth kid. Her parents were awesome and supportive of her. It was nice to see. A mom and a dad: a solid Black family. It was inspir-ing. They had been together for years. A sound foundation. There were tough scenes with Jordan and me. In one I had to scold her, and I felt weird about doing it. It was always happy and fun vibes on set with the cast. So when it came time for my character, Richard, to be an asshole, I had to dig deep.

I was nothing like Richard. It was the first role where I had to play something so far from myself. There's one scene in the show where I had to have an outburst at a memorial, and I had to be drunk doing it. I was nervous about pretending to be drunk. I thought, *Man, I hate watching movies and you see actors playing drunk and it's such bullshit, a terrible portrayal of someone inebriated.* I was nervous about looking phony, so I went to Luca and I said, "Hey, I think I want to drink a little bit for this."

He said, "Oh, you want the bottle? I got you."

He gave me a bottle of Black Label whiskey. I drank damn near half of that bottle and I got blasted, almost too drunk, but not too drunk where I didn't remember my lines. That was the key.

I went out, and before we started the scene Faith was watching me because she knew I asked for the liquor and she could tell I was fucking saucy. I just smiled at her with this goofy-ass grin. They started the scene. I got through it completely, fully in it. I lost myself. Everything I had, I gave it. I left it in the room on the first take. Right when I finished and they yelled, "Cut!" the strangest thing happened—and something tells me this doesn't happen often to people on set: Everybody in the room, cast and extras included, clapped and cheered for me. It was such a validating feeling. I don't think up until this point I even felt I was all that great of an actor. I gained a lot of confidence after that.

We did that scene three times. At the end, Faith, Chloë, and Alice all came up to me showing me love. I have so much respect for all three of those women, I put them all up on a pedestal, and to have them all honor me in that way was overwhelming. I went to bed with a big smile on my face. Chloë said I killed it. Chloë is a queen. She's a master thespian, and she fucked with the performance. I was nervous about that scene all night before. I knew that Chloë was gonna be in the scene and that if she thought it sucked it was gonna be written on her face. I was so scared. All I could think about was Chloë: *What does Chloë think?* When she came over showing love, I thought, *Oh thank God.*

Timmy Chalamet visited while I was in Italy filming the show just to see me. He stayed in the villa I was renting for a couple days and we bonded. I played Timmy "Willing to Trust" before it was gonna come out and he cried. He felt that shit. That's always my thing: to play Timmy music before I drop to see what he thinks. I love doing that. Him and Jaden—they're the compass to let me know if I'm on the right track.

They're always gonna shoot me straight. They pretty much love every-thing I do, but there's levels to the shit. Sometimes Timmy rocks his head, but sometimes he'll get up and go, "Oh shit!" I kind of study their reactions, and the one for "Willing to Trust" was a big one. That's how I knew it was special.

That same year when I was filming *Bill & Ted Face the Music*, Dean stopped by the set. I had him come out because the original movie was a key part of our childhood, and I knew he would get a kick out of it. He got a chance to meet Alex Winter, Keanu Reeves, and William Sadler. We all took a pic together. I was even able to get him into the movie as a background extra. I'll never forget sharing that moment with my big bro.

I needed to be willing to trust to bring love in my life. Sometimes when I was in Paris I would see Lola, who was working as a designer at Louis Vuitton. We'd connect, I'd go over to her house, and we'd talk or kick it. I was getting to know her, but it didn't seem possible. What, was I going to date her? She lived in Paris. She had a life there. It didn't seem like anything real. So I tried my best not to get my emotions too wrapped up in it.

Around that same year, Rocky and I started to talk again and get serious. Coachella was when we first kicked it, and she was very stand-offish with me because of how I was before, and she had a right to be. But my goal with Rocky at this time was to prove to her that I was a new man, a man reborn, and I could make her happy. So that's what I threw all of my attention into. The first time we met up, I was not in a good place, but at this stage in my life I was doing much better, and I wanted to make up for that. That was my motive: to try to figure it out with her. She didn't want to be with me for a while, or to say that we were boyfriend and girlfriend. But rehab changed me. It made me face my demons in a way that I never had before, and actually talk about things that had been troubling me that I never spoke about to anyone. So I was unpacking trauma and facing my own bullshit. The treatment, them talking to me, the medication, getting off the drugs, definitely helped, because there was no way I could have gotten out of that otherwise. Eventually, Rocky and I became a couple again.

In the beginning of 2020, I moved to Woodland Hills from Los Feliz. I needed a new place. I hadn't found my dream home yet, but I needed to get out of Los Feliz. I had outgrown that house. It was becoming madness. I always had clutter everywhere, accumulating far more stuff than I could store, and it was getting out of hand. I was trying to fight living in a real mansion, but I finally gave in.

By 2020, Rocky and I had broken up again, this time for good. For her it was about trust. I'd put her in positions before where she couldn't trust me, and I couldn't shake her out of that. I was miserable about it. One thing that I was always good at was using my pain to make millions of dollars. So I decided to write an album. But not just any album: *Man on the Moon III: The Chosen*. My label had been asking me to do *Man on the Moon III* for years, and I kept on telling them to stop asking me. Now I was ready. I was supposed to do one more album, but when I asked for another *Man on the Moon* and more millions and they asked for another album on top of that I agreed, and I might have made twenty songs in around two weeks.

I explicitly asked Dot to be the executive producer, and he and I were just creating at that point. He started making music with the concept of the album in mind. We had sessions with different producers for the tone of the album, and we were able to bring Plain Pat, Mike Dean, and Anthony Kilhoffer back—guys who had made key contributions to the first two albums. I had to do it with Dot because of all the history. He had been so close to my story for years, and I knew he could stay as true to it as possible.

Man on the Moon III was a very important album. It was me trying to finish the trilogy ten years on. The whole time I was thinking about how much of a disaster it could be. But I knew I had incredible taste, and I knew that I'd be able to do something tasteful. Just as I did on the previous two, I let my heart be the guide. I was in the zone. It was my first solo since 2016, my return to form, a *Man on the Moon* album. I had a lot to prove. It was a very ballsy move to say I was gonna do a *Man on the Moon* album after a decade. But I had confidence. I knew that muthafucka was gonna go up.

It was just me cooking with Take a Daytrip and Dot in the studio, whipping shit up. I'll never forget when we made "Tequila Shots"—the way it came together. So beautiful. Take a Daytrip and Dot produced magic in the studio, bro. Dot did "Another Day," and those chords are powerful as fuck. He's a bad muthafucka with some keys and chords and coming up with melodies, finding the right shit for me to sing on top. He has a special knack for that. Our musical chemistry is fucking magnetic. We had something to prove on that album, all of us. If I could pull this off, I would solidify myself in the culture with a fucking amazing hip-hop trilogy.

COVID hit and disrupted everything. The world coming to a stand-still made me comfortable with the idea of continuing the trilogy. Returning to the Moon Man was essential. The character always represented individuality, me being one of one. But the concept was a reminder to others that I was still a presence to be reckoned with in the music space. I wanted to compete. I had created such an important legacy that people, no matter what, were going to stop and pay attention. That album was one of the first to drop into the unknown of the COVID landscape. It was a signal that there was room to release new music again.

During the COVID winter I had a little part in the black comedy *Don't Look Up*. I was super, super excited to jump in and work with Adam McKay, the director behind some of the great 2000s comedies like *Anchorman: The Legend of Ron Burgandy* and *Step Brothers*. There were so many great actors in the movie—Leonardo DiCaprio, Cate Blanchett, Meryl Streep, Jennifer Lawrence, Jonah Hill, and on and on—and it was the first movie that Timmy and I did together too. When I was doing my performance scene with Ariana Grande, Leonardo DiCaprio and Jennifer Lawrence were there. I've known Leo since the beginning of my career, just from hanging out and kicking it. He came up to me and we were talking, between takes. He was like, "Yo, man, I see you doing your thing, doing more movies."

"Yeah, man, I'm trying. I'm trying," I said.

"No, man, you're doing it. I see you."

It was so energizing to be acknowledged by someone at the peak of the industry. When I was doing my scenes, I could hear Adam laughing in the background, just enjoying what he was seeing. And that would let me know my performance was working. It was a small role but one of the best times I've had on set. Ariana was such a sweetheart. Working on a song with her was fulfilling. We recorded our parts separately, but it was just nice how we were able to find a way to make me fit. I was nervous about my place in the song. But Nick Britell, the composer who worked with *Moonlight* director Barry Jenkins, with McKay on other films, and on the hit HBO series *Succession,* brought me to his house and we cooked it up. He was so supportive and made me feel comfortable. Collaborating with so many awesome people on one project was incredibly eye-opening.

When *Man on the Moon III* was released, on December 11, 2020, it debuted at number two in the first week with 144,000, my best week in years for a solo, and even doing slightly better than *Kids See Ghosts.* I felt so fucking accomplished. We would have had the number one if Taylor Swift hadn't dropped her surprise album that same night. I was so sick, man. I literally got robbed of my first number one of my career. But it was a success befitting my defining trilogy.

In 2021, I got the offer to be the musical guest on *Saturday Night Live.* The show shaped my point of view so dramatically that I had to do it justice. I immediately thought, *Man, how can I have an impact onstage, a memorable moment?* It hit me: *I want to pay homage to Kurt, because Nirvana's was one of my favorite performances in the show's history.* I was like, *I know what I'm gonna do. I'm gonna wear a sundress with flowers on it like the one he wore on the cover of* The Face *magazine.*

I hit up Virgil Abloh, and I was like, "Bro, I want to wear a dress on *SNL* just like this," and I sent him some references.

He was like, "All right, I think I got some patterns."

And within seconds, he was texting me prints to use. He was on it. We made the dress in like two days. Everything about the process just felt right. That didn't stop me from feeling nervous leading up to the performance. I was like, *Oh my god, what am I doing? I'm fucking nuts.* But it was fucking rock and roll. When I came out onstage with it during the break, I heard somebody in the crowd go, "Ow!" Then as we were getting set up, people were clapping, and I thought, *This could work out.*

As soon as the song started, I was lost in it. It was such a beautiful moment, and I felt so strong standing there in that dress. After the performance, a lot of people didn't get it. But there were way more that did. I had so many people in my DMs calling me brave, saying that it was the dopest shit—celebrities, fans, old friends I hadn't heard from in a while. It made me feel like I made the right choice. I just wanted to go up there and be myself and show love to one of my favorite artists.

Having expanded my comfort zone as a performer, I needed to continue to move outside of it as an actor. In February 2021, I flew out to New Zealand to shoot my very first feature horror movie, *X*, directed and written by Ti West. I was a huge fan of Ti. In 2016, I met him for dinner because I wanted to connect. It was at a time when I didn't know you could do that. My agent told me, "Cudi, you know, you can just meet directors," and I said, "Holy shit, for real?!" and Ti West was the first director I wanted to meet. We met at Soho House and I saw his movie *The House of the Devil*, and it blew me away.

I loved the retro vibes and thought it was super genius. It was dope that he'd kept me in mind all those years later and thought of me to play Jackson Hole and to produce it with my production company, Mad Solar. We were trying to find projects to get started with, and this was one of our first movies outside of *Entergalactic* that we were doing.

When I was in quarantine the first day in New Zealand, I thought, *OK, I can't be sitting in this bitch and not do nothing, not have nothing going on; I'm gonna go crazy.* I needed to have something to do. So I finally decided to conjure up my clothing line. I had started working on it in 2016. We started making some samples, and the samples came back shitty. I thought, *Fuck this, what am I doing?* And I got discouraged. *Maybe I shouldn't be doing this.* But ever since then it had been something in the back of my mind. At this point, I had a full vision. I came up with the name instantly: Members of the Rage. We talked with Nigo from Bape about the logo. Everything came together in two weeks, the whole vision for the brand.

X freaked me out in a lot of ways because of the explicit content. Looking at the script, I was trying to imagine how we were going to shoot this shit. I had never done anything like what this movie was asking me to do. I never had to be butt naked on camera before. So I was being brave. I thought, *I gotta do this. I've always wanted to do a horror movie. Let's just do it.*

My homies on set were Brittany Snow, Jenna Ortega, and Martin Henderson. Brittany, Martin, and I became our own little crew, and I vibed with Jenna. She didn't hang out with us when we were going out as a group, but toward the end of filming she and I were the last few people who had scenes, so we got a chance to hang out, and she's the coolest kid. I have this big-bro nurturing mentality, and I felt as if she needed somebody to look out for her. She was eighteen years old at the time; usually eighteen-year-olds have their parents stay on set with them, but she was out there on her own. I was worried about her—being so young and in this business. But she's so strong and so focused and knows her shit, man. Stands up for herself. She was a very impressive eighteen-year-old. I was not that impressive at her age.

On the last day of filming, Jenna and I went out into the city to hang out and get a drink. In New Zealand you only have to be eighteen to drink, so Jenna was kickin' it. We were going to different bars. We had this guy that was kind of hosting us and showing us around different spots. He hit me after he left and told me, "Yo, I left a little something in there for you"—because he got me some weed before because I wanted to smoke before I went to bed. When I looked in the package there was a little bit of cocaine in there, but he had no sense of what I'd gone through. I stared at it for about twenty seconds and I thought to myself, *Now, you can use a tiny bit of coke and no one would know, and it'd be fine.* And I immediately thought, *I would know.* Took that baggie, put it back in the package, texted the dude: "Come get the shit, bro. Nah, we ain't partying like that," not because I was tempted to do it, because I didn't even want that shit in my room. I didn't want that kid to have the story that he left coke with Kid Cudi. That let me know that I was past that point in my life. That was the universe's test to see if I'd overcome that, and I didn't crave it anymore.

CHAPTER 24

I walked in Virgil's final show. It felt surreal like the first time—almost fake—but for other reasons. Virgil wasn't there. His spirit was, but you could feel his absence, the emptiness.

I woke up November 28, 2021, as if it were any other day. I was getting my shit together and I was talking to Lola on the phone as she came home from work. We were talking about Virgil, as we often did, how awesome he was, and how he was such a sweet person, and then Dennis started calling me. Lola got a call at the same time. She told me, "Hey, babe, I think I gotta take this."

I said, "Yeah, Dennis is calling too. I'll call you back."

I answered and Dennis told me: Virgil died.

My heart was crushed. My brain was confused. I had talked to Virgil the day before because he wanted me to walk in this show that he had in Miami. My world was turned upside down. I couldn't understand. Then the reports came out about what he was dealing with: He'd been diagnosed with cardiac angiosarcoma, a rare cancer, and kept it secret for two years. This man was going through hell and he was still responding to text messages, still in good spirits.

November 26, 2021, at 10:28 a.m., I texted Virgil: "Hope you had a great Thanksgiving with the fam. So thankful to have you in my life. Love you, brother."

He responded: "Mad love for you, my G."

I called Lola back and she was hysterical. It was hard watching her break down like that. Virgil uplifted and supported Lola. He gave her a shot at being a designer. He brought us together. He was always a part of our conversations.

The last time I saw Virgil was Halloween that year at this Circoloco party. He was DJing and he said, "Watch what I do next," and "Pursuit of Happiness" came on. He smiled at me, the crowd was hype, and next thing I knew he was gesturing for me to go up on the stage and stand up on the table where the turntable was—it was a lip where I could've fell and busted my ass, but I said, "Fuck it, let's go for it," and he helped me get up. It was so powerful, just raging with the fans. That was the last moment we shared. The pain is going to be forever. It's not going to be anything compared to the pain that his family feels. But Virgil's legacy will live forever in the people he touched, the worlds he built, the boundaries he dissolved.

The memorial was one deserving of such a seismic cultural footprint. It was set up at this museum in Chicago. Everybody was there: A$AP Rocky, Tyler. Dennis came with me. We were all awkwardly sitting there waiting for something, and we came to find out that Kanye was holding up the memorial because he was outside signing autographs. I don't think he realized how disrespectful that was. It was the most fucked-up shit anyone could've done: make a moment like this about them.

When Pastor Rich was wrapping up the memorial, he had all of Virgil's close friends come up onstage. Kanye was there and he gave me a hug. I hadn't seen him in forever and he was crying, emotional. I didn't know what those tears meant. I didn't know if Kanye was crying because he was sad about Virgil or because he regretted talking shit about him. It could've been a lot of things coursing through him.

There was one point where he tried to nudge Pastor Rich and tried to speak, but Pastor Rich turned and with his eyes said, *No.* Kanye backed up. He was salty. So salty you heard about it for the next couple of years in rants.

In the summer of 2022, I did my deal with Twentyfourseven to start my clothing line, Members of the Rage (MOTR). I met with Giacomo Piazza, the head of Twentyfourseven, told him about my vision, and he fucked with it. He was totally open to collaborating with me, bringing me on board, and being the machine behind my brand.

When I started designing my own clothes, I started to wear a lot more bright colors showing the light that I was feeling at the time. I was dying my hair. I wanted to create clothing that was a true embodiment of who I was but also made people feel like superstars. I wanted something for people that love to dress up and go out to an event, who need an outfit for the party or for the performance.

It wasn't long until I had my first showroom in Paris during Fashion Week. I was on a high. I designed the showroom to look like my closet: pink-painted walls, green Astroturf, checkerboard ceilings, blue railings for clothes racks. It was the most hyped shit in the building.

Jenna Ortega came to show support. She's the sweetest human being. So happy to have her in my life. Every project I do I like to take one or two friends, and she was one I took from *X* for sure. To see her come out by herself to support me was everything.

I did my first interview for Vogue.com with Amy Verner. I was very nervous, but upon meeting Amy I was immediately relaxed—not only was she a fan of mine, but she liked what she saw in the collection. I knew I wasn't gonna get skewered. I ended up finding out later that it was one of the most viewed stories on the website that year. When I did my second collection in Paris, it could have been a disaster— everybody was looking for the sophomore slump—but we fine-tuned the things that we established in the first season. I was tweaking and getting better and making some cool shit that I wear. The goal for the clothing line was truly to stop shopping. Or at least stop shopping as much. I'm always gonna want to buy some shit, but I wanted to spend less and wear my own shit. My guiding principle was designing clothes I want for myself.

In the summer of 2022, I also went to Mexico City to film this action movie, *Silent Night*, with John Woo. I'd been itching to do an action film. It was at the top of my fucking list and I was so eager to get it on. Doing a movie without dialogue seemed challenging, but the way it was written everything made sense and felt right. I had to do this stunt where I slid on my legs to shoot these dudes and then stood up. The next day I was struggling to walk. I didn't train at all beforehand. I did a little bit of work, but I wasn't working out at the time. I went into that shit cold and I should not have done that. As someone excited about taking on the action gauntlet, I should've been more prepared. That's me, though: Sometimes I just run off into shit.

A few months later, I was back on tour. It was the best on-the-road experience I've ever had. The energy of every show was electric. The kids showed up to fuck with me. Each night I was so fucking happy seeing their faces, selling out arenas after fourteen years in the industry. Every crowd, every single fucking show, was fucking madness. I realized then that I want to tour as long as I can. Doing a greatest hits tour in my sixties would be ill. I could do this shit for a long time. I could stop making albums right now and go on tour for the rest of my life and kill it.

Rocky was with me on tour sometimes. She came out on a couple dates. We were still trying to work it out, I guess, or trying to be friends. I was confused. I didn't know what she wanted. I was the best I had ever been in my life and she was benefiting from my energy. Every year I was getting better and better, and I adored her. But as far as being an item, we had too many problems. I didn't know if it was ever gonna work. I was not that positive about it.

As a part of the tour, in September, I did Moon Man's Landing, my first festival, in Cleveland. Close to twenty thousand people showed up. Seeing the love from the city, seeing everybody come out, no problems, no arrests, no brawls. It was peace. From what I saw online, it seemed like kids had a good time.

During the festival, I found out that somebody had leaked my entire *Entergalactic* album weeks before it was to come out. I had been at odds with a producer on the project. He was publicly talking shit about me on Twitter. I suspected that he had something to do with it, but I don't know for sure. I was upset in the moment, but then I was like, *Fuck that guy.* Nobody could ruin this monumental achievement.

The show finally came out on Netflix on September 30, 2022, and we had a premiere in New York. It was such a beautiful moment to share with everybody—my mom was there, all my friends. It was powerful. My childhood dream made real. I dropped it that day for one reason: It was Virgil's birthday. I wanted to dedicate it to him to honor all of the hard work we put in, all the creative energy expended, everything we were able to build together. It was both a tribute and a eulogy. He was gone, but his legacy was eternal, and I was hell-bent on carrying it on.

CHAPTER 25

While I was taking a trip to Tokyo for the holidays, I broke it off with Rocky for good. I knew that she wasn't ever going to be what I needed. When we first started dating back in 2013, I was such a mess it was hard for me to see her with 20/20 vision, but from 2019 on I was watching that girl. I was studying her every fucking move, and it took me up until that moment to realize that she was the worst girl for me and I would be wasting my time if I gave her even one more ounce of my energy. So I let her go.

I ended up hanging out with Lola during New Year's in Tokyo. It was perfect. Exactly what I needed. Somebody I always vibed with. Somebody pleasant. Somebody sweet. We had never spent more than a day together. Now that I was done with Rocky, I could seriously court Lola and actually see it through. Maybe there was a way it could work.

Around the summer I started to think about my life and what I wanted for myself. I knew I wanted to start a family, have more kids, and enter that level of growth. I was tired of linking up with girls and having one-night stands. I had slowed down that lifestyle. When I was single back in the day, I used to kick it, but as I got older I stopped wanting to give my time to so many people. I was linking up with chicks hoping they would be the one or hoping it would be something, but it could never be anything. It just wasn't magic.

Lola, when it came down to it, was the only person. I was still trying to better myself and get my life in LA established.

As the year went by, I was trying to feel her out and see:

"Hey, would you ever move to LA?"

She was like, "I would do that."

I said, "For real?" I couldn't believe it.

She said, "Yeah," and that started to get me thinking. I wasn't ready to fully commit because, as a man with needs, I hated long-distance relationships. I just know me. So for a while in 2023 I was kind of going with the flow. But now I had a different mindset. Before, my relationship with Lola was just a friendship. There was never a conversation about us being together. Now I wanted it to be a reality. I wanted to see it through. Talk of potentially moving to LA made it all real for me. At that point I started to see her as my woman.

I was at this place where I realized, *Scott, you have a choice to make. You know God has given you what you ask for. He's given you the light. You're in a much better place, no more darkness. Lola is right here. You asked her if she would move to LA; she said yes. Make a decision. What do you feel? Does this feel right?* When I sat and thought about it, it couldn't get much righter. *Go for it. Take the chance.* I'm so happy I did. I'm so sure of myself, as sure as I was about moving to

New York and becoming an artist, the same certainty. I just knew: This girl can make me the happiest man in the world. We can live happily ever after.

I conquered the loneliness before, and now I was ready. It was like God gave me that test. He knew that I was leeching on to these women. I had to find that self-fulfillment before I could be complete enough to be in a partnership. With Rocky, I was too busy trying to fix something from pre-rehab, someone who knew a whole other Scott. She couldn't relate to who I'd become. What I needed was somebody that could appreciate the Scott that I was. And that was Lola.

I was feeling so energized and inspired. In November 2022, I started working on *INSANO*. I knew exactly what I wanted to do: give people a fucking experience. I needed a quarterback—that perfect executive producer that could help me get the right vibe. It was my dude Jean Baptiste. We started linking up and he began to feed me hundreds of beats at a time. I would sit down and pick the best of the best. I wanted the album to feel like an event, so I had Drama host it. He came through and brought his signature energy, which elevated the project.

By August, I was done with *INSANO* and had the album turned in. It was inspired by seeing Kendrick Lamar perform live that fall in Paris. I was awestruck by his show: the energy behind the records, seeing him rocking muthafuckas all the way out there. I thought, *Oh man, we gotta get to the arenas in Paris, first off. Number two, we need to conjure up some shit that evokes this type of emotion. We need to conjure up something that will have muthafuckas losing their shit every song, singing every word.* So that was my motivation. I was like, *I want to make this album for live shows. This is for the arena.*

INSANO (NITRO MEGA) came immediately on the heels of *INSANO*. After the first album, there was simply no stopping. I was in beast mode. The album warranted a different take, one with a lot more classic Cudi vibes. Given my range, I can do so much shit, so many different types of music. *INSANO* and *INSANO (NITRO MEGA)* back-to-back proved it. That same month, I had my first Calvin Klein campaign go live all around the world. It was something I had wanted since first starting my career as a little scrawny fucker. Not sure what the fuck I was thinking, believing I was about to get in a Calvin Klein ad in 2009. But a kid could dream. And his dream got him a campaign eventually—that and working out with his trainer.

Shortly after starting *INSANO*, I got an email from my agent that I had an offer to be in the Knuckles TV show on Paramount+. I had done the theme song for the second Sonic movie, shot a music video, and ended up meeting Sonic producers Toby Ascher and Neal Moritz, the latter a producer behind the *Fast & Furious* franchise. They were telling me that they had a role and asked me if I would be open to doing it. I told them hell fucking yes. They were a ways away, but I told them when it comes together to keep me in mind.

A year went by and they reached out. I spent a month in London shooting the show. It was so much fun to work with Adam Pally and the rest of the cast. It was another one of those surreal experiences. I was a huge fan of the Sonic movies. I'd been a fan of the character since those days playing *Sonic 2* on Sega as a kid. I saw the first one and thought about how cool it would be to be in one, and there I was getting a chance to be a part of it. I also got to be funny. And I got to do some action. I was gonna be fighting Knuckles, squaring up and interacting with something that was not there. I'd always wondered how actors do it. The stages and the sets were super elaborate. I did a lot of my own stunts and wirework, getting thrown around a room. I ran into Idris Elba at Jeymes Samuel's house and I was telling him how I was doing my own stunts and he looked at me crazy like, "What are you doing? You know they've got guys for that?"

I replied, "I just want to do it, man."

He kept looking at me like I was nuts. I get it. In a few years, I might be looking at a younger man the same way. One day my back ain't gonna be working for me in the same ways and I ain't gon' move as quick.

Doing the stunt choreography, I learned that I do have some athletic ability. I always tell people I'm not an athlete, but to do what I do onstage, there's athleticism that comes into play. When I was doing the stunt work, and working through the physicality of it, I was surprising myself. I thought, *Man, with training, I can pretty much do anything.* When it came time to shoot, we were locked in. I knew where my beats were. I knew where to throw a punch, where Knuckles would be, and how to react from his punches. The whole thing felt like a dream. And then, when it came out, watching it was a bonus—seeing the way real and digital came together. I'm hopeful to get back in the Sonic universe again one day.

Dreams were coming true left and right that year. The director M. Night Shyamalan hit me up about a movie he was working on called *Trap*. We had already been friends—I visited his house in Philly one summer, had dinner with him and his family, and just connected. M. Night is one of my favorite directors ever. I think he's a genius and a mastermind. It was just nice to have that friendship with him. Of course, I wanted to work with him. But I wasn't in his ear, like, *Hey, man, we got to do a movie.* It was like, *Hey, this is a great friendship, and I want to direct one day, and maybe I could learn some things from him and get some pointers.*

So when he reached out one day and told me, "I'm working on this movie, and I am doing it with my daughter—she's starring in it, and she plays the pop star—and we want to have you on a song and have you perform the song in the movie," it was an immediate yes.

I reached out to Dot da Genius, my right-hand secret weapon, and we went out to Philly and worked with M. Night and Saleka, his daughter, and just cooked up something from scratch. At that point, I was just figuring, *Hey, I'm just gonna come on as this character and just do the song.* But then M. Night said, "I want to have some backstage moments of you maybe yelling at your assistant or something." It was already established that he would be like a gay pop star, but I took it to an extreme when I got to set. I thought, *OK, I'm going to make him such a diva.*

When we were shooting, I got to my wardrobe like, *Where is he?* I was looking for my friend Josh Hartnett, who was starring in the movie. I'm looking for him, and then he's looking for me at the same time. I can't see him but I hear him say, "Where is he?"

Turn around.

I'm like, "Yo!"

He's like, "Yo!"

We gave each other a big hug. He's such a good dude. It had been years since I'd seen him. We had just lost touch. Life happened. It wasn't anything personal. But it was beautiful, man. Being reunited with Josh was a sweet feeling, and what made it even better was he was enjoying every single one of my takes for the movie.

When I came to set, they asked me if I wanted a wig, and I was like, "No, I'm just gonna wear my regular hair." Then I thought about it when I was in makeup. I didn't want to look like myself playing this character. I wanted to fall into a real character and have people see me as a different person. So they pulled out the blond bussdown, and I was like, *Yes, yes, let's do it.* I'll never forget when they put it on me for the first time. I was just looking in the mirror like, *Oh my god, I'm so pretty! This hair is ridiculous.*

I was improving a lot of stuff in my scenes and just trying different things. M. Night was loving it. Every take that we did, he would come from behind the monitors just laughing his ass off. I was doing something new each time. My assistant fucks up my kombucha order in the scene and we went online and searched different names of flavors. *Honeysuckle sour kombucha.* Sounds great. *Feral fig.* Let's do it. When a director gives me the freedom to be as goofy as I want to be and just have fun with it, that's when I shine. Not every director will trust you enough and give you that grace to explore.

I'll be getting compliments about *Trap* till I'm like eighty years old. People are just going to keep discovering that movie. And it's going to bring so many people joy. I was in the movie for only like three minutes, but they were all unforgettable.

As the end of the year approached, my mind was made up that I was going to ask Lola to marry me. I took a private jet to Portland to pick up the ring. I had it custom made and I had it rushed. My boy Alexandre Arnault, who I met at the Kendrick Lamar show in Paris, helped me get a custom design, an eleven-carat diamond platinum ring. Huge stone. It was a quest to get the ring. I wanted Lola to understand that this shit was not a game for me. The size of the ring represented the size of my investment in the relationship. And then it hit me: *I'm about to propose to this girl.*

Every time I was with her, I was so happy. She was perfect, a delight to be around and the most agreeable person I'd ever met. We'd only had three arguments total. They were all things that we were able to talk through. That's one thing about me: I need to be able to communicate with my woman. She was always down to work through it. She wasn't going to walk away. In a moment you might feel like that's what you need to do to protect your heart, but Lola didn't want to run away from me, and I didn't want to run from her, no matter what we said. We know there are going to be more problems, hurdles we're going to have to get over. But we're a team. Communication is key. As long as we've got that and we know we are teammates and we love each other, we'll go the distance. I believe that.

CHAPTER 26

By the end of the year, I had planned everything. I was like, *OK, I'm going to do the proposal in Kyoto*—Lola loves Kyoto; I've never been—*I'ma set it all up.* My man Verbal from Teriyaki Boyz hooked me up with someone that set me up in some temples. We could go visit and walk and do some sightseeing and have wonderful dinners. I had it all planned out.

December rolled around, Lola was going to meet me in Kyoto, and we were staying at the Aman, which is one of my favorite strings of hotels ever. Always awesome to stay there, no matter where I'm at in the world. I pulled up. The people were so welcoming. I took this little golf cart to my villa. I came to my room and then I checked my bag and made sure that the ring was there. I wanted it to be a Tiffany ring; I had to pull out the blue box.

Lola got there. Everything was magical. Nothing else mattered except that moment. I was with my lady. The next day we walked through the garden, checking out temples. I had this whole thing set up where I would do the proposal in the garden and there was a temple I rented and no other people were there. I flew my camera guy and my videographer out to film it. They were hiding in the bushes when we got there. The temple was a super elegant, beautiful, stunning place that looked like a fairy tale. It was a quiet, lovely day. I came up with this line that I wanted to say—I wanted to have like an opening into the proposal—I had to have one, right? It had to be a little smooth.

So I said, "Babe, it's really a beautiful day." She agreed.

"Not as beautiful as you, though."

She was like, "Aww, babe."

She kissed me. From that point on, I went blank and started to speak from the heart. I told her I loved her so much, she was my best friend, and I wanted to spend the rest of my life with her. Then I got down on my knee and asked her if she would marry me. She said, "Yes," with the quickness. I thought she was going to say something about the size of the ring because she wants me to be a little bit more conservative with my spending. I know with her, not only is she gonna hold me down, but she gon' help me keep some money in my pocket. You need a woman like that. But she didn't trip over the ring—I mean, she tripped over the ring but like not in that way.

The photographers went out to get the moment and they missed it. We were kissing and then they were peeking out, not sure if they should come out, so the only pictures I have are after the actual proposal. But it's OK because if they came out before she would have known something was up and it would have ruined it. She had no clue I was going to propose, but I asked her after if she knew what was up and she said she had noticed something. As we entered the temple, there were two lanterns with our names on them in Japanese. She thought that was strange, but she didn't know what it meant.

I called my mom. She and Lola started crying on the phone together. It was so sweet. Lola called her mom. She had the flu, and I felt bad for her, but she was happy for us. We had the support from our parents, and afterward I had it all planned so we had sake with all different types of desserts. A lady was playing this harp behind us while we were eating sweets. It was super fly. I was proud of myself. I'd never set up anything like this before. I felt like I did the damn thing.

We spent New Year's in Tokyo. I performed at 1 OAK. Shit was madness. I had the best time. We'd hung out the year before for New Year's in Tokyo, and she was not drinking. She was trying to stay sober to be on her best behavior. I told her this year she had to get lit. No trying to be cool. Let loose around me. She's so free around her friends. I wanted her to feel that comfortable around me. So she got lit. I was lit too, and it was beautiful. We had so much fun. Lola's so cute when she's a little drunk. As a French-Italian woman, she is self-conscious about her English. But when she drinks she's not in her head about that and she has a lot to say.

Later that week, it was time for a different nerve-racking moment: the Creative Arts Emmys. *Entergalactic* was nominated. We were up against some titans—*The Simpsons, Rick and Morty, Bob's Burgers*— but I felt optimistic about it. We had already won one leading into that for animation. I wore a suit from MOTR that I was preparing to debut in a couple days. It was made of this pattern I created with colored pencils, embellished with different types of crystals and stitching. It's a gorgeous piece, and the kind of thing I want to do more of.

The thing that was intense about the Emmys was that I had to present three awards. I did it once, but I got pissy drunk and embarrassed myself—I went out with Drake and Jeremih before the Emmys back in the day. I was so scared that I got wasted, so that's probably why I'd never been asked back to do it. This time, I presented without a problem.

Then it was time for our category. I was sitting there and my mom had my hand. They said the names of all the nominees in the category, the cameras were on me, and I was right smack-dab in the front in the second row, and they called, "*The Simpsons.*" I immediately felt the pain. My heart sank. I wanted to win it. It was a bummer. We deserved that win. But it was motivation. I left knowing I would be back. One day, I'll make something great enough to be honored. A nomination is like winning for me—first thing I ever put together, first thing I ever produced—and we did win something. That's huge. I knew it was more fuel to the fire.

A few days after the Emmys, *INSANO* dropped. I was stepping into a new chapter with some new flavor. There was something inside of me that knew that people were gonna be into it. I had this whole thing planned where I would put up these thirty-foot statues in different places around the world. They were playing music and the eyes were glowing. It was like a light show damn near—on the water in Long Beach, in New York, in Paris. It made a lot of noise. It was exactly what I wanted. It was supposed to be like an homage to Michael Jackson's statue for his *HIStory: Past, Present and Future* album.

I saw that Page Six had this story about the statues being Satanic. I thought that was funny. The public likes to throw that at people a lot;

they have with me throughout my career. They were reaching. I was trying to create an experience for my rollout, nothing more. This is how some people in the world are—just unbelievably simpleminded. Every once in a while, I'm reminded of that, whether I'm wearing a dress or doing something different. Sometimes it makes me sad. But fuck it. Fuck them. If you've ever listened to my music, I talk about God a lot; everybody knows I'm a God-fearing man. I've been dealing with demons and I've been fighting them. I've been trying to walk the path of light. Anyone who sees otherwise doesn't know me, hasn't been paying attention, and doesn't know what the fuck they're talking about.

When the album came out, the response was overwhelmingly positive. It seemed like I was able to achieve something new and give people something that they haven't heard from me after eleven albums. That's the shit—still being able to reinvent yourself after sixteen years.

On January 14, I had to fly to Paris for my showroom for Members of the Rage. We were debuting our Fall/Winter 2024 collection, and I was so fucking excited. I knew that we were doing something epic. The collection finally had balance. It was in perfect harmony and it set the tone for what MOTR could be. Giacomo was texting me samples throughout the process, and I could tell he was proud. He took a chance on me and I've been able to deliver. The collections kept getting better and better. I was pushing myself each time, drawing a lot more. The goal is to try to make some cool shit, and so far we've been able to do that. People started wearing the brand. I saw homies rocking the shit: Westside Gunn, Moneybagg Yo, my youngin Hit-Boy, all reppin'. It's a beautiful thing to see love out there, man, for something else I'm doing that's not music. This is a form of validation. I know the designs are good, but when you see other people get it too it confirms that. MOTR is only for the flyest of individuals.

I've never had a personal stylist ever, except for individual photo shoots. I don't believe in it. You have to know how to dress yourself. You have to know how to put fits together. Something about that is so much iller. For the most part, I go to stores myself and shop by myself. I go in like everybody else and buy shit, and I be putting shit together. You know, not everybody got style. A lot of muthafuckas got somebody that got a fit for them and they put it on. They couldn't do that shit on they own. But I pride myself on being the nigga out here with that drip. It's in me. Niggas could never fuck with me with that fashion. I am one of the freshest niggas out here. And that's one of the reasons why I started my brand, because I wanted to keep flexing that notion. My taste level is exceptionally high.

I brought my mom to Paris with me to meet Lola's mom. We all went out to dinner and it was sensational. Something that I learned at that dinner that night: Love is a universal language everybody understands. Lola's mom doesn't speak English that well, and she couldn't understand everything we were saying. Lola had to translate—some things her mom picked up on; others she didn't. But one thing she did understand was that I truly loved her daughter and I was going to take care of her, and that she was gonna be safe with me. My mom was living with me, so it was important for Lola's mom to meet my mom as well. After that dinner, I know she was reassured. At some point, they held hands and they started crying. It was so powerful—understanding emotions no matter the language.

Lola moved back to LA with me on January 26, and after the first week I was like, *This is the best decision I ever could have made.* I never had a girl living with me. It was all new. Yet she fit so perfectly. She was cooking—I ain't never had a girl cook for me in this way. She was throwing down. They say the way to a man's heart is through their stomach, and I was in love. Cooking was like the icing on the cake. I felt like I was the man she needed too.

All of the stuff that I'd been through got me to that place: finally, being able to receive the love and see it. Part of that was me knowing my worth and knowing that I was a good man. Loving myself and not really needing a relationship as a crutch, but more as a bonus in my life. Before Lola, I needed the women in my life to prop me up. I didn't love myself; I wasn't positive. But with clarity I was able to realize: I deserve someone that I'm happy with all the time, that I don't argue with all the time. Someone that's my best friend, truly.

Lola being in my life brought completion to the whole cycle of post-rehab internal growth. The only piece that I was missing was a companion. She was not only the perfect companion, but she was peace in my life that I just hadn't felt with a woman before.

I love every little quirk about her. She inspires me; she uplifts me; she supports me in every single endeavor I have, whether it's writing a movie, or with fashion. She's a fashion designer, and she encouraged me the whole time: "No, you're a fucking dope designer. Don't let nobody make you feel any different." Things like that were priceless. She's a master in her craft, so it's like I found my equal in creativity too.

Her being a strong woman, being there for me in ways that no other woman has been, was romantically and creatively enriching in a way I'd never experienced. She isn't in it for anything else but me. Not the fame. Not the money. Me. A question that every man in my position asks himself is: *If I lost it all, would my girl still stay with me?* A lot of people might say, "No, she wouldn't." But I know, if I lost it all today, if I had to lose my legs, she would be pushing me around in the wheelchair and would be happy that she's still with me. She'd never been to America for longer than seventeen hours before moving for me. It was still a foreign place when she came to live here. But my home became her home, and being with her has come to feel like home.

Lola was with me when I turned forty on January 30, 2024. At more than one point in my life I didn't even think I would make it to forty. It was so unreal to me that I got there.

I threw a huge party and about two hundred of my friends came out. So much love in the room. I had Bill Bellamy host. Clipse came out—my man Pusha and his brother Malice have always supported me, and they did some of my favorite songs of theirs. Busta Rhymes came out and killed it; he's literally one of the best, if not the best, hip-hop performers in the game. Brad Roberts, from the Crash Test Dummies, performed two of my favorite songs from his debut album, and the ten-year-old Scott in me freaked out. It was a crazy fucking moment. Timmy came out and spoke. Jaden spoke. My mom gave this speech, and I'd never heard her speak about me like that. Maybe she talked about me like this to her friends, but I had never heard her say anything like that. I don't want to repeat what she said, because I don't even feel worthy. But nobody's ever talked about me like that before. It was nice that I heard it and everybody in that room heard it. And the beautiful thing about that whole night was that Lola was there to share it with me. That party was definitely one of the top three moments in my life.

When I was younger, I could never imagine myself older than thirty. I needed to throw this big rager of a birthday party because I felt like it needed to be a celebration. Like, who knew? I think people for sure thought that I was going to kill myself at some point. There were times I wasn't sure I wouldn't. It just felt like such a huge relief for me.

People really showed out. I realized that so many care. It was nice to look around the room and see so many different faces from so many different walks of life, so many different parts of my life, all mingling and getting to know each other—and to know that I was the common thread that connected them. The party felt like a representation of something I'd been seeking my whole life, something I'd been searching for in my music—which my music had now led me directly to: community and interconnection. My songs gave voice to a certain kind of social out- lier, and now those same outsiders were a collective. Watching those people celebrate me felt like the ultimate payoff for my work. I have the most support ever, and I probably always have, but I never knew it. In that moment, it was crystal clear: *Scott, even all them times when you felt low and you were struggling, you had love.*

As I looked around the room, surrounded by everyone I cherished, celebrating a milestone that often felt so very far out of reach, I thought about the days spent alone in my room as a kid—all the dreaming and scheming of what my life could be, dancing in my door's reflection. Draw- ing and pretending I was in a music video were glimpses into a future that always felt possible. And now my reality was even better than the one I imagined. At my loneliest, my most isolated, music always felt like an escape, a way to access my creativity and touch people. In the end, it guided me from the little room in Shaker Heights to this grand one: in a crowd of friends and family from across my roller coaster of a journey.

When I think about my life, every single person I met was for a pur- pose. Every loss, every bit of pain that I felt as a kid, every heartbreak, every fight, every friendship that only lasted a few seasons, every one was there for a reason—they were all characters in my story. My life feels like *The Truman Show*. Every season there are new cast members; sometimes they stick around. I thank every person I ever interacted with who showed me love, held me down, embraced my goofiness, my strangeness, never judged me, and fucked with me all day. I love each and every one of y'all muthafuckas.

When I came out, there was nothing that sounded like me, and I created a whole new lane for generations to come. The doors I helped open created the boundless, genreless space where artists don't have to be defined by their small town or the way their music is supposed to sound—whatever that may mean, whatever limiting form it takes. I could have stopped with *Man on the Moon II* and I still would have had an undeniable impact.

A lot more people got honest with their music after me. I made it cool to be vulnerable. But I wouldn't be who I am if it wasn't for God, my mom, my siblings. I wouldn't be anything. Even in my darkest hour, I always felt that God was close, and He shepherded me through. I was a broken man who healed. I was trapped in the blanket of darkness for a long, long time. Alone in a room. I eventually found the light. I know there will be more days when I don't feel like myself, but I know how to get through it now. I won't crumble. I won't let shit ruin me or ruin the relationships I hold dear. I know how to talk to people. I know how to squash shit, to get past things. I'm a new man. Forty years old and I feel like a brand-new muthafuckin' man—who's just getting warmed up.

THE END/THE BEGINNING

The room I grew up in in Shaker Heights wasn't very big, but in many ways it was. It was a gateway to other worlds. When I was in there alone, I could see the possible futures for myself. It was there where, above all, I imagined a gravity-defying artist. At first, the imaginings were a coping mechanism for flying solo, a means of entertaining myself and realizing that I was one of a kind. But when death came calling, I'd retreat there and try to remake the world as I wished it to be.

Sketching and writing poems were my only outlets, ways to express what I was feeling and design something new. Then came music, another environment onto which I could map out my mind, in hopes of reaching someone. Mounting losses clouded my soul, but my art was free from the restrictions of my personal reality. Eventually, my ingenuity and vision *could* materially change the world around me. It gave my family and me a whole new way of life, it opened other avenues to tapping my creativity, and it helped people all around the world through their solitude. But music and success alone couldn't rescue that skinny kid from Ohio from a lingering sense of neglect.

The power of my mind's eye was always formidable, but I never could have imagined this. I thought the dark cloud would follow me forever. The threat of losing someone dear to me, or dying myself, always loomed. It took years to realize how those unresolved issues were affecting me. I feared getting too close, being misunderstood, not being a great dad or partner. There were moments I worried I would never fill that hole in my heart.

Now I stand on the other side of those doubts as a restored man. A man aware of his blessings. It wasn't the fame that brought me to my nirvana; it was all the wonderful, sincere people who my music led into my life. In all my time searching for life in outer space, I never thought I'd find peace and love on earth.

Acknowledgments

There are so many people in my life who have inspired me, helped me, been true friends. People I can always count on. There are too many to name, so I'm just going to say this: To the ones who know, to the people who met me anywhere along my journey, any interaction big or small that changed me and made me the man I am today: I love you unconditionally. To the people I haven't seen in a long time or have lost touch with: I miss you and I hope that one day I can find you again so that we can reconnect.

About the Author

SCOTT MESCUDI (a.k.a. Kid Cudi) is a Grammy Award–winning artist, actor, designer, and cultural trailblazer who transformed the sound—and soul—of modern music. His debut album, *Man on the Moon: The End of Day*, redefined hip-hop and paved the way for a new era of emotional vulnerability and sonic innovation. In 2022, he released *Entergalactic*, a visionary album accompanied by an Emmy-winning animated film on Netflix, further establishing his reputation as a boundary-breaking storyteller. On-screen, he's earned acclaim for his roles in *How to Make It in America*, *Westworld*, *Don't Look Up*, *X*, *Knuckles*, *Happy Gilmore 2*, and more. In 2023, he debuted his fashion label, Members of the Rage (MOTR), at Paris Fashion Week, expanding his creative influence into the world of high fashion. More than a multihyphenate, Scott is a generational voice whose influence spans music, film, fashion, and mental health advocacy—cementing his legacy as one of the most impactful and enduring artists of our time.